WORLD PEACE

VOLUME ONE

POVERTY AND PEACE

Suresh Chandra Mallick
Pritam Mallick

I.

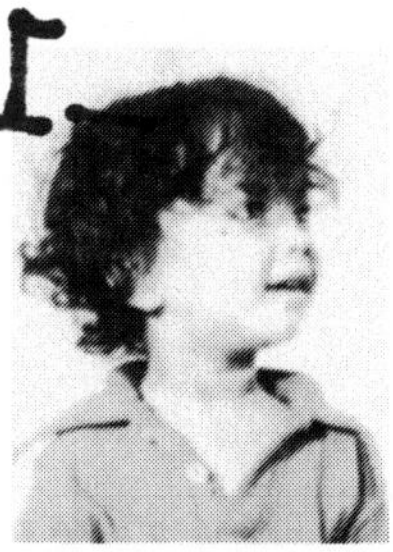

POVERTY AND PEACE

Institute of Development Studies and Policy Research, Pritam Bhawan, 93, Dharma Vihar, Khandagiri, Bhubaneswar - 751030 (Orissa), INDIA

ISBN: 978-81-924851-0-2

First Edition

2018

Price: US $

Dedicated to

Mr. Bill Clinton
42nd President,
The United States of America

PROLOGUE

The study is intended to achieve WORLD PEACE by challenging the dismal factors, which cause crises in the world. The manuscript on World Peace – Volume One incorporates 'POVERTY AND PEACE'. The study argues that by decreasing the number of the food insecure families of South Asia, West Asia, sub-Saharan Africa and Latin American countries, World Peace could be achieved. In the twenty-first century more than 1.3 billion people live on less than $1 a day and 2.8 billion of people live on less than $2 a day. These poor people continue to be blighted by abysmal poverty, under nutrition, ill health, educational deprivation, environmental degradation, voiceless, devoid of human rights and wide ranging social inequalities. They are born in debt, live in debt and die in debt. They live in unhygienic areas without safe drinking water, without transport and communication facilities, without employment opportunities, and their children manage without schools, teachers and family members without health care centers, medicines and doctors. Most of them have neither touched money nor saved money. They are alive to suffer and die unknown and unseen. Poor can realize the intensity of poverty himself.

In this book, we have suggested the ways by which poverty could be reduced in all the low-income countries and World Peace could be established at the earliest. We have classified poverty on the basis of families, localities, regions or availability of funds rather than measurement of poverty through different formulae (chapter-1). Research studies on poverty have been analyzed and summaries have been incorporated to draw meaningful conclusions for policy prospective (chapter-II). The study suggests that rural poverty is the biggest challenge to the world community. Moreover, reduction of poverty can be addressed through effective government and governance, availability of micro-credit, creation of employment opportunities, ensuring food security, investment in agriculture, investment in human capital, invitation of foreign funding institutions, availability of debt relief, sustainable environment and a number of other factors. Achievements or weakness of heavily indebted poor countries (HIPCs) and other countries are discussed for references (chapter- III). Chapter IV incorporates various 'Committee Reports' with valuable suggestions for the benefit of different countries, which can be incorporated in amendment of laws and inclusion of poverty reduction programs. The world organizations and international donors have adopted Millennium Development Goals for reduction of poverty (Ch. V).

The chapter-VI highlights that the greatest obstacle in realizing world peace is poverty of people spread over all the nations. These people are hungry, and are devoid of human rights. The governments, rich people and rich countries neglect the poor. The funds allocated for them are not properly utilized by the corrupt administration. So a topic on 'hunger threatens world peace', committee reports on hunger, Millennium Development Goals Report, food for peace and charitable dining halls are emphasized to reduce poverty for the purpose of establishing world peace. We are confident that poverty can be reduced and starvation-deaths can be completely checked, if funding institutions donate one-third of their donations directly to the poor people and the rest to the public or private institutions. Our ultimate aim is world peace where terrorism is completely wiped out and no one dies through starvation (chapter- VII). We are indebted to all authors for their views, which have been incorporated in this manuscript for a greater cause of World Peace. We have extensively used search organizations like Goggle and Yahoo, and studied the reports of the World Bank, IMF, UNDP, G8 countries, profiles of south Asian countries and sub-Saharan Africa, proceedings of international seminars. We are grateful to World Atlas Organization for permitting us to use country photos in our manuscript. We are indebted to all, who have published news items and reports on poverty and peace. We are grateful to thousands of poor people of Orissa, whom we have contacted for studying their problems. They have narrated about their life, food pattern, sufferings and ultimate aim to us, which can be neither explained by us nor believed by the rich people and developed countries.

Even the poverty economists cannot measure income and expenditure of the poor and hungry people. Perhaps they are alive because they do not want to live longer. They are alive to suffer further.

We are indebted to all authors, publishers, researchers and Committees cited in this manuscript. All the views, commissions and omissions in the text are entirely the authors' responsibility. We shall appreciate for constructive criticisms aiming at improvement of the subsequent editions of the book. Our hearts will be filled with joy even if a small step towards World Peace and Poverty Reduction is contemplated through this endeavor.

June 1, 2018 Suresh Chandra Mallick

ACRONYMS

ABM	:	Anti-Ballistic Missile
ACIAR	:	Australian Center for Agricultural Research
ADB	:	Area Development Bank
ADS	:	Area Development Schemes
AIDS	:	Acquired Immune Deficiency Syndrome
AIPCR	:	Association Mondiale de la Route
APEC	:	Asia- Pacific Economic Co-operation
ASEAN	:	Association of South East Asian Nations
ASISTAP	:	Advisory Support, Information Services and Training – Asia and the Pacific
BC	:	Before Christ
BJP	:	Bharatiya Janata Party (India)
CD	:	Conference on Disarmament
CESR	:	Central for Economic and Social Rights
CGAP	:	Consultative Group to Assist the Poorest
CIDA	:	Canadian International Development Agency
CJI	:	Chief Justice of India
CROP	:	Comparative Research Programme of the Poverty (Norway)
CAADP	:	Comprehensive African Agricultural Development Program
DAC	:	Development Assistance Committee
DC	:	District of Columbia
DDC	:	District Development Committee

DFID	:	Department for International Development (U.K.)
EIP	:	World Association for School as Instrument of Peace
ESAF	:	Enhanced Structural Adjustment Facility
FAO	:	Food and Agriculture Organization (of U.N.)
FONCODE	:	A Social Compensation and Development Fund
FY	:	Financial Year
GCSP	:	Geneva Center for Security Police
GDP	:	Gross Domestic Product
GIPRI	:	Geneva International Peace Research Institute
GNP	:	Gross National Product
G-7	:	Group of Seven
GTZ	:	Gesellschaft fur Technische Zusammenarbeit –Germany
HIPC	:	Heavily Indebted Poor Countries
HIV	:	Human Immunodeficiency Virus
IADP	:	Integrated Area Development Program
IBRD	:	International Bank for Reconstruction and Development
ICCPR	:	International Covenant on Civil and Political Rights
ICSID	:	International Center for Settlement of Investment Disputes
IDA	:	International Development Association
IDT	:	Impress DesaTertinggal
IFAD	:	International Fund for Agricultural Development
IFC	:	International Finance Corporation
IFI	:	International Financial Institution
IFRTD	:	International Forum for Rural Transport and Development
ILO	:	International Labour Organization
IMF	:	International Monetary Fund
IPB	:	International Peace Bureau
ISD	:	Initiatives for Sustainable Development
IT	:	Information Technology
ITDG	:	Intermediate Technology Development Group
ITO	:	International Timber Organization

ITTO	:	International Tropical Timber Organization
JBCI	:	Japan Bank for International Cooperation
JCGP	:	Joint Consultative Group on Policy
JICA	:	Japan International Cooperation Agency
LLDC s	:	Least and Less Developed Countries
MAP	:	Multi-Country HIV/AIDS Program
MIGA	:	Multilateral Investment Guarantee Agency
NAB	:	New Arrangement to Borrow
NABARD	:	National Bank for Rural Development (India)
NEP	:	New Economic Policy
NGO	:	Non-Government Organization
NJC	:	National Judiciary Commission
NVP	:	Net Present Value
ODA	:	Official Development Assistance
OECD	:	Organization for Economic Cooperation and Development
OECF	:	Overseas Economic Cooperation Fund
OTCA	:	Overseas Technical Cooperation Agency
PAAP	:	Poverty Alleviation Action Plan
PAF	:	Poverty Alleviation Fund
PAP	:	Poverty Alleviation Program
PIARC	:	The World Road Association
PREDES	:	Reconstruction and Development Program
PRGF	:	Poverty Reduction and Growth Facility
PRSP	:	Poverty Reduction Strategy Papers
RD	:	Rural Development
RER	:	Real Exchange Rate
RNF	:	Rural Non-Farm
SAARC	:	South Asian Association for Regional Cooperation
SAPS	:	Special Assistance for Project Sustainability
SANGAT	:	South Asian Network of Gender Activities and Trainers
SDA	:	Special Development Assistance
SDR	:	Special Drawing Rights
SDC	:	Swiss Agency for Development and Cooperation
SEWA	:	Self Employed Women's Association
SHG	:	Self Help Group

SIDA	:	Swedish International Development Agency
SIDBI	:	Small Industries Development Bank of India
TAI	:	Tomato Agro-Industry
TRUGA	:	Training for Rural Activities
UNCDF	:	United Nations Capital Development Fund
UNCED	:	United Nations Conference on Environment and Development
UNDF	:	United Nations Development Fund
UNDP	:	United Nations Development Program
UNFPA	:	United Nations Population Fund
UNICEF	:	United Nations Children's Emergency Fund
UNIDIR	:	U. N. Institute for Disarmament Research
UK	:	United Kingdom
UNO	:	United Nations Organization
USSR	:	Union of Soviet Socialist Republic
VDC	:	Village Development Committee
WDR	:	World Development Report
WFP	:	World Food Program
WFS	:	World Food Summit
WIPSA	:	Women's Initiative for Peace in South Asia
WMD	:	Weapons of Mass Destruction
WSSD	:	World Summit for Social Development
WTO	:	World Trade Organization
ZOP	:	Zone of Peace

+++++

CONTENTS

Prologue
Acronyms
Contents
Introduction

I. Poverty – A Challenge: 18- 32
Severity of Poverty, Natural resources and poverty, Poverty in India, Poverty in Ethiopia, Causes of poverty and Conclusion

II. Research Studies on Poverty: 33 - 78
Government, Micro–credit, Employment Generation, Food security, Agriculture, Human capital, Foreign funding Institutions, Non-government organization, Governance, Debt Relief, Other important studies and Conclusion

III. Heavily Indebted Developing Countries: 79- 130
Income Classification, Poverty Reduction Strategy Papers, Benin, Burkina Faso, Ethiopia, Gambia, Kyrgyz Stan, Mali, Mauritania, Mongolia, Nepal, Zambia and Conclusion

IV. Reports of Committees on Poverty Alleviation: 131 – 173
Kyrgyz Stan experience, Dhaka Declaration, Washington Consensus, Poverty Reduction in Malawi, Philippines Experience, Addis Ababa Conference, Pacific Human Development Report (Suva Declaration), Promoting Social Agenda in Latin America and the Caribbean (Santiago de Chile Declaration), Poverty Alleviation in Rural Indonesia, Mongolia issues on Poverty, Zimbabwe's Poverty Alleviation Action Plan, Poverty Alleviation Program in Mexico, Promoting Community Development in Sudan, World Conference on Women, DAC Development Partnership Strategy, World Food Summit, Initiatives for Sustainable Development towards the 21stCentury, Kyoto Initiative, G8 Köln Communiqué, and Conclusion

V. World Organizations and International Donors: 174 -260
United Nations Development Program, The World Bank, International Monetary Fund, Japan International Co- operation Agency, Department for International Development (UK), Canadian International Development Agency, Australian Aid, IFAD and Conclusion

VI. Poverty Hinders World Peace: 261- 313
Hunger Threatens World Peace and Security, Task Force on Hunger 2005, Millennium Development Goals 2000, Millennium Development Goals Report 2009, Fight Poverty to End Insecurity 2009, G-8 summit Italy 2009, Global Monitoring Report 2009, G-20 Leaders Statement: the Pittsburgh Summit 2009, Food for Peace Program, Charitable Dining Halls, and Conclusion

VII World Peace is Possible 314 – 347
Difficulties in Poverty Reduction Programs, Views of the president, World Bank, Suggestions of the Secretary General, UNO, Views of the Researchers, Author's Suggestions: Food Security, Bank Account, Group Insurance Scheme, Debt Relief, Basic Needs, Rural Connectivity, Rural Agricultural Markets, Employment Opportunities, Land Reform, Environment, Favourable Price for Cereals, Measure of Peace and Conclusion

Author Index – 348- 352
Subject Index- 353 - 355

INTRODUCTION

The world population has crossed 7 billion on October 31, 2011. In 2006, 854 million people were hungry, 1.3 billion people lived on less than $ 1 a day and 2.8 billion people lived on less than $ 2 a day. An estimate released on October 14, 2009 by FAO, highlights that 1.02 billion people are undernourished. Over 100 million children miss out primary school education each year. 11 million children die each year from preventable diseases; 6 million children under the age 5 die each year from hunger and malnutrition; 33,000 children die every day. Moreover 529,000 women die of pregnancy and childbirth complications each year or one woman every minute. Almost half the births in developing countries occur without the aid of a skilled birth attendant. Each day HIV / AIDS kill 6000 people. Tuberculosis causes 9 million cases each year and it kills 2 million people a year, 5480 people each day. It is a fact that 1.1 billion people have no access to safe drinking water and 2.4 billion people don't have access to adequate sanitation.

Fighting poverty is vitally important in any campaign to free the world from hunger for two reasons. First, most of those who go hungry do so because they possess less or no land, land productivity is low, or they are unemployed for most part of the year, or they suffer from diseases, live as squalors, or possess less longevity. They are hungry because they do not possess purchasing power to purchase even the subsidized food-grains. Each poor has borrowed beyond his capacity. The unscrupulous moneylenders or influential person of his locality has grabbed his landed property illegally. A poor man sells manual labor to maintain the family members. The poor are illiterate and untrained. They live in low-income rural areas of the world; the hungry people are also found in slum areas of the sub-Saharan Africa, South Asia, and Latin American towns.

Poverty has caused migration of people to towns and cities within or outside the country with or without Passport or Visa for search of employment. The second main reason for stressing the significance of poverty studies is its impact on the society, state, country and the world. Each individual needs peace, security, food, recreation, and pleasure and is satisfied with own religion. However, our beautiful world is facing many challenges each day. On any given day, twenty or more armed conflicts are being fought around the world mostly in poor countries. On the other, the rich countries invest millions of dollars for defense research and have produced huge quantities of arsenals to destroy the entire world within few minutes.

Reduction of poverty is possible through mutual understanding, faith, cooperation, partnership, pro-poor policies and direct assistance to the poor. As long as the low-income countries depend upon the high-income countries for assistance for poverty reduction, unnecessary programs would be imposed on the poor countries. Then it becomes a trade, a burden and a problem for poverty reduction. It is possible that we can reduce the number of poor people; reduce severity of poverty, feed the hungry and increase life expectancies of the poor and can achieve world peace.

Chapter I

POVERTY – A CHALLENGE

I sit on a man's back, choking him and making him carrying me and yet assure myself and others that I am sorry for him and wish to lighten his load by all possible means except by getting off his back. - -Leo Tolstoy

Poverty is sin. Poverty is pain. Poverty is punishment. Poverty is disease. Poverty chokes the voice of poor. Poverty compels a mother to sell her son. Poverty forces a patient to perish without medicine. Poverty increases diseased, hungry and pessimistic squalors. Poverty increases under-five mortality, child labor, school dropouts, early marriages and health hazards. Poverty increases the risk of insecurity, inequality and exclusion. Poverty of women causes human trafficking and discrimination. Poverty breeds poverty and converts this beautiful world into a land of misery, distrust and violence. Poverty is darkness, deprivation and destitution.

The poor are people who may have lost their land, or their job or the support of other family members through death or illness. Poor people may have inherited their parents' poverty perhaps because they belong to a particular caste or tribe. Poverty is not about income alone. Social, political and even seasonal factors affect happiness of people from time to time. Some poor people particularly women and children are more vulnerable to sufferings. The poor are numerous in areas where the land is less productive; drinking water is scarce; communications are poor or where certain castes or tribes predominate. The poor migrate from rural areas to urban areas for employment.[1]

The poor people have expressed their assessment on the causes of poverty. These are:

(a) Lack of income and assets to attain basic necessities - food, shelter, clothing and acceptable levels of health and education
(b) Sense of voiceless and powerlessness in the institutions of state and society
(c) Vulnerability to adverse shocks, linked to an inability to cope with them.[2]

Dr. Malcolm S. Adiseshiah[3] has defined "poverty as deprivation". Deprivation has four essential features.
First, it is deprivation of the basic necessities of life - food, clothing and housing from which all other accompanying deprivations flow - educational and intellectual deprivations, cultural and moral deprivation, in what anthropologists have come to call the culture of poverty.
Second, deprivation means being deprived of what one is entitled to. Everyone is entitled, has a right,

---

[1]An Introduction to DFID INDIA, DFID Draft Report P.2

[2] The World Bank Report 2000-2001 P.34

[3] Dr. Malcolm S. Adiseshiah (1988), "Poverty: its what, why and how", Yojana, 32 (1 & 2), Government of India, New Delhi P.15

and to a decent standard of living, and deprivation negates this entitlement and right.

Third, there are various degrees of deprivation...

Fourth, deprivation involves its antinomy, which is abundance. That is, many are deprived because some have abundance; many are denied their entitlements because some have more than their entitlements.

The dictionary meaning of poverty is: 'state of being poor, existing in too small amounts, and state of being inferior'. Hence, it is necessary to search for that shrinking world where people suffer from hunger, malnutrition, disease, illiteracy, and inadequate medical facilities and without shelter. Our aim is to fight against poverty worldwide, which can render world peace, prosperity and development. There exists intra and inter variations in social, economic, geographical, religious, historical and cultural factors amongst countries.

There prevail infightings, insurgency, corruption, hunger and clash among religions in most of the low-income countries. The debt burden of Heavily Indebted Countries continues to grow; these countries pay more in installments than what they receive as grants; and they are placed in debt bondage. The budgetary allocation on education and health care is less than debt servicing in all low-income countries.

There are about 78 countries, which encounter the following problems:

(a) Higher pay and pension of government officials that has crossed the state gross domestic product;
(b) Expenditure on populist measures;
(c) Corruption in project work;
(d) Occurrence of frequent natural calamities;
(e) High cost General elections;

(f) Inaction of planning and monitoring machinery in government departments;
(g) Entry of tainted politicians in administration and
(h) Lethargic jurisprudential procedure

A number of poor countries have abundant natural resources like mines and minerals, oil deposits, forests, rivers, and cultivated land. Now, these countries have plenty of cheap and abundant labour force, technical know-how, and easy credit facility. Yet these countries are unable to utilize the funds for productive purposes. Unless the natural resources are utilized in productive ventures; the output is properly marketed; the low-income countries cannot achieve economic growth. The governments can hire expertise; can make viable projects for progress; can generate surplus funds to repay back the debt and utilize the surplus funds for welfare of the society and people.

Severity of Poverty

The Global Monitoring Report 2009 has explained that even at the MDG halfway point, around 75 million children of primary school age were not in school; 190,000 children under five died every week from preventable disease; 10,000 women died every week from treatable complications of pregnancy; more than 2 million people died from AIDS annually, close to 2 million from tuberculosis, and about 1 million from malaria; around 1 billion people suffered from hunger; about 2 billion people were undernourished; and about half of the developing world lacked access to basic sanitation — grim numbers that would be far lower if the world were on track on the Millennium Development Goals.

Most of the one billion food-insecure people reside in sub-Saharan Africa, Latin America and South Asian countries. These people need food; they are hungry. If immediate steps were not taken up, they would fall prey to untimely deaths through starvation, disease, diarrhea or suicide. There are additional 300 million people, who spend less than US $ 1 per day. They reside in small houses without safe drinking water, without health care and without roads. They have less or no land and are unable to avail schooling facilities for their kids. Additional 1.6 billion of poor people live on less than US $ 2 a day. They can prosper through pro-poor planning, availability of credit, employment opportunities, and peace and security in their locality and in the country.

Natural Resources and Poverty

Ayittey opines that Africa, where most of the world's 41 Heavily Indebted Poor Countries are located, is awash in natural wealth, from diamonds, gold, and oil to arable agricultural land. The continent has abundant natural potential. This potential, however, remains largely unrealized. Citing examples such as Russia, some argued that such resources are more a curse than a blessing, but that arguments do not explain the lack of development capacity. Different countries have become developed through utilization of resources. He makes the important distinction between African people and the leaders of African nations. It is not the African people who squander development opportunities. Too often, it is African leaders, who seize both native wealth and foreign aid, are successful in plunging their countries into war and they plunder their money, through the exploitation of resources like diamonds and stealing massive amounts of foreign aid. Ayittey [4] delineates four institutional pillars that are essential for lasting development in Africa: independent judiciaries, an

---

[4] George Ayittey, *Africa in Chaos* (New York: St. Martin's Press, 1998) and Ayittey, "How the West Compounds Africa's Crises," *Intellectual Capital*, June 29, 2000, located at http://207.87.15.232/issues/Issue 387/item9858.asp, quoted from Denise Froning, ibid.

independent central bank, free media, and neutral armed forces.

Ruchir Sharma[5] explains that historical evidence on the role of natural resources in economic development is terribly mixed. While some of the leading industrialized economies, starting with United States in the nineteenth century and later Australia, Canada, Sweden and Norway, all relied heavily on the export of natural resources to develop their economies, more recent experience suggest that oil riches can wreck havoc on a country's economic and political systems. Oil can be poison for a variety of reasons, ranging from oil-induced sloth to waste and corruption. Countries largely dependent on oil revenue often end up being run by authoritarian regimes that gain their power by controlling oil assets. Money flowing through weak structures leads to perverse outcomes. Only those countries that have strong institutions in place have been able to avoid the resource curse, such as Norway and Botswana of late. The US was able to exploit its natural resources to be held privately and yet reserve the right to intervene and prevent monopolies. Russia's economic fate will really dictate in which the debate over oil tilts.

Joseph E. Stiglitz[6] says abundant natural resources can and should be a blessing not a curse. We know what must be done, but what is missing is the political will to make it so. There is a curious phenomenon that economists call the *resource curse* – so named because, on average, countries with large endowments of natural resources perform worse than countries that are less well endowed. Yet some countries with abundant natural resources do perform

[5] Sharma, Ruchir "When the bountiful is not beautiful", *The Economic Times*, Kolkata, dated August 10, 2004, P4

[6]Stiglitz, Joseph E., "The Resource Curse Revisited", The Economic Times, Kolkata, dated 12.08.2004, P4

better than others, and some had done well. Why is the spell of the resource curse cast so unequally? Thirty years ago, Indonesia and Nigeria – both dependents on oil – had comparable per capita income. Today, Indonesia's per capita income is four times that of Nigeria. A similar pattern holds true in Sierra Leone and Botswana. Both are rich in diamonds. Yet Botswana averaged 8.7 per cent annual economic growth over the past thirty years, while Sierra Leone plunged into civil strife. The failures in the oil-rich Middle East are legion. Economists put forward three reasons for the dismal performance of some richly endowed countries:

First, the prospect of the riches orients official efforts to seizing a larger share of the pie, rather than creating a larger pie. The result of this wealth grab is often war. At other times simple rent–seeking behaviour by officials, aided and abetted by outsiders, is the outcome. It is cheaper to bribe a government to provide resources at below–market prices than to invest and develop an industry. Therefore, it is no surprise that some firms succumb to this temptation.

Second, natural resource prices are volatile, and managing this volatility is hard. Lenders provide money when times are good but want their money back when, say, energy prices plummet. (At the old adage has it, banks only like to lend to those who do not need money). Economic activity is thus even more volatile than commodity prices and much of the gains made in a boom unravel in the bust that follows.

Third, oil and other natural resources, while perhaps a source of wealth do not create jobs by themselves, and unfortunately, they often crowd out other economic sectors. For example, an inflow of oil money often leads to currency appreciation – a phenomenon called the **Dutch Disease.**

He further explains that secret bank account not only supports terrorism, but also facilitates corruption that undermines development. Moreover, oil money helps someone else's economy.

Poverty in India

The general perception is that African countries are the poorest countries and people living in Africa are poor. But the maximum poor people live in India and not in African countries. It is a fact that as many as 26 countries of African continent have 410 million poor people.

The 'Oxford Poverty and Human Development' organization (with assistance of the UNDP) has estimated that 421 million of poor people live in eight Indian states. These states are: Orissa, Bihar, Chhattisgarh, Jharkhand, Madhya Pradesh, Rajasthan, Uttar Pradesh, and West Bengal.

If we consider the total number of poor people in all the 30 states and union territories of India, it would rank the poorest country in the world. Yet the government is satisfied with the GDP growth of the country, which is pegged to 9 percent per annum. India is both the biggest democracy and the highest loaned country in the world. The hungry people face more health hazards. The country has achieved excellence in scientific achievement and has created a number of millionaires and billionaires. So both the policy for poverty alleviations is being wrongly operated and the corruption in administration has overpowered the planning and implementing agencies.

Thousands of poor farmers in India have committed suicide over the past decade as changes in India's agricultural policy set off a widening spiral of debt and despair. The farmer suicides became rampant since 1997.

Vandana Shiva tells that the corporate seed control had its direct impact on indebtedness of the farmers.

The globalization process in agriculture works with farming communities across India, which ceded control of the seed supply to the corporate chemical industry -- leading to increased production costs for the struggling farmers -- as well as falling food prices in a global agricultural economy. An estimated 200,000 farmers have taken their own lives in India over the past 13 years, according to Indian government statistics.[7]

Every third hungry person in the world is an Indian and every third Indian (340 million) goes to bed hungry.

The Arjun Sengupta Committee report says that 836 million Indians live on less than 20 INR per day. The National Sample Survey Organization estimated that nearly 19 per cent of Indian rural population lived on less than 12 INR per day. But the leaders in the Indian Parliament argue for **'Growth Mirage', 'Resurgent India' and 'Shining India**' slogans.

The fact is the World Bank has misled the country with 'Structural Adjustment Policy' and heavy loan for 'Infrastructure Development' of village roads. The excess loan has made the leaders, bureaucrats, businessmen, and even the general public susceptible for corruption. The sixth plan pay scales, supply of cheap rice, and wheat at subsided rate, and anti-poverty programs have maximized corruption, inequality, and spread of Maoism in the country. Purchase of voters in general elections through free food, drinks and cash has made democracy at a crossroad. Poverty has caused the growth of Maoists and Naxalites in about one-third of total geographical areas in the country. The peace loving country is fast

---

[7]Vandana Shiva told CNN's Christiane Amanpour.

moving toward a 'No Peace' country. Unless poverty is rooted out, all the southeast countries would become terror countries. The result is: there is a rise of 'no work culture' and increase of decisive forces in the country. Corruption is a way of life in the country. Justice is a utopian thought in India.

Poverty in Ethiopia

According to the United Nations Human Development Index, Ethiopia and its 75 million residents sit almost at the bottom of a ranking that measures standards of living, education levels, and life expectancy. Out of 208 countries, Ethiopia[8] received an HDI ranking of 202 in 2006. What does poverty look like in this Horn of Africa country? Agriculture is by far the largest activity, providing 80 percent of Ethiopia's employment and contributing 42 percent to the country's gross domestic product. Yet, coffee farmers are among some of the country's poorest people, earning little for their efforts while shouldering price fluctuations that leave them struggling to feed their families. Poverty also plagues countless herders, many of whom live in the more arid zones where irregular weather wreaks havoc on their pastureland and water sources. Almost 81 percent of Ethiopia's people live on less than $2 a day. That in turn limits their access to a whole range of necessities and critical services such as clean water and health care. The UN's Human Development Report notes that in 2002, 78 percent of the population did not have sustainable access to an improved source of water. In 2006, one of the consequences of lack of clean water hit home: an outbreak of acute watery diarrhea left 279 Ethiopians dead and sickened 28,880 others. Dirty water carries the microorganism that can cause that illness.

---

[8] CIA–the World Fact Book –Ethiopia / Www. Harvardhumanaitarian.org / Www Oxfam America Org

Only 2.6 percent of Ethiopia's gross domestic product (GDP) was spent on public health. Between 1990 and 2004, the country had just three doctors for very 100,000 people. Women suffer particularly from this shortage, delivering the vast majority of their babies without the benefit of medical care. Between 1992 and 2003, skilled health providers attended only 6 percent of births. The consequences of this broad neglect are devastating. The average life expectancy for an Ethiopian is just shy of 48 years. When natural disasters repeatedly strike a vulnerable population, robbing people of their sources of food and income and destroying their homes, the setbacks can be long-term and for some people, insurmountable. They quickly exhaust whatever savings they may have had and sap to depletion the support of family and friends, who may well be in equally hard straights. In any given year, 5 million Ethiopians face chronic food shortages and depend on aid to survive. Shortages of the basics—food, water, and pastureland—can spark conflict. Ethiopia has witnessed bursts of violence this year, too, triggered by politicized relationships among herders in the Borena and Guji zones and a dispute over land—so critical in a harsh environment where people need every patch of pasture and pocket of water to survive. The conflict forced the displacement of more than 90,000 people.

Solutions to all of this are challenging, particularly in a country where half the GDP is based on agriculture—much of it relying on increasingly erratic rainfall and poor cultivation practices. Compounding Ethiopia's economic problems is the country's system of land tenure by which the government owns the land and leases it to tenants. The system discourages entrepreneurial enterprise because the land can't be used as collateral for loans. Among the programs, Oxfam works on peace building, drought management and strengthening of livelihoods.

Causes of Poverty

Cohen and Soto have attempted to explain why single factor explanations of the poverty of nations were usually found to be unsatisfactory. Poor countries outside Africa, for instance, have an income per head, which stands at about one-third of the rich countries per head. Yet each of the three items of the Solow model, namely human capital, physical capital (appropriate weighted) and total factor productivity, are each equal to about 70 per cent of the corresponding levels of the rich countries. But 70 per cent to the power of three is 35 per cent. Multiplying small or relatively benign handicaps can yield dramatic effects on a country's income. The paper then moves on to explain each of the three items. It argues that the ***Lucas paradox*** on why capital is scarce can readily be solved. Once market prices rather than PPP prices are used to assess the return to capital mobility, and on the same ground it argues that PPP calculation bias downwards the TFP of poor countries. It then argues that human capital is lower in poor countries because of the fact that the returns to human capital are non-concave, so that the marginal propensity to turn one additional year of life expectancy into higher education is lower in poor countries than in the rich. The message of hope is that "transpiration" strategies a la Singapore may work elsewhere.[9]

There are a number of factors that result in poverty and results of poverty further strengthens the intensity of poverty. These are:

(a) Indebtedness

---

[9]Cohen, Daniel and Soto Marcelo, "Why are Poor Countries Poor?", A Message of Hope which involves the Resolution of a Becker / Lucas Paradox", CEPR ***Discussion Paper***, Center for Economic Policy Research, September 2002

(b) Unemployment of peasants for most of the days in a year
(c) Absence of remunerative prices for cereals and other agricultural produce
(d) Poor repaying capacity of loaned farmers
(e) Natural calamities
(f) Declining cottage industries
(g) Illiteracy
(h) Landless peasants and share croppers
(i) Absence of regulated markets
(j) Suicides by farmers
(k) Unproductive expenses in social functions

Poverty grows each year. So the World Summit for Social Development (1995) and the General Assembly of United Nations made three main commitments:

(a) To estimate overall and extreme income poverty;
(b) To set "time-bound goals and targets" for substantial reduction of overall poverty and the eradication of extreme poverty; and
(c) To implement national anti-poverty plans to reach their targets.

Hence, a new global strategy clearly needs to be mounted with more resources, a sharper focus and a stronger commitment. The international community has to squarely face the task of reforming the global enabling environment to accelerate poverty reduction. Developing countries, weighed down by external debt, starved of private capital and technology, blocked from rich country markets and faced with declining official development assistance cannot be expected to go into battle with reinforcements. They are being encouraged to launch a full-scale campaign against poverty while their budgets are being put on a **"poverty diet"**.[10]

---

[10]UNDP poverty Report 2000, chapter 1 P.2

Successful development is possible when the following conditions are fulfilled. These are:

(a) An improvement in living standards and access to all basic needs such that a person has enough food, water, shelter, clothing, health, education, etc;
(b) A stable political, social and economic environment, with associated political, social and economic freedoms, such as (though not limited to) equitable ownership of land and property;
(c) The ability to make free and informed choices that are not coerced;
(d) Be able to participate in a democratic environment with the ability to have a say in one's own future;
(e) To have the full potential for what the United Nations calls Human Development:

At a poverty line of $1.25 a day, the revised estimates find

(a) 1.4 billion people live at this poverty line or below
(b) This is more than the previous estimate of 984 million with the older measure of a $1 a day in 2004
(c) In 1981, the estimated number of poor was also revised upward, from 1.5 billion to 1.9 billion
(d) The World Bank notes "the incidence of poverty in the world is higher than past estimates have suggested. The main reason is that (previous data) had implicitly underestimated the cost of living in most developing countries."
(e) The data also does not reflect the recent global food crisis and rising cost of energy, which is feared will bring another 100 million into poverty.

(f) Accounting for the increased population between 1981 and 2005, the poverty rate has, however, fallen by about 25 percent.
(g) While this at least sounds encouraging, it masks regional variations, and perhaps most glaringly the impact of China:
(h) China's poverty rate fell from 85 percent to only 15.9 percent, or by over 600 million people.[11]

Conclusion:

The anti-poverty plans and programs should focus on food security and employment opportunities. The income measurement of poverty should not be compared among the developed, developing and transition countries before 2015. The classification of poverty and poverty mapping will assist the planners for reduction of poverty in different countries and pave the way for peace, prosperity and development.

A poor man is income-poor and he needs assistance to cross over the poverty line with humanitarian approach. Poverty has posed a challenge to the World Organizations and the governments of all the countries. All the institutions, planners, economists and general public are worried to solve the problem of poverty. It has caused a threat to the human civilization in the 21st century.

We need to reduce poverty in all the countries at the quickest possible time to establish peace everywhere. It is possible and achievable. Let us hope that our beautiful world is free from boundary disputes, insecurity, tensions, hunger, terrorism, irreligious attitudes, social injustice and inhumanity. The present civilization must be strengthened to guarantee food security and peace to all.

[11]Anup Shah, "Poverty around the World", 2011

Chapter-II

RESEARCH STUDIES ON POVERTY

There is enough in this world to meet at every individual need but there can never be enough to meet even a single individual greed.

-Mahatma M K Gandhi

A number of economists, planners, sociologists, anthropologists, statisticians, funding institutions, donor countries and highly indebted poverty countries, social workers and non-government organizations have undertaken research studies to identify the factors influencing occurrence of poverty in different communities, regions and countries. They have also suggested the ways to alleviate poverty in a scheduled time frame. But the world leaders who gathered in Monterrey (Mexico) in March 2002 to discuss regarding "how to fight poverty" were confused to find out the best ways for fulfilling the targets. In their opinion, the vast majority of people living in Africa, Latin America, Central Asia and West

Asia are no better off to-day than they were in 1989, when the fall of the Berlin Wall allowed capitalism to spread world-wide at a rapid rate. Globalization or the fast-paced growth of trade and cross border investment has done far less to raise the incomes of the world's poorest people. The economic integration has failed because of trade barriers imposed by developed countries. Moreover, annual private capital flows to the developing world fell from $ 300 billion in 1997 to just over half that level in 2001. The stock and bond markets showed reverse after the Asian financial crisis of 1997, drawing more money out of developing countries than they put in. Corporate foreign investments also declined after 1997.

George Soros observes that the trend of globalisation is that the surplus capital of the periphery countries is moving to the centre, which is the United States America. He suggests that an international pool of US$27 billion may be created to finance development program of the poor countries.[12]

Aiyar reports that interest and amortisation (repayment of principal) of old aid have consistently exceeded fresh inflows in India since 1995-96, with the result that the dollar flow has turned negative. In most of the countries this would be regarded as a disaster.[13]

So the question arises whether we are moving in the right direction? Why more than 1.2 billion people are in extreme consumption poverty? Why south Asia or sub-Saharan Africa is still in absolute poverty? What

---

[12]George Soros (2002), "Globalization Hasn't Done Much for World's Poor", UN Poverty meet, Times of India (New Delhi), Dt. 22.03.2002 P.13

[13]Aiyar, S.S.A (2002), "Who needs Foreign Aid from the World Bank and IMF Any Way", Sunday Times, of India (New Delhi), Vol. X (13), March 31, 2002 P.15

has been done to fulfill the commitments of Social Summit in Copenhagen (1995) and General Assembly of the United Nations (2000)? Why hunger continues to be a global tragedy? Why one billion people are still acutely malnourished? Could the World Bank, the United Nations Development Program, the OECD Countries and other funding institutions are able to reduce poverty by 50 percent within the target year 2015?

In this chapter, we put forward the research findings of eminent scholars, institutions, Universities, research organizations and countries for further analyses and conclusions. If the government accepts some of the suggestions and includes the proposals in government policies and programs and provide budgetary support, poverty would be minimized, which can strengthen the world peace movement.

The Government

The developing countries where squalors reside en-mass, the Government should appraise relevant trade off in the context of a poverty alleviation program. In the matter of rising public deficits and shrinking public resources, geographical targeting, poverty mapping, investment in agricultural research and strengthening the growth potentials of the country must be emphasized. The central planning process must aim at increasing the mobilization of domestic savings, and use of domestic and foreign resources. The developing countries should provide better market infrastructure for the poor farmers to dispose off their saleable surplus. The Government should provide adequate support for increasing livelihoods, food security and societal welfare. The first step of the ruling elite must be to create interest in the welfare of the poor people.

We like to highlight the suggestions of the researchers rather than to abridge their entire study/studies. Much money has been spent to study the causes of poverty and solution thereof. The past research experience will be the guiding factor in future planning for poverty alleviation programs.

Khanna (1989)[14] has observed that Government of India introduced a couple of poverty alleviation and rural employment programs for electoral ambitions of the ruling party. The rise of prices of essential commodities and inflation caused harm to the poorest of the poor.

Tanzi and Chu (1989) have reported that Latin America could restore fiscal discipline and stabilization for resumption of economic growth. But they apprehended that poverty alleviation in Latin America was not likely to be achieved in near future. They suggested that Government policy should promote a more equitable distribution of income and inferred that high domestic inflation leads to high social costs.[15]

Levy Santiago (1991) suggested that Mexico could fight with poverty through (a) compilation of research on poverty indices, nutrition, fertility, incentives and related topics for the design of poverty alleviation programs. The government should undertake (b) measuring the magnitude and regional composition of extreme poverty; and (c) by making a concrete policy proposal to deal with extreme poverty.[16]

---

[14] Khanna,Kailash C," Budget 1989/90: Fiscal Jugging? India", ***Bulletin for International Fiscal Documentation***; 43(6), June 1989, pp. 277-79.

[15]Tanzi,Vito and Chu,Keyoung, "Fiscal policy for stable and Equitable Growth in Latin America," ***International Monetary Fund Working Paper***: WP/89/93, November 1989, pages 41.

[16] Levy Santiago, " La Poborezaextrema on Mexico : UnaPropuesta de political (with English Summary)", ***Studios- Economics*** : 6 (1), Jan- June 1991 pp. 47-89

Echeverri (1992) contends that rigid social hierarchies privileged the position of local elite and provided them with the capacity to distort implementation or generate powerful opposition to each of the rural antipoverty programs. They cause the programs to face the challenge of finding the means to deliver program benefits to the poor while circumventing these obstacles.[17]

Cornelius (1995) has suggested that better targeting of the poor would generate a significant reduction in the incidence of poverty.[18]

Mitchell (1995)[19] has advocated that the aims of transfer policy, and the instrument used to affect these policies, vary significantly across countries. Moreover, within each country there are tensions between effective goals (minimizing poverty and inequality) and efficiency goals (maximizing the impact of given levels of resources). This paper develops a series of measures, which capture these cross-national differences in order to examine whether there are trade-offs between efficiency and effectiveness of goals, and whether these patterns can be related to a wider understanding of different welfare state regimes. The findings suggest that there is a strong trade-off between efficiency and effectiveness, when considered in relation to the

---

[17] Echeverri Gent, John, "Public Participation and Poverty Alleviation: The Experience of Reform Communists in India's West Bengal", ***World Development***; 20(10), October 1992, pp. 1401-22.

[18] Cornelius, Peter k, "Cash Benefits and poverty Alleviation in an Economy in Transition: The Cash of Lithuania", ***Comparative Economic Studies***; 37(2), summer 1995, pp. 49-69.

[19] Mitchell, Deborah, "Is There a Trade-off between the Efficiency and Effectiveness Goals of income Transfer Programs?" ***Journal of Income Distribution, 5*** (1), 1995 pp.111- 35

income inequality goal, while the evidence is mixed in relation to the poverty alleviation goal.

Chand and Shomme (1995) studied the simulation effect of poverty alleviation and financial programming which could reduce the adverse effects on poverty. This could improve the balance of payments but initially there would be higher fiscal deficit and inflation.[20]

Killick (1995) has opined that in the developing countries, the principal responsibility for achieving anti-poverty objectives must lie with national governments but they do not always display much concern with the poor. However, the international financial institutions must share the responsibility and could do more to design structural adjustment programs within a cost-minimizing framework. The principal policy tasks are to formulate a long term anti -poverty strategy and ensure that adjustment policies are consistent with that, without detracting from the imperative of adapting the economy to changing circumstances.[21]

Liu et al (1996) [22] have suggested that trade liberalization, currency devaluation, tax reform and target income support can achieve greater economic efficiency and alleviate poverty without incurring sizeable and external debts in Philippines.

---

[20] Liu,Aying; Yao,Shujie and Greener,Robert, "A CGE Model of Agricultural Policy Reform in the Philippines", ***Journal of Agricultural Economics***; 47(1), January 1996, pages 18-27

[21]Killick, Tony (1995),, "Structural Adjustment and Poverty Alleviation", ***Development and Change***; 26(2), April 1995, pp. 305-331.

[22] Liu,Aying, Yao,Shujie and Greener,Robert,"A CGE Model of Agricultural Policy Reform in the Philippines", ***Journal of Agricultural Economics***; 47(1), January 1996, pp. 18-27.

Baker (1997) analyzed the characteristics and causes of poverty in fifteen Caribbean countries and reviewed various poverty alleviation efforts, including the different coping mechanisms that many households have adopted. On the basis of analysis, he has presented recommendations on how policies and programs could be designed to be more effective in reducing poverty. [23]

Chilowa (1998)[24] has examined the donor-supported structural adjustment programs in Malawi and has observed that these programs have not impacted favorably on livelihoods, food security and the general welfare of the poor. This resulted from the prescription of wrong policy packages and limited attention to poverty alleviation policies. He has emphasized the policies should address towards production constraints and non-economic barriers to broad-based economic growth. The state should manipulate agricultural produce marketing and agricultural prices to improve the food security situation at the household level.

Rao et al (1998) have observed that inter governmental fiscal arrangements have played an important role in ameliorating poverty in many countries. In their opinion, successful poverty alleviation generally requires both capacity improving and safety net policies, and both types of policies may, to some extent, be implemented through, or affected by, inter governmental transfers. The general transfers enable all provinces to provide a given basket of public services at a given tax price by offsetting their revenue and cost disabilities. The

[23] . Discussion paper No. 366, Washington, D.C., World Bank pp. XXI, 206

[24] Chilowa, Wycliffe, (1998),"The Impact of Agricultural Liberalization on food security in Malawi", Food ***Policy***; 23(6), December 1998, pp. 553-569

specific transfers ensure the minimum levels of those public services to the poor throughout the country.[25]

Alam (1999) has reported that Bangladesh has successfully implemented structural adjustment measures to improve the efficiency of the economy and strengthen the growth potential of the country. The main objectives of the structural adjustment programs have been to sustain a high rate of growth of GDP and contain inflation while improving the viability of the balance of payments and making progress in regard to poverty alleviation. The structural adjustment program achieved higher and more efficient investment, increased the mobilization of domestic savings, and improved the utilization of external assistance and controlled fiscal and current account deficits.[26]

Weyland (1999) has explained that Chile could maintain economic stability through cautious economic policies of the Aylwin and Frei administrations. The administration maintained economic stability, fueled sustained growth and coped with inflows of foreign capital. Chile achieved successes in macro-economic policy, export development and poverty alleviation but faced challenges in high social inequality and difficulties in financial globalization.[27]

---

[25]Rao et al, (1999), " Fiscal Decentralization and Poverty Alleviation in a Transitional Economy: The Case of Viet Nam", ***Asian Economic Journal***, 12 (4), Dec. 1998, pp. 353-78

[26]Alam, Rouful (1999), "Impact of structural Adjustment and Stabilization Programme on Bangladesh", ***Journal of Economic Cooperation among Islamic Countries***; 20(2), April 1999, pp. 89-96

[27]. Weyland, Kurt TI (1999), "Economic Policy in Chile's New Democracy", ***Journal of Inter American Studies and World Affairs***; 41(3), fall 1999, pp. 67-96

Svensson (1999)[28] has concluded that the long-run growth impact of aid is conditional on the degree of political and civil liberties of the recipient country. Aid has a positive impact on democratic countries otherwise foreign aid is utilized to satisfy the Government's own non-productive goals. He laments that on average, aid is not channeled to more democratic countries, even though there are large cross-country differences between major donors.

Dashwood (1999) has expressed that anti-poverty programs in Zimbabwe, introduced since 1991, have either proved inadequate or failed completely for lack of interest on the part of ruling elite and unresponsive rich people.[29]

Bigman and Fofack (2000) have strongly opined that geographical targeting and detailed poverty maps are essential for poverty alleviation programs.[30]

Bardhan and Mukherjee (1998) have identified that local elites, local corruption, lack of accountability and limited ability to monitor the anti-poverty programs by the Government restrict the trade-off in poverty alleviation programs.[31]

---

[28]Svensson, Jakob, "Aid, Growth and Democracy", ***Economics and Politics***; 11(3), November 1999, pp. 275-297.

[29] Dashwood, Hevian S, Social Welfarism, "Poverty Alleviation and Political Stability in Zimbabwe", ***Canadian Journal of Development Studies***; 20(3), 1999, pp. 567-592.

[30] Bigman, David and Fofack Hippolyte, "Geographical Targeting for poverty Alleviation: An Introduction to the special Issue", ***World Bank Economic Review***; 14(1), January 2000, pp. 129-145.

[31] Bardhan, Pranab and Mookharjee, Dilip, "Expenditure Decentralization and the delivery of public services in Developing countries", University of California, Berkeley,

Micro-Credit

Poor families need credit. Earlier they were debarred of credit from banks because of formalities of the banks like surety bonds, collateral security, credit worthiness etc. Micro-finance is potential bell weather for women's empowerment. In India, a number of self-help groups (SHG) were created in the 1980s to provide credit facilities to the poor especially for women. Now international donor agencies like Ford Foundation, United Nations Development Fund, and Swiss Agency for Development and Cooperation (SDC) have extended liberal grants to SHGs as seed money. Moreover, the institutions like National Bank for Rural Development (NABARD) and Small Industries Development Bank of India (SIDBI) have increased their lending activities to SHGs in India. However, the lending rates of SHGs are not cheap, and they charge up to 30 per cent to individual borrowers.

Grameen Banks of Bangladesh have made remarkable progress in micro-finance. But it relied on subsidies for 17 years before becoming financially viable. The Self-Employed Women's Association (SEWA) of Ahmadabad (India) offers low-interest micro-loans and raises the wages, education and standard of living of the women; it serves.

In the world arena, RESULTS Educational Fund -an U.S. based non-governmental organization (NGO) held a three-day micro-credit summit in Washington, DC on February 2-4, 1997. The World Bank, IFAD, Citicorp, Chase Manhattan and American Express supported the summit. The summit started a global campaign to finance 100 million of the world's poorest families by 2005 for self-employment. The

---

Centre for International and Development Economics Research (CIDER) ***Working Paper***: C98/104, December 1998, pages 55.

World Bank launched its own micro-lending program through "Consultative Group to Assist the Poorest" (CGAP) for the globe's poorest citizens, particularly women in 2001. But other economists have opined that these entities may simply lend legitimacy and greater financial clout to an exploitative form of organized money lending.

Wahid[32] (1994) has reported that the Grameen (rural) Bank of Bangladesh has adopted a mechanism under which credit can be provided to the poorest of the poor on a group liability basis instead of any collateral. The recovery rate is very high and credit program has significantly improved the socio-economic conditions of the borrowers. But the Grameen (rural) Bank is not yet a viable institution.

Rahman (1996) has reported that Grameen (rural) Bank of Bangladesh's success story is currently imparting necessary technical assistance in terms of field training through dialogue programs, monitoring and evaluation services etc. to the replicates.[33]

Ismail and Ahmad (1997)[34] have reported that the financing of micro-enterprises (such as pawnshop loans) in small amounts and with low risk is popular among the marginal groups in Malaysia.

Khandker (1998) has suggested that experiences of micro-finance programs in Bangladesh may be

---

[32] Wahid, Abu N. M,"The Grameen Bank and Poverty Alleviation in Bangladesh: Theory, Evidence and Limitations", ***American Journal of Economics and Sociology***; 53(1), January 1994, pp. 1-15.

[33] Rahman, A., "Rural Development from Below: Lessons Learned from Grameen Bank Experience in Bangladesh", ***Journal of Socio Economics***, 25(2), 1996, pp. 189-223

[34] Ismail, Abdul Ghafar and Ahmad, Nor Zamias,"Pawnshop as an Instrument of Micro enterprise Credit in Malaysia", ***International Journal of Social Economics***; 24(11), 1997, pp. 1343-52

replicated in other countries and the limitations of micro-finance be noted for final conclusion.[35]

Karim and Osada (1998) have found that about one-third of Grameen Bank members were already dropped by their sixth year of membership. It seems that the dropouts neither rose out of poverty nor economically graduated leaving the ultimate objective of poverty alleviation in question. It was also found that dropouts had adversely affected the profits of the program. They have suggested that the provision of childcare, expansion of marketing facilities, managerial training, and the creation of full or part time jobs within the program may reduce the number of dropouts.[36]

Evans et al (1999) undertook a population survey of over 24,000 households in Bangladesh to study the impact of micro-credit schemes as a means of poverty alleviation. The study revealed that although three-quarters were eligible for micro-credit, less than one-quarter participated. The participation rate in micro-credit is higher among poorer households. The study identifies lack of female education, small household size and landlessness as risk factor for non-participation.[37]

Goheer (1999) has analyzed the bleak picture of stagnant economic growth in Pakistan in the 1990s,

---

[35] Khandker, Shahidur R, "Fighting poverty with micro credit: Experience in Bangladesh", Oxford and New York: ***Oxford University Press for the World Bank***, 1998, pages xii, 228.

[36]Karim, M. Rezaul and Osada, Mitsu, "Dropping Out: An Emerging Factor in the Success of Micro credit-Based Poverty Alleviation Programs", Developing ***Economies***; 36(3), September 1998, pp. 257-288.

[37]Evans, Timothy G. et al, "Demystifying No participation in Micro credit: A Population-Based Analysis", ***World Development***; 27(2), February 1999, pp. 419-430.

raising poverty levels and chronic plight of womenfolk in the society. A situation analysis of the role of formal and informal finance in the pursuit of poverty alleviation shows the bias of the formal finance towards the rich. It also reveals that major credit demand of the rural poor is being met by expensive and unsteady informal sector. Inability of the poor to serve collateral has been identified as a major hurdle in reaching the poor. He has observed that Grameen Bank (of Bangladesh) model is propagated to make a case for an effective and sustainable institutional mechanism of combating gender focused poverty in Pakistan.[38]

Rajasekhar[39] (2000) opines that there is widely held beliefs that micro-finance is a key strategy for poverty alleviation and women's empowerment. Government officials, donors and NGOs link micro-finance to poverty alleviation and women's empowerment directly. Access to credit is seen as vital to women's ability to earn an income, which, in turn, is seen as central to their wider status and autonomy. He has concluded that micro-finance programs do not automatically lead to poverty alleviation and women's empowerment on the basis of his studies of two NGOs in Kerala (India). He has identified several problems that NGOs face during micro-finance programs.

Fujita (2000) undertook intensive economic survey in two villages in Bangladesh. Major findings include: Informal credit flows basically from the poor to the

---

[38] Goheer, Nabeel A., "Poverty in Pakistan: Increasing Incidence, Chronic Gender Preponderance, and the Plausibility of Grameen-Type Intermediation", ***Pakistan Development Review***; 38(4), winter 1999, pp. 873-893.

[39] Rajasekhar, D., "Micro-finance Programmes and Women's Empowerment: A Study of Two NGOs from Kerala", *Journal* ***of Social and Economic Development***; 3(1), Jan.-June 2000, pp. 76-94.

rich mainly in the form of long-term credit with land mortgaging; Trickle down effects of the Green Revolution and the development of off-farm job opportunities generate savings among the poor, which are circulated in informal financial channels. The Grameen Bank provided "advancements for future savings" among the poor and thus basically succeeded in poverty alleviation by encouraging hard work resulting in saving, not by promoting micro-enterprises per se. He has concluded that the Grameen Bank is basically effective for poor people who have fairly regular non-farm income sources; but it is not effective in helping the abject poor or economically backward rural areas.[40]

Rankin (2001) has addressed the emergence of micro-credit programs as a preferred strategy for poverty alleviation worldwide. The author has praised the Government of Nepal, as micro-credit program constitutes social citizenship and women's needs in a manner consistent with neo-liberalism. Drawing on ethnographic research, the paper also considers the progressive and regressive possibilities in the articulation of such constructed subjectivity with local cultural ideologies and social processes.[41]

In short, micro-credit program has assumed greater importance in all the developing countries of the world for the purpose of poverty alleviation and women's empowerment. Researchers have also suggested that this program should aim at or include childcare, female education, expansion of marketing

---

[40] Fujita, Koichi, "Credit Flowing from the Poor to the Rich: The Financial Market and the Role of the Grameen Bank in Rural Bangladesh", ***Developing Economies***; 38(3), September 2000, pp. 343-373.

[41] Rankin, Katharine N, "Governing Development: Neo-liberalism, Microcredit, and Rational Economic Woman" ***Economy and Society***; 30(1), February 2001, pages 18-37.

facilities, managerial training, low interest rate and promotion of micro-enterprise for checking dropouts. The Grameen (rural) Bank of Bangladesh is the beginning but not an end itself.

Employment Generation

Haggblade et al (1989) [42] have observed that agricultural growth, through a network of consumption and production linkages; can generate sizable income and employment multipliers in the rural non-farm economy. In Asia, those linkages have proven beneficial for poverty alleviation as well as national economic growth.

Ravallion (1991) has suggested that one way to reach the poor more effectively is to build incentives for self-selection for poverty alleviation scheme. Labor-intensive rural public works projects have the potentiality to reach and protect the poor, as well as to create and maintain rural infrastructure. The limited evidence for South Asia suggests that few non-poor persons want to participate, so that both direct and indirect transfer and stabilization benefits to the poor can be sizable. These benefits can, however, be rapidly dissipated by a badly conceived and executed projects; the details of how projects are selected, designed, and financed are crucial to success in both the short and long run.[43]

Von-Braun et al (1992) have reported that during structural adjustment, capital costs increased relative to labor costs, which favored labor-intensive technology in 13 African countries. They have opined

---

[42] Haggblade, Steven, Hazell, Peter and Brown, James "Farm-Non-farm Linkages in Rural Sub-Saharan Africa", *World* ***Development***; 17(8), August 1989, pp. 1173-1201

[43] Ravallion, Martin, "Reaching the Rural Poor through Public Employment: Arguments, Evidence, and Lessons from South Asia", ***World Bank Research Observer***; 6(2), July 1991, pp. 153-175.

that food insecurity; lack of employment, environmental degradation and poor infrastructure can be addressed simultaneously through labor-intensive employment programs. Moreover, these programs will ensure poverty alleviation and prevent famine. They have concluded that poverty works must be integrated into national planning, where both local government and the private sector can play key roles.[44]

Gaude and Watzlawick (1992)[45] have also supported labor-intensive investment policies. They have emphasized for design and implementation of small-scale, needs-oriented basic infrastructures.

The United Nations Centre for Human Settlements (Habitat) and ILO (1995) identified the possibilities of employment generation and poverty alleviation in poor communities through shelter, infrastructure and services provision.[46]

Deepak Lal (1995)[47] has advocated that the minimum wage is an instrument for poverty alleviation. This minimum wage is a well–intentioned policy, though

---

[44] Von-Braun, Joachim; Teklu, -Tesfaye; Webb, -Patrick, "Labour-Intensive Public Works for food security in Africa: Past Experience and Future Potential", ***International Labour Review***; 131(1), 1992, pp. 19-33.

[45]Gaude, J. and Watzlawick, H., "Employment Creation and Poverty Alleviation through Labour-Intensive Public Works in Least Developed Countries", ***International Labour Review***; 131(1), 1992, pp. 3-18.

[46]United Nations Centre for Human Settlements- (Habitat), International Labour Office, "Shelter provision and employment generation", ***Nairobi: United Nations Centre for Human Settlements (Habitat)***; Geneva and Washington, D.C.: International Labour Office, 1995, pages xxii, 249.

[47] Lal, Deepak, "The Minimum Wage", ***University of California***, Los Angeles, Department of Economics Working Paper: 723, January 1995, pages 24.

inefficient and inexpert, interference with the mechanisms of supply and demand still stands.

Malik (1996) has observed that informal sector plays an important role in urban poverty alleviation through employment creation and income generation. He has further indicated that the role of informal market in poverty alleviation can be enhanced, if the productivity and earnings of its participants are increased.[48]

Arena and Aneka (1998) have described the socio-economic conditions of return migrant women in the informal labor markets – both farm and non-farm in the Anambra State of Nigeria. Human capital and demographic characteristics play major roles in determining access to farm and non-farm sectors.[49]

Mallick et al (1995)[50] observed that retail trade of rice, vegetables, fruits, poultry birds and fish increases off-farm income and creates employment opportunities both in rural and urban markets in Angul district (Orissa) India. Poverty alleviation is possible through retail trade with low investment, which could be available through micro-credit facilities. Women empowerment is also possible through retail trade. The poor can create self-employment opportunities and earn his/her livelihood with dignity.

---

[48] Malik, Muhammad Hussain, "Urban Poverty Alleviation through Development of the Informal Sector" ***Asia Pacific Development Journal***; 3(2), December 1996, pp. 31-48

[49] Arene, C. J. and Aneke, G. C., "The Position of Return Migrant Women in the Informal Farm and Non-farm Labour Markets in Nigeria", ***Indian Journal of Labour Economics***; 41(1), Jan.-March 1998, pages 119-124

[50] Mallick, SC, R.K. Samal and Pritam Mallick, "Economics of Retailing of Agricultural Commodities in Orissa", Ind. Jour Agril. Marketing, Conf. Spl. 1995 pp. 178-179

Gupta[51] (2000) has examined the implications of economic growth for poverty and employment in India. The paper finds weak links between economic growth and poverty alleviation. He concludes that no macro policy of market led growth will be successful in dealing with the problem of either poverty or employment in India. The author suggests that appropriate social, demographic and economic policies will have to be developed to upgrade the skills of the poorer sections of the population to a reasonable level to enable them to enter the mainstream market activities.

Ruben and Marrit (2001) have analyzed the role of non-farm income of rural farm households in Honduras. Income from non-farm wage and self-employment represents 16 to 25 per cent of farm household income and is especially important for middle and higher income group of farmers. Non-farm wage labour is geographically concentrated in northern region and self-employment is developed in southern region. They have suggested that suitable policies should be promulgated to enhance non-farm employment, investment in education, training, and technical assistance to reduce labour intensity in agricultural production. Moreover, they have emphasized on public investments and credit services to improve access to non-farm activities.[52]

In short, non-farm employment adds to total income of the households for a better living. This is possible through education, training, technical assistance, and public investment, credit services and suitable social, demographic and economic policies of the

---

[51] Gupta, S. P, "Trickledown Theory Revisited: The Role of Employment and Poverty", ***Indian Journal of Labour Economics***; 43(1), Jan.-March 2000, pages 25-34.

[52]Ruben, Ruend and Marrit Berg, " Non- farm Employment and poverty Alleviation of Rural Farm Households in Handuras", World Development, 29 (3), March 2001, pp. 549-60

Government. The minimum wage policy helps in poverty alleviation programs. Employment can be generated through construction of shelter, infrastructure and services provision. Labor-intensive employment programs can solve the problems of food insecurity, un- employment, environmental degradation and poor infrastructure, if public works is integrated into national planning. Even retailing of agricultural commodities can generate employment opportunities and earnings and will cause poverty alleviation.

Food Security

Besley et al (1987) have opined that the issue of targeting food subsidies to achieve maximum impact on poverty reduction in developing countries is one of great practical and policy significance. At the operational level, there exist many heuristics and intuitively justified rules of thumb that are used in policy discussions. Taking explicit account of the budget constraint and of preferences and technology, rules can be derived for re-targeting food subsidies to reduce poverty.[53]

Vyas (1997) [54] has observed that South Asian countries have made significant progress in alleviating poverty, but not in malnutrition. To achieve nutritional goals, the countries in the region will have to strengthen household food security, availability and access to health services, and quality of care. A comprehensive approach is needed while pursuing the goal of poverty alleviation and the achievements should be constantly reviewed.

---

[53]Besley, Timothy and Kanbur, Ravi , "Food Subsidies and Poverty Alleviation", ***Oxford Applied Economics Discussion Paper***: 27, June 1987, pages 36

[54] Vyas, V. S., "Poverty Alleviation and Nutrition Enhancement in South Asia: The Missing Links", ***Asian Journal of Agricultural Economics***; 2(2), 1997, pp. 101-108

Islam[55] (1997) has hypothesized that there exists relationship between long-term poverty, famine and human deprivation. In South Asian countries, the poverty alleviation programs are affected by the combination of social, traditional and political conditions prevailing in those countries.

Breslin et al (1997)[56] have reported that poverty and malnutrition are major problems in South Africa, especially among black people in rural areas. The poorest are heavily dependent on social pensions, remittances, low wages, and piece jobs and, to a very small extent, household agriculture. Industrial safeties nets are weak and do not necessarily help the vulnerable to overcome their poverty. This article draws on the experience of Operation Hunger, a South African NGO founded in 1980, to examine the impact of poverty alleviation programs on the recipients.

The article reviews the strategies employed by the government and NGO to strengthen vulnerable household's food aid, public works and agricultural programs drawing on Operation Hunger's experience in these areas. The article concludes that targeting, monitoring and evaluation, and piloting development programs are crucial, and stresses the importance of NGOs in this regard.

Agriculture

Ahmed (1988) has analyzed the ex-post evaluation of the socio-economic impact of Green Revolution for an

---

[55] Islam, Nurul, "Hunger, Famines, and Poverty: A Few Considerations of Political Economy", ***Asia Pacific Development Journal***; 4(1), June 1997, pages 27-38.

[56] Breslin, Edward D., Delius, Peter and Madrid, Carlos, "Strengthening Institutional Safety Nets in South Africa: Sharing Operation Hunger's Insights and Experiences", ***Development Southern Africa***; 14(1), February 1997, pp. 21-41.

ex-ante assessment of the likely impact of the bio-revolution. He has linked the scientific character of the bio-revolution with its socio-economic consequences and assessed its impact on green revolution. The bio-revolution's possible effects on direct and indirect employment and on specific poverty groups are analyzed.[57] The article suggests how present developments in this technology could be steered in a direction more helpful to the poor (e.g. liberating farmers from their dependence on agro-chemicals) and away from currently strong anti-poor trends (e.g., growing corporate power and institutional protection for proprietary rights and secrecy).

Travers and Ma[58] (1994) have studied agricultural productivity and rural poverty in China. A variable elasticity model of the aggregate agricultural production function was used to assess the potential impact of proposed poverty alleviation interventions. The findings suggest that some scope remains, under current technologies and prices, for improving peasant income through further intensification of machinery and fertilizer use, but not by further irrigation development.

Coxhead and Warr (1995) have examined the impact of technical progress in agriculture on changes in measured poverty and aggregate welfare in a developing country, Philippines. Using a small general equilibrium model, the economic components of an observed change in poverty can be isolated to expose the significance of inter-sector-linkages and the economic roles of change in relative commodity and

---

[57] Ahmed, Iftikhar, "The bio revolution in agriculture: Key to poverty Alleviation in the Third world?" ***International Labour Review***; 127(1), 1988, pp. 53-72.

[58] Travers, Lee and Ma, Jun, "Agriculture productivity and Rural Poverty in China", ***China Economic Review***; 5(1), Spring 1994, pp. 141- 159

factor prices. Variation in the measured rate and distribution of poverty alleviation depends somewhat on the choice of poverty measure, but more substantively on structural assumptions and the effects of policy interventions in agricultural markets.[59]

Faruqee (1998) has reviewed past trends in total factor productivity in agriculture in Pakistan and found stagnation in agricultural productivity mainly due to resource degradation, failure to adopt technical change and poor farmer incentives. The paper argues that future growth through productivity increase requires major changes in system, policies and institutions dealing with the agricultural sector. These changes are crucial for agriculture because this sector will remain the key sector for achieving growth with poverty alleviation and environmental protection in the next century. The appropriate role of the government should be limited for encouraging the development of a smoothly functioning market through institutional and regulatory reforms that facilitate private sector activities and market efficiency.[60]

Ahmad and Qureshi (1999) have reported that agricultural productivity can be increased through managerial skills, farmers' education, an effective agricultural extension system and provision of timely inputs.[61]

---

[59]Coxhead, Ian and Warr Peter G, "Does Technical Progress in Agriculture Alleviate Poverty? A Philippine Case Study ", ***Australian Journal of Agricultural Economics***; 39(1), April 1995, pages 25-54

[60] Faruqee, Rashid, "Pakistan's Agriculture in the 21st Century", **Pakistan Development Review**; 37(4), winter 1998, pp. 245-53

[61] Ahmad, M and Qureshi S.K., "Recent Evidence on Size and Land Productivity: Implications for public policy",

Human Capital

The World Bank (1990) identifies and analyzes major obstacles to internal and external efficiency of formal systems of vocational and technical education in Bangladesh; possible reforms to upgrade and improve these programs; and alternative non-formal approaches to vocational training and education. The World Bank estimates the efficiency of the formal systems with negative rates of return to investment, as graduates of programs cannot find jobs in their field. But the non-formal vocational and technical education has shown potential. The efficiency of internal and external efficiency of formal programs could be improved through training of teachers, administrators and improving the management of programs.[62]

Psacharopoulos et al (1997)[63] have concluded that investment in education is critical for economic growth and poverty alleviation. Such investment is typically being financed by the state. Yet in many countries families contribute privately for education of their children. In an era of stagnating public budgets for education, the private financing of education gains importance for a country's investment in human resources. But the private education is highly selective and affordable only by the rich. In Bolivia - a highly indebted poor country, there is a remarkable willingness of households to pay for private education for their children.

Pakistan Development Review, 38 (4), Winter 1999, pp. 1135-52

[62]---------,"Bangladesh: Vocational and technical education review", **A World Bank Country Study,** Washington, D.C. 1990, pages xx, 105

[63] Psacharopoulos, George, Arieira, Carlos R and Mattson, Robert, "Private Education in a Poor Country: The Case of Urban Bolivia", **Economics of Education Review**; 16(4), October 1997, pp. 395-406.

Saugestad (2000) have reported that members of the less well off community, compared with the better-off families, enjoy fewer benefits in education. They have concluded that households with better access to credit and basic infrastructure facilities invested more in education of children in Philippines. This insight suggests how the design of poverty-alleviation expenditure programs might be improved in rural Philippines.[64]

Foreign Funding Institutions

Tendler (1989)[65] has observed that programs funded by Foreign Funding Institutions for alleviating poverty, in most of the cases, do fail rather than succeed. The Foreign Funding Institutions focus narrowly on a particular trade or activity in the beginning; use credit as an entry point; start by brokering loans rather than lending directly; and have leadership linked to powerful institutions. Participants are generally engaged in the economic activities supported by the programs; marketing channels exist; and powerful consumer groups are often in favorof production by beneficiary groups. Though these findings seem obvious, few programs funded by donors' display these characteristics, suggesting that donors choose programs and organizations more carefully and not limit their funding to the non-governmental sector.

Clements (1993) has explored the nature of the poverty alleviation problem from the prospective of international development funding agencies. These

---

[64]Saugestad, Sidsel, "Dilemmas in Norwegian Development Assistance to Indigenous People: A Case of Study from Botswana", **Forum for Development Studies**; 6(2), November 2000, pp. 205-234.
[65]Tendler, Judith, "What Ever Happened to Poverty Alleviation?" **World Development**; 17 (7), July 1989, pp. 1033-44.

agencies have been poorly structured to promote the interests of the poor. Agencies such as the World Bank and the U.S. Agency for International Development (USAID) can achieve better results by creating independent units devoted exclusively to poverty alleviation. These units should immerse their staff more completely in local societies, with lower pay scales and longer hours of duty.[66]

West and Tarazona [67] (1998) have analyzed the developmental impact of the Multilateral Investment Guarantee Agency (MIGA), a member agency of the World Bank group that provides political risk insurance to qualified foreign investors in developing member countries. The MIGA carries out advisory and technical programs for governments of these countries to improve their ability to attract foreign investment. MIGA-supported projects bear impacts on social development and poverty alleviation.

Saugestad (2000) has analyzed the Norwegian support to the Remote Area Development Program in Botswana. It includes background on Norwegian international commitment to the development of indigenous peoples, and explores the way these principles have been handled in a concrete case of development assistance. The analysis demonstrates how emphasis on poverty alleviation may lead to welfare policies. But the process of client selection comes in opposition to other development objectives such as empowerment .The Norwegian involvement was too brief .The paper notes that the support should be more consistent and professional

---

[66]Clements, Paul, "An Approach to Poverty Alleviation for Large International Development Agencies, "**World Development**; 21(10), October 1993, pages 1633-46.

[67] West, Gerald T and Tarazona, Ethel I. "MIGA and direct investment: Evaluating developmental impacts", ***Washington, D.C.: Multilateral Investment Guarantee Agency***, 1998, pages x, 86.

experience gained in Norwegian–Saami relations should be used for poverty alleviation.[68]

Rasiah and Shari (2001) have reported, "The World Bank has inferred that liberalization holds the key to growth, poverty alleviation and redistribution." Using Malaysia as an example, this paper argues that growth; poverty alleviation and redistribution in the country were achieved under circumstances of both interventionist policies as well as market coordination. Throughout the New Economic Policy (NEP) period (1970-90), strong incentives were offered to both import substitution and export oriented manufacturing sectors and the state made strong forays into the market to redress poverty and inequality. The paper also argues that poorly coordinated government intervention generated substantial unproductive rent seeking.[69]

Non-Government Organization

Arellano and Petras (1994) have studied the role of NGOs in poverty alleviation in Bolivia. It is reported that NGOs became increasingly involved in implementing development projects in Latin America. The NGOs played central roles in efforts to alleviate poverty associated with structural adjustment, consolidation of neo-liberal economic policies, and reorganization of the state. International donors have shown enthusiasm for working through NGOs in the area of poverty alleviation. However, it is not clear that NGOs are more successful in overcoming poverty than state agencies. Both the state agencies and

---

[68]Saugestad, Sidsel, "Dilemmas in Norwegian Development Assistance to Indigenous People: A Case of Study from Botswana" **Forum for Development Studies**; 6(2), November 2000, pp. 205-234.
[69] Rasiah, R. and Shari, I. (2001), "Market Government Malaysia's New Economic Policy", ***Cambridge Journal of Economics,*** *25 (1), pp 57-78*

NGOs have undermined the grassroots organizations representing the interest of poor people in implementing the development programs.[70]

Cleary (1997) has studied the international NGO campaigns in four countries with authoritarian governments. He examined Indonesian examples of international NGO advocacy, including NGO opposition to a Dam Project and a proposed Scott Paper investment. The researcher studied the role of NGOs in democratic community building through civics in South Africa; with regard to macro-economic policy making and poverty alleviation in Sri Lanka; and Philippines NGO responses to increased political process. He has considered how decisions were reached and how projects were identified and implemented. Then he drew broad conclusions that contribute to the debate about NGO accountability.[71]

Shaw (1999) has illustrated that in 1991, the World Bank moved to streamline the Sri Lankan welfare sector by funding a poverty alleviation project which promoted the role of non-government organization (NGO) and decentralized government agencies and replaced traditional consumption-oriented transfers with an emphasis on household self-reliance through productivity activity. The project design was based on a model that depends for its success on key conditions – guaranteed political independence and a well-developed NGO sector – which did not exist in Sri Lanka in the early 1990s. Additional problems included management deficiencies and failure to

---

[70] Arellano Lopez, Sonia and Petras, James F," Non Governmental Organizations and Poverty Alleviation in Bolivia", ***Development and Change***; 25(3), July 1994, pp. 555-568.

[71] Cleary, "The role NGOs under authoritarian political systems", International ***Political Economy Series, New York: St. Martin's Press***, London: Macmillan Press, 1997, pages xii, 274.

provide key supports for production-related poverty reduction.[72]

Governance

Graham (1992) has reported that the Emergency Social Fund (ESF) of Bolivia was very effective because of its demand-based approach, efficiency, and transparency with its rapid results. Hence, similar programs were attempted in Latin America and Africa. Critics question the program's ability to provide permanent poverty alleviation or to target the poorest sectors, and its institutional position outside the public sector. The study analyses the impact of the ESF on politics, adjustment process, institutions, non-government actors and the poor. The study seeks to enhance efforts to protect the poor during adjustment through political sustainability of the process.[73]

Sverrisson (1996) studied the politics and governance of poverty alleviation programs in sub-Saharan Africa and Latin America. The World Bank's fundamental objective is sustainable poverty reduction in the developing world. The article examines changing institutional architecture of SAP related anti-poverty "Safety Net" interventions looking in particular at the relationship of Poverty Alleviation Programs (PAPs) to the governance agent of the Bank, and the political implications of different PAPs.

The interest in poverty alleviation can be interpreted as a rhetorical device, or a bolt-on addition to the Structural Adjustment agenda as the perceived need

---

[72].Shaw, Judith, "World Bank Intervention in the Sri Lankan Welfare Sector: The National Development Trust Fund", ***World Development***; 27(5), May 1999, pp. 825-838.

[73] Graham, Carol, "The Politics of protecting the poor during Adjustment: Bolivia's Emergency Social Fund", ***World Development***; 20(9), September 1992, pp. 1233-51.

for economic liberalization remains paramount in the overall strategy. A successful PAP can contribute towards the political sustainability of adjustment, whether by compensating loser in the adjustment process, or building new conditions to support liberalization governments. However, the complexity of achieving such a goal can be underestimated and the political benefits over estimated, which can be counterproductive politically and in terms of poverty alleviation.[74]

Lieten (1996) has examined the achievements of Left Front Government in West Bengal, which has held office since 1977. He has opined that specific class-related politics like land reforms, minimum wages and other policies have helped to improve the socio-economic position of different classes. The government of West Bengal (India) has increased the moral conduct, education, family planning and women empowerment in the state. The rural development policy has a positive impact on the rural masses.[75]

Debt Relief

Fischer (1987) has observed that since August 1982, the international debt crisis has dominated economic policy making in the developing countries, economic relations between the debtors and creditor countries, and dealings of the multilateral institutions with the

---

[74] Sverrisson, Alan Sturla, "The politics Governance of poverty Alleviation Programs: Comparative Case Studies in Sub-Saharan Africa and Latin America", ***European Journal of Development Research***; 8(2), December 1996, pp. 129-156.

[75]Lieten, G.K., "Development, Devolution and Democracy: Village Discourse in West Bengal", ***Indo Dutch Studies in Development Alternatives***, vol. 18. New Delhi, Thousand Oaks, Calif. and London: Sage Publications, 1996, pages 252.

debtor nations, and private sector decisions on lending to the developing countries. Three classes of solutions are described and evaluated. These are: Procedural reform and changes in the nature of the claims on the existing debt creation facility, or new institution to deal with the overhang of existing debt. The other measure is debt relief either in direct negotiation between creditors and debtors and/or in conjunction with the creation of a facility.[76]

Corden (1988)[77] has illustrated the principal reasons that are based on the "investment-capacity" and the "default-forestalling" arguments. Debt relief is reduction of the present value of the contractual debt. The paper provides an analytical basis for various debt relief proposals that do not require finance or guarantees from creditor governments. It explains for the considerable amount of relief in the form of rescheduling and concerted lending that has already taken place. The free rider problem and the extent the market may overcome it, is discussed.

Houben[78] (1995) has reviewed commercial bank debt restructuring based on the recent experience of Bulgaria. While the deal is shown to have generated substantial debt relief at a remarkable low cost, several lessons are drawn that may be of broader relevance to countries restructuring bank debt. As, from time to time, it has been suggested that Bulgaria should have held out for more favorable

---

[76] . Fischer, Stanley, "Resolving the International Debt Crisis", *National Bureau of Economic Research Working Paper*: 2373, September 1987.
[77] Corden, W.Max, "Is Debt Relief in the Interest of the Creditors", ***International Monetary Fund***, ***Working Paper***, WP/88/72, August 1988, page 17
[78] Houben, Aerdt, C.F.J., "Commercial Bank Debt Restructuring the Experience of Bulgaria", *International Monetary Fund Papers on Policy Analysis and Assessment*: PPAA/95/06, April 1995, pages 23.

treatment, or that it should now seek further debt reduction, the likely costs of these options are identified. Looking ahead, key policy issues are discussed that will determine growth prospects and debt sustainability over the medium term. It is argued that the deal's success remains to be underpinned in particularly by judicious fiscal and debt management policies.

Boote and Thugge (1997) have described the debt burden of low-income countries and the traditional mechanisms that have been implemented by the international community to alleviate this burden. While these mechanisms are sufficient to reduce the external debts of many Heavily Indebted Poor Countries (HIPC) to sustainable levels provided these countries implemented sound economic policies, they are likely to be insufficient for a number of countries. To deal with these cases, the World Bank and the IMF have jointly proposed and implemented the HIPC Initiative. The paper describes this initiative and suggests that it should enable HIPC to exit from the debt rescheduling process. [79]

Ghani and Zang[80] (1997) have studied fiscal and debt management in Ethiopia. The problem of debt overhang facing a number of low-income countries has received considerable international attention in recent times. The international development community has begun to recognize that options would need to be seriously explored aimed at providing debt relief to those countries where debt is

---

[79]Boote, Antony R, Thugge, Kamau, "Debt Relief For Low Income Countries and the HIPC Initiative", *International Monetary Fund Working Paper*: WP/97/24, March 1997,pages 23

[80] Ghani, Ejaz; Zang, Hyoungsoo, "Fiscial and Debt Management in a Severely Indebted Low-Income Country", *Journal of Economic Research*;2(1), May 1997, pages 135-48

not sustainable. This paper builds on the Branson (1990) model of debt sustainability and applies it to a severely indebted low-income country, Ethiopia. It provides a simplified framework where debt sustainability (both domestic and external) is an integral element of macroeconomic stability. Interactions between different policy variables (such as debt, fiscal and interest rate policies), and outcome variables (such as GDP growth), as well as international economic conditions (international interest rates) jointly define if the country is on a sustainable debt path. Equations on debt sustainability can be easily estimated under this framework, and in this sense, it provides a good starting point for examining debt sustainability.

Christou et al (1998) have studied the optimal path of foreign public debt that can support politically unanimous (Pareto welfare improving) economic growth under uncertainty. The feasibility of the plan depends on whether the maintenance of political consensus in the debtor country requires additional loans that are high relative to the country's outstanding debt. If a program is feasible, then the creditors will have an incentive to preserve political support for the plan, in case of adverse developments, by offering debt relief. Unlike the certainty case, where only total debt matters, uncertainty makes also the timing of debt repayments critical for economic development.[81]

Stephens (1998) analyzed the causes of the reduction in trade finance in South East Asian countries post-1997, with a particular focus on the role of export credit agencies. It concludes that while such agencies did not cause or prolong the problem, they did contribute significantly to a solution. The paper also

---

[81] Christou Costas, Dellas, Harriis and Belessakos, Elias, "Foreign Debt and Economics", *Review of International Economics*, 6(1), February 1998, pp. 1-14

suggests some implications from events in South East Asia for both traditional debt-relief mechanisms and for the architecture of the international financial system.[82]

The OECD Development Assistance Committee (1999) reviewed the development cooperation policies and examines the overall framework of Japan's changes in the policy directions and organization. The committee studied aid management; issues in the health, education, environment, water and sanitation sectors; issues of basic human needs, poverty, and gender equality; aid intervention aimed at issues of governance and corruption. It also incorporated Japan's aid evaluation and aid effectiveness; the coherence between Japan's development assistance (ODA); Japan's contribution to multilateral institutions; the instruments of Japan's ODA and its geographical, country-income-group, and sectoral distribution; Japan's tying procurement policies; and its debt relief to poorer countries.[83]

Elbadawi (1999) has hypothesized that African countries should start thinking through undertaking an orderly transition from the current high dependence on foreign aid for financing economic and social development. Aid dependency should be reduced not because the international development community believes it will eventually happen, but because such dependence on foreign aid could substantially impair Africa's export competitiveness and therefore derail the continent's export oriented development strategies. A combination of further

---

[82] Stephens, Malcolm, "Export Credit, Trade Finance and South East Asia", *International Monetary Fund Working Paper*: WP/98/175, December 1998, pages 52

[83] OECD Development Assistance Committee," Japan: 1999", Development Co-operation Review Series, no. 34. Paris and Washington, D.C.: Organization for Economic Co-operation and Development, 1999, pages 109

debt relief, reforms of the current aid regime and enhanced policy environment should allow a managed transition to a mixed menu of official development assistance (ODA) and private capital flows. However, the attempt by Africa to increase its share of investments from international private capital markets should be firmly anchored to the basic tenets of an export-based development strategy. To provide the basis for these policy conclusions, the author has estimated the relationship between ODA, real exchange rates (RER) and nontraditional exports for a panel of 62 developing countries, including 28 from Africa. Unsustainable ODA flows were shown to have caused substantial partial RER overvaluation in many African and non-African countries. Moreover, exceptionally high aid-dependent African countries have either experienced, or are likely to experience, overall RER overvaluation. Conditional on absence of RER overvaluation-a proxy for good policy environment of relevance to export performance-a robust Laffer curve - type relationship exists between aid and non-traditional exports through the misalignment of RER relative to its equilibrium. The Laffer curve relationship justifies a "precise" concept of aid dependency, based on the extent to which excessive ODA flows exceeded the threshold beyond which more ODA actually hinders rather than helps export expansion. According to this concept, several African countries were characterized as being "aid dependent".[84]

GraciaAldaz (1999) has reviewed the aid provided by Spain for development. The discussion addresses the activity of the various agents and their responsibilities, along with non-reimbursable co-operation instruments, i.e., humanitarian aid, food aid, technical co-operation programmes, investment

---

[84]Elbadawi, Ibrahim A., "External Aid: Help or Hindrance to Export Orientation in Africa?"Journal of Africa Economies, 8(4), December 1999, pp. 578-616.

projects and the operation in connection with debt relief. Finally, it suggests certain perspectives for our non-reimbursable co-operation and points out that the enactment of the Act on International Co-operation for Development affords an excellent opportunity.[85]

Dent and Peter (1999)[86] described Jubilee 2000-a campaign aimed at releasing low-income countries from the burden of un-payable sovereign debt. It discusses the problem of debt and poverty; the genesis, history, and growth of Jubilee 2000 and the debt situation of fifty-one low-income countries that are the focus of the Jubilee 2000 debt-remission campaign. It incorporates efforts made so far by the World Bank and the Paris Club to deal with the problem of debt; the boundaries and criteria of Jubilee debt remission; conditionality for remission; benefits and costs of the remission.

The report explains debt problems in Nigeria, Malawi, and Nicaragua; non-economic benefits from cancellation for creditor as well as for debtor countries. It explains a parallel between Jubilee 2000 and the antislavery movement in the nineteenth century. Moreover, tactical considerations and means of implementing the Jubilee; the future of the campaign beyond the year 2000; the origin and development of the campaign for debt relief cancellation and the critique of the International financial institution, 1983-93 are discussed. They explained the approach to debt in faiths other than Judaism and Christianity, Jubilee 2000 campaign and a criticism of World Bank philosophies and policies.

---

[85] GraciaAldaz,Jesus, "Non-reimbursable Co-operation", *Information Commercial EspanolaRevisited de Economia*; O (778), May-June 1999, pp. 103-118

[86]Dent, Martin and Peters, Bill, "The crisis of poverty and debt in the third world" Aldershot, U.K. Brookfield, Vt. And Sydney: Ashgate, 1999, pages xii, 284

Moreover, management of international financial institutions, possibility of a grand concordat between debtor and creditor countries, and the reform of United Nations and Bretton Woods's structures are discussed.

Daseking and Powell (1999) have studied the history of debt relief. In their opinion the low-income country debt crisis had its origins in weak macroeconomics policies, and official creditor's willingness to take risks unacceptable to private lenders. Payments problems were initially addressed through non-concessional re-scheduling and new lending that maximized financing while containing the budgetary costs for creditors. This led to an unsustainable buildup in debt stocks. More recently, debt ratios have improved, reflecting both adjustment and substantial debt relief. The paper estimates debt relief initiatives since 1988 have cost creditors at least $30 billion, and possibly much more. This compares with the estimated costs of about $27 billion under the enhanced HIPC Initiatives.[87]

Hayri (2000) has developing formulae for sovereign debt by incorporating strategic debt relief games into a model of debt pricing under continuous time uncertainty. Two types of debt relief for sovereign borrowers are considered: debt reductions and exit deals. The formulae provide a good fit to the data and generate plausible predictions in a simulation analysis. The paper also examines how the availability of credible commitment mechanisms affects the amount of debt reduction. Compared with the time-consistent equilibrium, creditors would want to commit to a larger, later debt reduction while the

---

[87] Daseeking, Christina and Powell, Robert "From Toronto Terms to the HIPC initiative: A brief History of Debt Relief for Low-Income Countries" *International Monetary Fund Working Paper*, WP/99/142, October 1999, pages 29.

debtor would rather have an earlier, smaller debt reduction.[88]

Nasution (2000) [89] has analyzed the meltdown of Indonesian economy. He has observed that three sets of factors came together to cause the economic meltdown in Indonesia in 1997: negative external shocks (financial contagion, adverse terms of trade); weak fundamentals (financially fragile banks, over-reliance on foreign loans by corporations); and incompetent management (overly rigid exchange rate, inadequate prudential supervision). When the crisis unfolded, the government was paralyzed by indecision over adoption of a currency board, reduction of large state-guaranteed investments, and implementation of economic deregulation.

The IMF's insistence on abrupt bank closures accelerated the bank-run, and its insistence on abrupt fiscal tightening deepened the output collapse. Recovery to sustained growth will require re-capitalization of banks, improved monitoring of the financial system, and prudent regulation of capital inflows, external debt relief, and greater flexibility in the exchange rate, comprehensive microeconomics deregulation, and better macroeconomic management.

Cheru (2000)[90] has linked the HIPC initiative to the HIV / AIDS epidemic in Zambia. He has opined that besides being a global public health emergency, the HIV / AIDS epidemic has become the foremost

---

[88] Hayri, Aydin, "Debt Relief", *Journalof International Economics*; 52(1), October 2000, pp. 137-152

[89] Nasution, Anwar, "The Meltdown of the Indonesian Economy: Causes, Responses and Lessons" ASEAN Economic-Bulletin; 17(2), August 2000, pages 148-62.

[90]Cheru,Fantu, "Debt Relief and Social Investment: Linking the HIPC Initiative to the HIVIAIDS Epidemic in Africa" *Review of African Political Economy*; 27(86), December 2000, pp. 519-535.

contemporary threat to the development of many African countries. Past achievements in economic growth, improved life expectancy and decreasing child mortality have been reversed by the rapid spread of the HIV virus. It is estimated that each day in Africa more than 5,000 people die from AIDS or HIV related illness, with the figure expected to climb to almost 13,000 by 2005. In the context of this unfolding humanitarian crisis, creditor nations and institutions should cancel outstanding debt immediately so that resources of affected countries can be directed towards containment of the epidemic, within broader strategies of poverty alleviation. Addressing this crisis should not be construed as an act of charity, but an obligation and a necessity. Linking debt relief to HIV/AIDS is one small but important step in the long march to eradicate poverty in the poorest developing countries.

Other Studies

The World Bank (1985) sanctioned 128 projects in ten countries (Brazil, India, Indonesia, Kenya, Mali, Morocco, Nigeria, Sudan, Thailand, and Turkey) during 1974-80. The aim of these projects was to bring effective and relevant low-cost technologies to small producers, and they reflect the Banks poverty alleviation policy in rural development. These projects supported research and extension programs in relation to different levels in the decision-making process within national systems by identifying country issues.[91]

Echeverri Gent (1992) studied the relationship between public participation and poverty alleviation in the West Bengal state of India .He has observed public participation is essential to making poverty alleviation programs responsive to the need of the

---

[91] -----------, "Agricultural research and extension: An evolution of the World Bank's experience", ***Washington, D.C.***, 1985, pages ix, 110

poor, but it requires a political process that adequately represents their interest. Yet as long as the poor remains poor, they are disadvantaged in securing equitable representation. This article highlights the problems stemming from this paradox of participation. It shows how implementing poverty alleviation programs through elected governing councils has simultaneously made policy more responsive to the poor while permitting the organizational interests of the ruling communist party to distort implementation. The article highlights the importance of political competition among parties and non-governmental organizations for maximizing responsiveness to the poor.[92]

Kaijage and Tibaijuka (1996) have studied rural poverty, inequality and exclusion in the context of issues relating to access to land rights and have examined the crisis of the traditional social safety nets and the failure of state provision of welfare in situation of acute distress in Tanzania. They have emphasized the design of policies for poverty alleviation and social integration.[93]

The World Bank (1996) has explored the effectiveness of Hungary's system of cash transfer programs in lifting people out of poverty and providing a safety net for those who remain poor. Steps should be taken for improving the efficiency of

---

[92] Echeverri Gent, John, "Public Participation and Poverty Alleviation: The Experience of Reform Communists in India's West Bengal", ***World Development***; 20(10), October 1992, pp. 1401-22.

[93] Kaijage, Frederick and Tibaijuka, Anna, "Poverty and social exclusion in Tanzania", Research *Series*, vol. 109, Geneva: International Institute for Labour Studies; distributed by ILO Publications Center, Waldorf, Md., 1996, pages x, 202

poverty alleviation programs focusing on their eligibility criteria and targeting effectiveness.[94]

Sen[95] (1996) has observed that in Bangladesh shift to non-farm occupations has been on balance, pro-poor in nature. This is seen both in terms of greater potentials for poverty alleviation in these activities, and in respect of their potentials for moderating overall rural income inequality. The other view, favoring a 'dynamic' characterization is lack of improvement in labour productivity in many rural non-farm (RNF) activities. This creates over-crowding at the lower end of productivity scale.

Khandker (1996) has illustrated that in labour surplus country like Bangladesh, rural non-farm (RNF) sector is important not only for poverty alleviation but also promoting overall economic growth. Micro-credit from Grameen Bank and other banks have played a significant role in relaxing this constraint and promoting RNF activities in Bangladesh. Household attributes, village characteristics, prices and wages have been found to explain a significant part of variations of the choice structure of the rural non-farm (RNF) activities. He opines that supply of affordable credit for the expansion of RNF production must be supported by appropriate skill development, market promotion, and other organizational supports.[96]

---

[94] ------------, "Hungry: Poverty and social transfers" ***World Bank Country Studies***, Washington, D.C., 1996, pages xvii, 85.

[95] Sen, Binayak, "Rural Non farm Sector in Bangladesh: Stagnating and Residual, or dynamic and Potential?" ***Bangladesh Development Studies***; 24(3-4), Sept.-Dec. 1996, pp. 143-180.

[96] Khandker, Shahidur R. "Role of Targeted Credit in Rural Nonfarm Growth", Bangladesh ***Development Studies***; 24(3-4), Sept. Dec. 1996, pp. 181-93

Khan (1997) has explored the connections between environmental damages, inequality and poverty in Bangladesh. Using the adjusted income distribution for either measurement modifies starting with a new concept of national income and its distribution, which takes ecological damage into account, standard measure of poverty and inequality. Under fairly conservative assumptions of modest environmental damages and a uniform distribution of the damages among the population, it is shown that both inequality and poverty worsen when environmental deterioration is taken into account. From a policy perspective, since there is no inevitable environmental Cuznet curve, developing countries like Bangladesh can enhance the poverty alleviation effects of growth by improving environmental quality through effective interventions.[97]

Chakraverty et al (1997) have explored the present and potential contribution of community forestry to sustainable forest and poverty alleviation in the terrain region of Nepal. They have introduced community forestry as an approach to common poor resource management. They have presented policy recommendations for bilateral development co-operation among forest administration, forest user growth and forest related industries.[98]

Berry (1997)[99] has expected that the participation of small scale enterprises in export production, directly

---

[97]Khan, Haider Ali, "Ecology, Inequality, and Poverty: The Case of Bangladesh", ***Asian Development Review***, 15(2), 1997, pp. 164-179.

[98]Chakraborty, RabindraNath et al, "Community forestry in the Terai region of Nepal: Policy issue, experience, and potential", ***Reports and Working Papers 5/1997***. Berlin: German Development Institute, 1997, pages v, 130.

[99] Berry, Albert, "Small scale Non agriculture Exports as a Route to Employment Creation and Poverty Alleviation", ***Konjunkturpolitik***; 43(3), 1997, pp. 275-298

or indirectly through subcontracting, can make an important contribution to employment to creation for relating low-income workers and thereby to poverty alleviation in developing countries. Achievement of this outcome will call for an increase in the density of subcontracting between large and small firm, improved conditions for the development of clutters of small firms, and generally easier entry and better support for small enterprises.

The World Bank (1998)[100] has studied the possibilities of rural development in El Salvador and developed a strategy for poverty alleviation. The strategy includes revitalization of agricultural sector by enhancing competitiveness, addressing the incentive frame work, the rural financial sector, agricultural research and technology transfer, rural and infrastructure and agricultural export diversification. The issues of rural non-farm employment access to basic services, and degradation of land must be considered for the strategy of poverty alleviation.

Baron (2000)[101] has reported that the Tomato Agro-Industry (TAI) is by far the most important agro-industry in Mexico in terms of export and employment generation. Most of the laborers employed by the TAI in North Western Mexico are temporary migrants coming from poverty stricken regions in southern Mexico. The main conclusion is that migrant income earned in the tomato fields and packing plants is fundamental for the bare survival in villages in poverty stricken regions. However, this does not provide a solution to poverty alleviation because migrant income is not sufficient to contribute

---

[100]--- "EI Salvador: Rural development study ", **World Bank Country Study**, Washington D.C., 1998, pages xviii, 221

[101]Barron Maria Antonieta and Rello Fernando, "The Impact of the Tomato Agro-industry on the Rural Poor in Mexico", **Agricultural Economics**, 23(3), September 2000, pages 289-97.

to capital formation in the migrating communities or to create the conditions for endogenous local development.

Orr (2000) has examined the impact of abolition of estate monopoly on cultivation of burley tobacco in Malawi effected in 1990.A nation-wide survey in 1993 showed that small holding households cultivating burley also grow hybrid maize, use more fertilizer and are more food secure. But resource poor households particularly those headed by women face land and labor constraints on burley adoption. Burley and hybrid maize increase the demand for hired labors but not enough to absorb the growth in the rural labor force. Orr has emphasized that majority of small holders with holding size of 0.5 hectares or less should be targeted for availability of technology and poverty alleviation programs.[102]

Jan Vandemoortele [103] (2005) in the face of the different views about the MDGs asks that we should not ask what we can do for the MDGs but what the MDGs can do for our cause – that is, the realization of fundamental economic and social rights. He suggests we can compensate for the slow start of the 1990s and still achieve the global targets by 2015. It is pessimism, skepticism and cynicism that are the three worst enemies of the global anti-poverty agenda. Its three best friends are the space to adapt and tailor global targets, an explicit focus on equity, and a quantum leap in imagination.

Lopez and Luis Serven (2006) have concluded that inequality hampers poverty reduction, not only because of its negative impact on the growth

[102] Orr "Green Gold: Burley Tobacco, Small holder Agriculture and Poverty Alleviation in Malawi", **World Development,** 28 (2) February 2000, 11.347-63

[103] Jan Vandemoortele, " Ambition is Golden: Meeting the MDGs" Development 2005, 48 (1), 5-11: doi:10.1057 / palgrave.development. 1100100

elasticity of poverty but, in most scenarios, also because of its negative impact on the inequality elasticity of poverty.

Second, for a given poverty line, the impact of growth on poverty is stronger in richer than in poorer countries, and hence the latter will find it harder than the former to achieve fast poverty reduction. Third, the share of the overall variance of poverty changes attributable to growth should be generally lower in richer and more unequal countries. And fourth, for given initial levels of development and inequality, the relative poverty-reduction effectiveness of growth and inequality changes depends on the poverty line – the higher the poverty line, the bigger the role of growth and the smaller the role of distribution change.[104]

Conclusion

In short, researchers have suggested a number of procedures to alleviate the sufferings of the poor in all the low-income countries and developing countries but poverty could not be reduced dramatically because of several pertinent factors. Poor people suffer because foreign aids and grants and borrowed funds of multilateral development banks or donor countries are misappropriated by the politicians–bureaucrats - contractor nexus.

The governments of Low-income countries utilize external funds for election purposes and invest in unproductive sectors.

Most of the poverty alleviation programs lack transparency and are managed by rich and powerful persons.

---

[104] Lopez, j. Humberto and Luis Serven, "A Normal Relationship? Poverty, Growth, and Inequality" World Bank Policy Research Working Paper 3814, January 2006, pp. 1-15

Pro-poor policies do not reflect in government budgets and the governments make plans without adequate research studies.

Micro-credit has boosted women empowerment but interest rate is too high. It is ineffective in helping the abject poor residing in backward rural areas.

Bio-revolution, use of machinery and fertilizer, policy intervention in agricultural markets, and higher agricultural productivity can reduce poverty.

Investment in human capital such as vocational, technical education and education of children can exert influence on poverty reduction in rural areas.

Funds released by Foreign Funding Institutions can stimulate economic development in a country and in the process can alleviate poverty through various welfare policies.

Funds not utilized properly become liabilities to the country.

The international donors prefer NGOs for poverty alleviation programs. The amount is simply wasted. Rampant corruption by the government officials and NGOs has resulted in making an army of millionaires in poor countries but vast majority of poor at grass root level have not been benefited.

Poor governance has encouraged corruption and mis-utilization of funds in all LDCs and developing countries.

The researchers have advocated for increasing farm and non-farm employment generation, food security and food subsidies for the vulnerable people. Hence, debt relief is the only possible way to reduce the fiscal burden on the economy and get rid of the debt trap.

Corruption has become synonymous with civilization. Funds available for poverty reduction are pocketed by few powerful entities. The resources, which could be utilized for betterment of the humanity, are spent for destruction of the society.

The media covers the vixen news and repeats the ugly events to train the young generation to become vindictive and revengeful.

There occur class conflicts, insurgency and wars in the name of religion.

When rich people greet the New Year with celebrations, it is a fact that 200,000 sick children below the age of five die each week in developing countries. Prevalence of infants and women malnutrition is common in all the developing countries. The HIV / AIDS pandemic are still a global health emergency. Sale of child, child prostitution and child pornography is common in many countries. The problems of malaria, refugees, drought and hunger, factional fighting, WTO rulings, avian flu, swine flu, earthquake, hurricanes Katrina and Rita, lack of drinking water facility and activities of terrorists challenge the very existence of our civilization.

And poverty still remains as the greatest challenge.

+++++

Chapter- III

HEAVILY INDEBTED DEVELOPING COUNTRIES

Like slavery and apartheid, poverty is not natural. It is man-made, and can be overcome and eradicated by the actions of human beings.
-- Nelson Mandela

The Heavily Indebted Poor Countries (HIPC) Initiative is the first international response to provide comprehensive debt relief to the world's poorest, most heavily indebted countries. Launched by the World Bank and IMF in 1996, the Initiative broke new ground by removing the debt overhang for countries pursuing economic and social reforms targeted at measurable poverty reduction, reducing multilateral debt, and helping countries exit from endless debt restructuring. [105] In 1998, HIPC Initiative made a major expansion with three key enhancements:

[105]Dev News Media Centre, The World Bank Group

(a) Deeper and Broader Debt Relief: External debt servicing will be cut by more than US $ 50 billion, more than twice the relief provided under the original framework. The World Bank itself will contribute nearly US $11 billion.

(b) Faster Debt Relief: The World Bank and other funding institutions are providing debt relief immediately at the decision point. As a result, the reforms are completed before time in many countries.

(c) Stronger Link between Debt Relief and Poverty Reduction

In September 1999, the World Bank and IMF endorsed a new framework for Poverty Reduction Strategy Papers (PRSP). The PRSP prepared by countries in collaboration with the World Bank and IMF, is a three-year strategy document aimed at integrating macroeconomic and sector strategies in achieving poverty reduction targets, form the basis for Bank and Fund concessional lending, and debt relief under the enhanced HIPC. PRSPs are designed to be:

(a) Country-driven with broad participation of civil society;
(b) Based on an understanding of the links between public actions and poverty outcomes; and
(c) Oriented to achieve outcome-related goals for poverty reduction

The enhanced HIPC Initiative has assisted 26 countries as much as $40 billion over time ($25.7 billion net present value NPV) by September 2002.HIPC initiative cuts the total external debt in these countries by two-thirds. In 10 HIPC countries education spending has increased to double. These countries are saving an average of $1.3 billion a year. Every HIPC country is investing more funds in education, health services, rural development, water supply, governance, institution building and rural roads through HIPC relief.[106] But the HIPC initiative has been criticized. They say that the most glaring problem with the HIPC initiative for debt relief is that it will not provide lasting relief from debt for the highly indebted countries. The HIPC process is aimed not at canceling debts, but at ensuring that they can be repaid. It has little to do with enhancing human development, reducing poverty, or even increasing economic growth in debtor countries. Rather, it is designed to massage debt figures down to a level where they would be deemed "sustainable" again according to the criteria of the International Monetary Fund. [107] The European Network on Debt and Development has also pointed out that the HIPC is unlikely to free up resources to tackle poverty for three main reasons:

(a). Threshold levels to measure debt sustainability are arbitrary and still too high and that sustainability is defined in economic terms and not in terms of human and social development.

(b) The debt reduction on offer is too small. They point out that Zambia and Niger will actually pay more after the initiative than they did before.

(c) The "piling up" of different sets of conditionality slows down the process. The PRSPs from the IMF and World Bank do not succeed in aligning macro - economic issues and poverty issues more closely than in the past and macro-economic frameworks haven't changed significantly as a result of PRSPs.

---

[106] Jan Bojo and R.C. Reddy (2001), "Poverty Reduction Strategies and Environment", the World Bank Group

[107] The Transfer of Wealth; Debt and the making of a Global South, Chapter 4, a publication of " Focus on the Global South" October 2000.

The IMF and World Bank have actually admitted that the HIPC initiative is backfiring in some cases.

Joseph Stiglitz, the former Chief Economist and Vice-President of the World Bank[108] resigned because he was convinced that the structural adjustment in HIPC initiative was misguided, which called for a more humble approach to macro-economic and a commitment to honor promises made in social sectors. Moreover, the policy of imposing conditions on countries seeking economic aid has failed. It is also reported that people have become disgruntled at the initiative claiming that the program is more in the interest of the creditors than the debtors are.

The present status of debt of the HIPC countries is more than four times their annual export earnings, and 120 per cent of GNP. Moreover, 1.2 billion people are under poverty line, with income of less than US $1 per day. The poor countries face natural calamities frequently and the number of people infected by HIV/AIDS is rising above millions. Hence, the governments of HIPC countries require assistance from their rich brethren for temporary relief, if not permanent recovery.

Income Classification

Economies are divided according to 2005 GNI per capita, calculated using the World Bank Atlas method. The groups are:

Low income = $875 or less;
Lower middle income = $876 - $3,465;
Upper middle income = $3,466 - $10,725; and
High income = $10,726 or more.

---

[108]The European Network on Debt and Development, "The Myth of HIPC debt relief", Salih Booker, The Mail & Guardian (a pan- African daily), December 12, 2000

There are 35 high-income countries with more than US $ 10,726 per capita income, 28 upper-middle income countries in the range of $3,466 to $ 10,725 per capita income, 59 lower-middle income countries in the range of $876 to $ 3,465 per capita income and 52 low-income countries with less than $ 875 per capita income. Moreover, there are other 20 countries for which income statistics are not available or unreliable. (194 countries)

The World Bank[109] has reported that as per **Atlas Methodology** classification, GNI per capita was US $ 580 in low-income countries, US $ 2,640 in middle-income countries, US $ 1918 in lower-middle income countries, US $ 5625 in upper middle-income countries, US $ 1746 in low and middle-income countries, US $ 1627 in East Asia and Pacific countries, US $ 4113 in Europe and Central Asia, US $ 4008 in Latin America and Caribbean countries, US $ 2241 in middle east and north Africa, US $ 684 in South Asia, US $ 745 in sub-Saharan Africa in 2005. But the GNI per capita was US $ 35, 131 in high-income countries and US $ 31,914 in European Monetary Union in 2005.

So it is evident that there is huge income disparity among the nations. The GDP per capita (PPP) of Bermuda is $69,900 and for Luxembourg it is $65,900 in 2005, while the GDP per capita (PPP) of Solomon Islands, Comoros, Somalia, Malawi and Gaza Strip is only $600 in 2005. The ratio of GDP per capita - Purchasing Power Parity (PPP) between the lowest and highest income generating country is 1:

---

[109]*Notes:* Classifications are set each year on 1 July. These official analytical classifications are fixed during the World Bank's fiscal year (ending on 30 June), thus countries remain in the categories in which they are classified irrespective of any revisions to their per capita income data. Taiwan, China is also included in high income. Source: http://web.worldbank.org

116.5. The reasons of such variations in income are many but we have to find out the solutions of this challenge. We are citing other examples: the GNI per capita of Norway is $59,590 as against $270 for Nepal and $470 for Bangladesh. Similarly, the above facts explain that the low-income countries particularly the South Asia and sub-Saharan Africa are the worst sufferers as more than three-fourths of world poverty population reside in these parts of the world. But the World Bank, International Monetary Fund and developed countries focus their attention to sub-Saharan Africa and neglect the South Asia. A hungry man of any country should be treated equally.

A hungry man is alive because he wants to die; he is alive because he anticipates that his children would earn food and construct a dwelling house for the family in future; and he is alive because he believes in God.

Poverty Reduction Strategy Papers (PRSP)

The countries can avail debt relief through preparation of Poverty Reduction Strategy Papers (PRSP). The principles of PRSP approach are (a) country–driven (b) Result-oriented (c) comprehensive (d) partnership and (e) Long-term Perspective. These are as follows:

(i) Country–driven: Country-ownership of a poverty reduction strategy is paramount. Broad-based participation of civil society in the adoption and monitoring of the poverty reduction strategy tailored to country circumstances will enhance its sustained implementation.

(ii) Result-oriented: An understanding of the nature and determinants of poverty, and the public actions that can help reduce it, is required for the formulation of an effective strategy. Medium- and long-term goals for poverty reduction including key outcome and intermediate indicators are needed to ensure that policies are well designed, effectively implemented and carefully monitored.

(iii) Comprehensive: Sustained poverty reduction will not be possible without rapid economic growth; macroeconomic stability, structural reforms and social stability are required to move countries to a higher path of sustainable growth. Poverty is multidimensional; specific actions are needed to enable the poor to share in the benefits from growth, increase their capabilities and well being, and reduce their vulnerabilities to risks. A poverty reduction strategy should integrate institutional, structural and sect oral interventions into a consistent macroeconomic framework.

(iv). Partnerships with Organizations: The development strategy of a government can provide the context for improved coordination of the work among the World Bank, IMF and that of regional development banks and other multilateral, bilateral assistance agencies, NGOs, academia, think tanks, and private sector organizations.

(v) Long – term Perspective: A medium- and long-term perspective is needed, recognizing that poverty reduction will require institutional changes and capacity building including efforts to strengthen governance and accountability and is therefore a long- term process. National and international partners' willingness to make medium-term commitments will enhance the effectiveness of their support for the poverty reduction strategy papers.[110]

There are 42 Heavily Indebted Poor Countries as named by the World Bank. These are Angola, Benin,

[110]The Myth of HIPC debt relief

Bolivia, Burkina, Faso, Burundi, Cameroon, Central, African, Republic, Chad, Comoros, Congo Dem Rep, Congo Rep, Cote d'Ivoire, Ethiopia, The Gambia, Ghana, Guinea, Guinea, Bissau, Guyana, Honduras, Kenya, Lao, PDR, Liberia, Madagascar, Malawi, Mali, Mauritania, Mozambique, Myanmar (Burma), Nicaragua, Niger, Rwanda, Sao Tome & Principe, Senegal, Sierra Leone, Somalia, Sudan, Tanzania, Togo, Uganda, Vietnam, Yemen Rep, and Zambia.

Let us study seven heavily indebted poor countries (HIPC) and three developing countries as regards their present status, plans and programs for sustainable achievements under HIPC initiative. Of course, the benefits can be realized after a gestation period. If the assistance were rendered with an aim to mitigate the sufferings of the resource poor brethren, the ultimate result would be the right road map to world peace. But if the assistance is mismanaged or politically motivated, the entire episode will force the HIPC countries to go into deep debt trap and internal insurgency leading to a point of no return.

Benin

The People's Republic of Benin (Formerly Dahomey) is located in West Africa. It is one of the smallest and most densely populated states in Africa. Benin achieved its independence on August 1, 1960. There were coups and counter-coups for nearly 30 years till the presidential selection was held in 1991.[111]

---

[111] Description of country reports such as Benin, Burkina Faso, Ethiopia, the Gambia, Kryrgyzstan, Mali, Mauritian, Mongolia, Nepal and Zambia are collected from different sources, (i) Country profiles, (ii) UNDP publications, (iii) World Bank Publications, (iv) Manorama Year Book 2000, Malayala Manorama, Thiruvananthapuram, India and (v) Maps were provided by: www.worldatlas.com

Benin tries to fight poverty by improving macro-economic policies, targeting interventions to the poor and setting up a comprehensive poverty monitoring system. Benin has created social change observatories such as Urban and Rural Observatories, Price Observatory and Labour Market Observatory. These observatories help the planners and policy makers for poverty reduction programmes. These observatories have produced a valuable database and a set of poverty profiles. The Benin System uses qualitative and quantitative surveys to monitor household living conditions. The qualitative surveys identify people's perception of poverty, wealth and personal welfare. The surveys identify poorer groups and areas. About 90 percent of non-agricultural labour force and about 40 percent of entire labour force are employed in informal sector. About 80 percent of rural women are illiterate. Benin emphasizes on economic growth through structural adjustment and anchoring its poverty programme in the perceived needs of the poor. Benin's external debt totals more than 60 percent of GDP and its annual budget deficit are entirely financed by external resources.

The Poverty Reduction Strategy Paper (PRSP) prepared by the International Development Association (IDA) and the International Monetary Fund (IMF) presents the government's objectives and priority measures for reducing poverty over the next three years. The main strengths of the PRSP are: (I) the comprehensiveness of the strategic framework; (ii) an effort to make explicit the linkages between policy actions and result indicators; and (iii) a detailed and comprehensive medium-term expenditure framework in line with strategic priorities.

The PRSP presents an action plan to improve monitoring and evaluation capacity to refine poverty diagnosis. PRSP includes (a) a national household survey on living conditions; (b) an annual cores welfare indicators questionnaire; (c) participatory poverty assessments; and (d) the establishment of a poverty map and departmental poverty profiles.

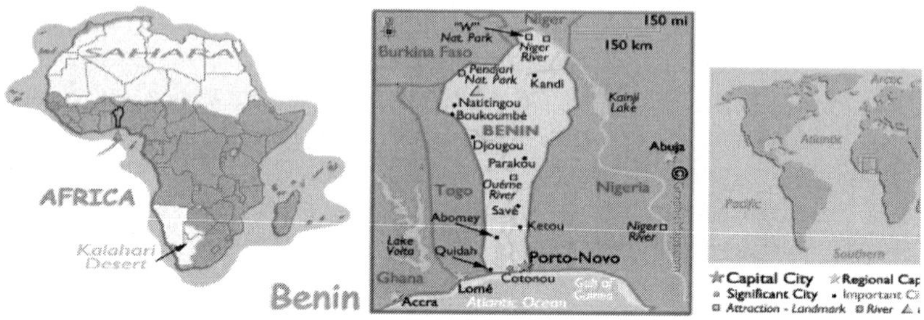

Benin

Benin's strategic framework of the PRSP rests on four main pillars and is coherent towards results. The four pillars for effective poverty reduction are as follows:

(a) Bolstering the medium-term macroeconomic framework
(b) Strengthening human development and environmental management, including improving the access of the poor to quality basic services (basic education, primary health care, water and sanitation, food security and nutrition, adequate habitat, and rural roads);
(c) Improving governance and institutional reforms, such as decentralization, public administration reforms and strengthening of the legal and judicial system; and
(d) The PRSP of Benin addresses most of the key policy issues and constraints in poverty reduction. The strategy underscores the government's commitment to reforms in public expenditure management and decentralization as means to improve results on the ground and enhance ownership. Successful implementation will require mastering of organizational and institutional challenges and accelerating structural reforms, especially with

respect to privatization, governance, and public sector management.

The PRSP is prepared on the basis of past trends, medium and long-term targets. It has identified the priority sectors like basic education, health, safe water, environment, agriculture, and transportation for sustainable growth. The PRSP has indicated to monitor the impact of governance, judicial reform, and cotton sector reform programs over a period of time. It expects that policy-targeting and greater dis-aggregating can successfully narrow down disparities among social groups, genders and locations or regions. The monitoring and evaluation program should be very effective for achieving the desired goals as it strengthens a data bank and assists in strategy making and policy design for different sectors, regions and the country as a whole.

The Third Growth and Poverty Reduction Strategy Support Programme (GPRSSP III) is aligned with the Bank's intervention strategy in Benin for 2005-2009, which focuses on "the diversification of production". The Programme is the continuation of the previous Poverty Reduction Strategy Support Programmes (PRSSP I and II), designed to complete the structural (privatization and diversification of the economy) and public finance (improvement of internal and external controls) reforms in order to accelerate economic growth and poverty reduction.

Since 1990, the African Development Bank (ADB) Group has financed a series of reform support operations that have enabled Benin to embark on a process of stabilizing public finance and significantly reducing internal and external deficits. The financing instrument used by the Bank to support these programmes was budget support prepared jointly with other technical and financial partners, including the World Bank, the International Monetary Fund and the European Union.

The people of Benin will be the main beneficiaries of the program and, more specifically, the poor to whom the government will allocate substantial expenditures by maintaining a good implementation rate of budget allocations to the priority sectors of the strategy (Agriculture, Health, Education, Water and Sanitation), as well as more efficient public resource management. Furthermore, economic operators will benefit from improvement in the business climate through the easing of procedures for starting businesses, facilitating access to land, combating corruption and granting tax benefits. The programme will help to mitigate the impact of the global financial crisis on public finance, and strengthen macro-economic stability.

As a result of global financial crisis, the budget deficit, which was about 167.5 billion CFAF in late December 2008, increased to 214.8 billion CFAF in 2009 and will reach 231.2 billion CFAF in 2010. A total of 41 billion CFAF will be required in 2009 and 52.4 billion FCFA in 2010 to fund identified activities. ADF budget support will be UA16.5 million (12.6 billion CFAF) in 2009 and UA 5.5 million (4.2 billion FCFCA) in 2010, representing 18 percent of the residual gap. (Tunis, 29 April 2009)

Burkina Faso

The Republic of Burkina Faso is a landlocked country surrounded by Mali, Niger, Benin, Togo, Ghana and Coted Ivoire. Its old name is Upper Volta. The country gained independence in 1960. It is an agricultural country with 80 percent of the population depending upon agriculture. The peasants of Burkina Faso grow extensively crops like sorghum, millet, yams, cotton, rice, and peanuts. Livestock is developed. The country is heavily dependent on foreign aid. About 2 million of citizens (out of 12 millions) have left the country for employment in Coted Ivoire and Ghana.

Burkina Faso is among the poorest countries of the world. In 1977, Burkina Faso ranked 171st among 174 countries according to human development index and recorded a human poverty index of 80 percent. About 45 percent of its population is poor. Still the country does not have a stand-alone poverty reduction strategy or program. The budgetary expenditure for basic social services was only 27 per cent in 1994, 24 per cent in 1995, 28 percent in 1996 and 35 percent in 1997. But debt service was to the extent of 48 per cent in 1994 and 1995, 42 per cent in 1996 and 35 per cent in 1997. Hence, it cannot make any progress in poverty reduction without debt relief. The country urgently needs debt relief and after which basic social services can be taken up for the welfare of the poor.

The 2008 UN Human Development Index places it 173rd out of the 179 countries listed, with over 70 percent of the population living on less than $2 a day. Many key development indicators are falling behind, even in relation to the average for Africa, and progress is hampered by high population growth of 3 percent per annum.

The poverty benchmark adopted for the Millennium Development Goals (MDGs) stood at 44.5 percent in 1994 but has remained stubbornly in excess of 40 percent, defying efforts to halve the rate by 2015. Literacy is another area failing to respond to investment, the rate was as low as 39 percent (for the 15-24 age groups) in 2007. The ratio of girls to boys enrolling in primary education is below 80 percent and completion rates are very poor. The government now provides free education in 45 priority provinces. A "needs assessment" for the MDGs conducted in 2007 suggested that an investment of $200 per capita of population is required every year until 2015. Delivery of development programs has been slowed by the capacity limitations of government institutions. For their part, the global donor agencies are devoting more efforts to combining their aid programs in order to increase efficiency of implementation.

Health and HIV/AIDS in Burkina Faso

An example of this joint aid resolve is the massive $1.2 billion commitment to water and sanitation by a consortium of development banks and bilateral agencies. Whilst there has been progress in the provision of safe water, about a quarter of the population lacks access. Sanitation has been seriously neglected and coverage remains under 30 percent. The donors have clearly identified this sector as a foundation for stabilizing the chronic health problems experienced in Burkina Faso. Over 5 million cases of malaria were reported in 2007, creating disproportionate demand on limited health services and causing the greatest number of deaths. Emergency vaccination programs feature at regular intervals in response to threatened outbreaks of polio, meningitis and yellow fever.

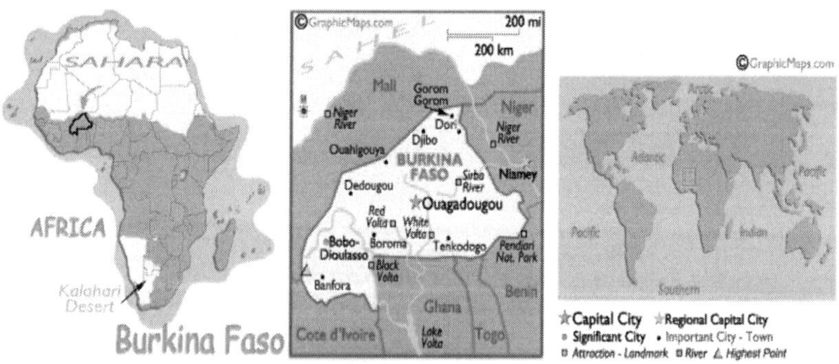

Burkina Faso

Rates of maternal and child mortality remain unacceptably high and the slow pace of improvement is far below that necessary to attain the MDG targets. For example, according to the World Bank, infant mortality fell from 107 only to 96 deaths per thousand births in the decade to 2005. A major cause is acute malnutrition, which affected over 35 percent of children aged under-five in 2007. A fifth of new mothers are themselves malnourished and only 56 percent of mothers had qualified assistance in giving birth in 2007.

The target to halt the spread of HIV/AIDS is the MDG for which Burkina Faso has demonstrated the most success. Prevalence fell to 2.7 percent in 2006, almost half the rate in 2003. Strategies to fight the disease have included co-operation with traditional healers whose influence in their respective communities makes them essential partners. Nevertheless, widespread poverty and illiteracy will continue to threaten the advances that have been made. Prevalence in the capital, Ouagadougou, is over double the national average. The strategic plan for 2006-2010 has the ambitious target of providing antiretroviral treatment to 90 percent of those in need.

Food Security in Burkina Faso:

Whilst the incidence of child malnutrition does not correlate precisely with the availability of food, the haphazard track record of Burkina Faso's food security is nevertheless a major factor. With 80 percent of the population engaged in subsistence rain-fed agriculture, the country is greatly dependent on predictable and steady rainfall. As in most of West Africa, reality rarely meets this need as the people of Burkina Faso suffer a succession of floods and drought, which create serious food shortages.

In 2007 the country experienced 8 major floods in the rainy season with inevitable results for the harvest. Forced to spend around three-quarters of their income on food, households were in no position to cope with the increase in prices that occurred during the first half of 2008. Urban poverty increased and food riots broke out in Ouagadougou and other cities. A coalition of trade unions and community groups organized a national strike. The government responded by reducing import and sales taxes, an approach criticized by the IMF, which favours more direct support such as school feeding and reduced fees for health and education.

In 2008 nature has been much kinder and the government itself reversed its policy of non-intervention in agriculture. Harvests yielded a substantial surplus over domestic needs. Rice production was three times that of the previous year. Prices in markets have fallen considerably but remain well above the levels prior to the 2008 crisis. It is too early to assess the impact on poverty but the government promises to continue its support for farmers in the shape of subsidized seed and fertilizer.

Climate Change in Burkina Faso:

The potential climate footprint of the rich on the poor is nowhere illustrated well than Burkina Faso. The 2008 review of the country's Poverty Reduction Strategy Paper (PRSP) refers to the "persistent vulnerability of many households to climate and price shocks". There is already evidence of increasing frequency of extremes of flooding and drought. The National Adaptation Plan of Action (NAPA) envisages that gradual temperature rise in the period to 2050 will result in net reduction in rainfall, less availability of water, a loss of crop production and drastic loss in pasture due to desertification.

The NAPA suggests that the priorities for adaptation are improved prediction of extreme weather events and investment in irrigation. The government already sponsors mass tree planting schemes in an attempt to counter the desertification that results from extensive clearance of forested areas for household purposes.

The Economy in Burkina Faso:

Burkina Faso is landlocked, chronically short of power, and over-dependent on cotton as the key source of foreign exchange. About 3 million livelihoods are linked directly or indirectly to the crop whose fortunes are highly vulnerable to world commodity prices and foreign exchange rates. Cotton prices are volatile but have been broadly in decline since 2003 and in real terms are at their lowest level since the 1930s. This slump has acted as a brake on economic growth in Burkina Faso and hampered investment in the cotton industry.

The primary cause of global overproduction and weak cotton prices is the US government's persistence in paying subsidies to cotton farmers, which at around $2 billion per annum are of similar order to the entire public expenditure of the Burkina Faso government. Although the World Trade Organization has upheld a protest from Brazil against unfair subsidies, the US has prevaricated over implementation of the ruling. Desperate for higher prices and yields, the Burkina Faso farmers are experimenting both with organic cotton and with genetically modified seeds, the two strategies inevitably raising difficult conflicts of interest.

Burkina Faso has been a slave to the economic prescriptions of the World Bank and IMF and, by the benchmarks of these institutions, has a stable economy with satisfactory rates of growth and inflation. Debt is also under control thanks to the debt cancellation package announced at the July 2005 G8 summit. Nevertheless, Burkina Faso remains highly dependent on foreign aid that accounts for almost half of the government's budget.

Politics in Burkina Faso:

Under its previous name of Upper Volta, the country gained independence from France in 1960. The name Burkina Faso translates as "land of honest men" and was bestowed by Thomas Sankara, the country's charismatic leader who took power in 1983 in one of a succession of post-independence coups. Sankara pursued a radical socialist agenda until he was overthrown and killed during the coup, which ushered in the current president, Blaise Campaoré, in 1987. For many years the Campaoré government permitted little more than token gestures to democracy and Burkina Faso was regarded internationally as a refuge for West African perpetrators of crime and violence. Political opposition to Campaoré stiffened considerably following the murder in 1998 of Norbert Zongo, a prominent journalist and government critic. A number of democratic reforms were brought in to appease public anger - these included the use of a simple ballot form to benefit opposition parties. Nevertheless, in the 2007 elections for the National Assembly, the ruling party, the Congress for Democracy and Progress (CDP), won dominant 73 out of 111 seats.

Campaoré has polished up his international image through acceptance of economic discipline and participation in regional conflict resolution. He enjoyed a landslide victory in the presidential election in November 2005 despite protests that he was standing yet again. The courts had ruled that a 2000 constitutional amendment limiting the head of state to two terms should not be applied retrospectively. The president has powers of making key appointments, including the Prime Minister, currently Tertius Zongo.

The constitution provides for the participation of civil society in Burkina Faso by guaranteeing the freedom to form associations, including trade unions. Representatives sit on the Independent National

Electoral Commission and were involved in preparation of the PRSP.

Human Rights in Burkina Faso:

Amongst international human rights observers, Burkina Faso has been unable to shake off the disquiet over the unresolved 1998 murder of Norbert Zongo. Despite the naming of six suspects by an independent commission of inquiry, subsequent investigations have been marred by gross irregularities and no prosecutions have been completed. Attempts during 2007 by local media to disclose the possible implication of the president's brother resulted in charges of libel against the editors concerned.

Burkina Faso is an integral component of West African networks of child trafficking. New legislation has imposed tougher penalties but convictions are notoriously difficult to secure. Law enforcement is also problematic in attempts to end the practice of female circumcision, for which the country is credited as one of the first in Africa to introduce a legal ban. However, despite extensive campaigning led by the wife of the president, the culture is deeply entrenched and possibly about 50% of women continue to suffer this cruelty. Broader aspirations of gender equality are far from fulfilled; the 34-member cabinet contained a single woman in 2008.

Conflict in Burkina Faso:

Tensions with neighbouring Ivory Coast date back to the 2002 outbreak of internal violence there between rebels in the north and the government. A long-established and substantial people of Burkina Faso migrant population found itself targeted by both sides and half a million people fled back to Burkina Faso whose government was accused by Ivory Coast of supporting the rebels. In the event it was Campaoré, who mediated an agreement in 2007 between the Ivorian factions, creating an uneasy but enduring end to violence.[112]

Ethiopia

Ethiopia is a mountainous country in Northeast Africa. Ethiopia is a land of contrast. She is the second most populous country in sub-Saharan Africa with a population of 67 million in July 2002. Ethiopia has reasonably good resource potential for development – agriculture, bio-diversity, water resources and minerals. Ethiopia is faced with complex poverty, which is broad, deep and structural. The proportion of the population below the poverty line is 44 per cent in 1999/2000. Thus, poverty eradication was and is the central development agenda of the government that guides its development activities.

The economy is mainly agricultural and pastoral. Ethiopia exports coffee, hides and skins, pulses and oilseeds. Gross Domestic Product of Ethiopia grew at an annual average rate close to 5 per cent during 1992/93 to 2000/01. The sectoral growth rate was 2.5 per cent for agriculture; 5.3 per cent for industry, and 6.3 for distributive services (transportation and communication trade and tourism) and 8.2 per cent in other services. GDP per capita has been growing by 2.4 per cent per annum from 1992/93 to 1999/2000. Ethiopia is in a position to attract foreign investment projects. During 1995/96 to 2000/01, 262 foreign investment projects received certificates, of which 56 have been operational.

In Ethiopia, school enrolment has increased from 35 per cent to 51 per cent and enrolment of girls from 26 per cent to 41 per cent during 1995-96 to 1999-2000. And infant mortality has been reduced from 110/1000 to 97/1000 during this period. Literacy rate in Ethiopia was 70.4 per cent in urban area, 21.8 per

---

[112] One World Net

cent in rural areas and overall literacy was 29.4 per cent (1999-2000). During 1995-96 to 1999-2000, food poverty households in rural areas have been reduced by (-) 12.6 per cent, but in urban areas it has increased by (+) 43.7 per cent and the overall food poverty households decreased by only (-) 6.7 per cent. The average family size in Ethiopia is 4.9. Prevalence of stunting, which is a reflection of long-run malnutrition is 57 per cent by 1999-2000 while severe stunting stood at 31.3 per cent during the same year. Both stunting and severe stunting are higher in rural areas than urban areas. In short, shadow famine is still continuing in Ethiopia till date. Unless food poverty is completely eradicated or checked in Ethiopia and other heavily indebted poor countries, the benefits of structural reforms cannot be called a mass based reform.

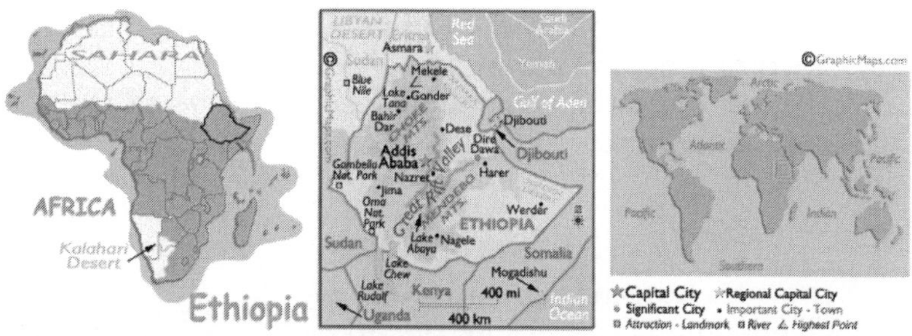

Ethiopia

Hence, the government of Ethiopia adopted a policy for both rapid economic growth and poverty reduction in October 2001. The government issued white papers on Rural Development Policies and Strategies, Capacity Building and Democracy in Ethiopia. The PRSP of Ethiopia has mentioned, "Gaps will be filled through learning by doing since PRSP is a process not an immutable blue print".

Sustainable Development and Poverty Reduction Program (SDPRP):

The SDPRP of Ethiopia has incorporated socioeconomic performance and poverty profile, analysis of growth and poverty linkage, major outcomes of the consultation process, and overview of Ethiopia's development challenges. The fundamental development objectives are to build a free-market economic system in the country. These are:

(a) The economy to develop rapidly;
(b) The country to extricate itself from dependence on food aid; and
(c) Poor people to be the main beneficiaries from economic growth

Major Thrusts:

(a) Overriding and intentional focus on agriculture as the sector is the source of livelihood for 85 per cent of the population where the bulk of the poor live. The government gives overriding primacy to the welfare of rural populace. Agriculture is also believed to be a potential source to generate primary surplus to fuel the growth of other sectors of the economy (industry),

(b) Strengthening private sector growth and development especially in industry as means of achieving off-farm employment and output growth (including investment in necessary infrastructure);

(c) Rapid export growth through production of high value agricultural products and increased support to export oriented manufacturing sectors particularly intensified processing of high quality skins/leather and textile garments;

(d) Undertaking major investment in education and strengthening the ongoing effort on capacity building to overcome critical constraints for implementation of development programs;

(e). Deepening and strengthening the decentralization process to shift decision-making process to the grass root population, to improve responsiveness and service delivery;

(f). Improvements in governance to move forward in the transformation of society, improve empowerment of the poor and set framework/provide enabling environment for private sector growth and development;

(g). Agriculture research, water harvesting and small scale irrigation; and

(h). Focus on increased water resource utilization to ensure food security

The overarching objective of the government's poverty reduction strategy is to reduce poverty and maintaining macroeconomic stability. The target is to reduce poverty by 4 per cent and GDP to grow by 7 per cent. This can be achieved through reforming legal system, enforcing contracts, ensuring property rights, maintaining peace and stability, and improving the functioning of public services. The government also takes steps on capacity building, devolution and empowerment, justice system and civil system reform and anti-corruption.

The PRSP has urged for reforms in fiscal policy, monetary policy and financial sectors. The salient suggestions are: inflation rate should be restricted to single digit preferably within 5 per cent; foreign exchange reserve to cover 4-5 months of import of goods and non-factor services. PRSP has also suggested for reduction of deficit in budget and more investment in food security, natural resources, education, health and roads; increasing tax revenue to 17.7 per cent of GDP; and availability of adequate domestic credit to the private sector.

The government of Ethiopia has built a strategy on four pillars (building blocks). These are:

(a) Agricultural Development Led Industrialization (ADLI);
(b) Justice system and civil service reform;
(c) Decentralization and empowerment; and
(d) Capacity building in public and private sectors

Such a four-pronged approach is believed to be effective in a fight against poverty and ensure sustainable development. ADLI and food security can be ensured through creation of employment, extension of credit, establishment of rural banks and co-operatives, non-peasant private sector in agricultural production, agricultural marketing and processing of agricultural products. The Civil Service Reform Program (CSRP) sought to build a fair, transparent, efficient, effective and ethical civil service to strengthen the public sector. The districts should be the center of socioeconomic development. This will provide a basis for meaningful participation by the people in local development programs. The districts will entail primary education, primary health care, rural water supply, rural roads, agricultural extension, small-scale irrigation, market infrastructure and cottage industries. Capacity building is necessary for development of human resources and institutions. Training of farmers, staff of institutions, technicians and civil servants can boost the economy.

Key Sector Measures and Crosscutting Issues

Ethiopia can achieve of progress and fight poverty through increased investments in the following sectors. These are:

(a) Agriculture
(b) Food security
(c) Education
(d) Health services

(e) HIV / AIDS
(f) Roads
(g) Water and Sanitation
(h) Gender and Development

The government is working towards effective mobilization and coordinated use of the resources of the public, private, NGOs and communities to ensure rapid, broad-based development and effectively attack deep and wide poverty, the most serious challenge that Ethiopia is facing. The government has transferred a number of responsibilities from regional governments to districts and municipalities. The government recognizes the donor communities and NGOs as important development forces and partners in development of Ethiopia. Development partners are also expected to facilitate market access, trade and foreign investment flows to Ethiopia to contribute to the realization of development and poverty reduction objectives of Ethiopia.

Debt Relief: Ethiopia has reached a decision point for enhanced HIPC relief in October 2001. The total amount of debt relief is estimated at US $1930 million, which accounted for 36 per cent of the nominal debt stock on July 7, 2001 or a common reduction factor of 47.2 per cent based on the estimated NPV of debt outstanding. The debt relief under the enhanced HIPC Initiative would supplement the federal and regional government's own effort to boost social spending by increasing budget allocation for education, health, roads, agriculture and natural resources. The allocation of resource from HIPC debt relief was 425 million Birr[a] in 2001-02, 778.9 million Birr in 2002-03 and 806.4 million Birr in 2003-04 and will be 689 million Birr in 2004-05. In other words, HIPC debt relief was 1137 million Birr for recurring

[a]Birr refers to Ethiopian currency unit equivalent to 100 cents denominations

expenditure and 2274.3 million Birr for capital expenditure in Ethiopia. [7]

The Gambia

The Gambia, the smallest African country, is a narrow strip of land in West Africa, extending inland from the Atlantic Ocean for about 48 kilometers on either side of the Gambia River and surrounded on three sides by Senegal. The Gambia became an independent state (formerly a British Colony) on February 18, 1965 and a republic in April 1970.

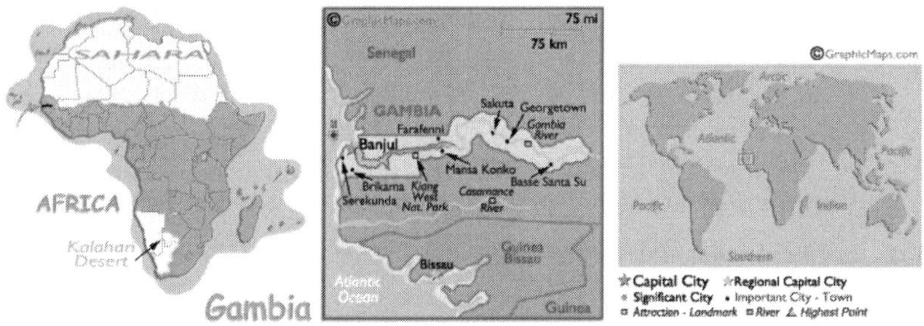

Gambia

The level of poverty in the Gambia, based on per capita consumption, the head counts index (the percentage of poor people), accounts for 58 per cent, according to the 2003 Household Poverty Survey. Reducing this rising poverty level continues to be a major challenge for the government. The statistics of the report, presented here Monday, gave the poverty gap as 25.1 per cent whilst the poverty severity accounts for about 13.9 per cent. Compared to previous statistics on poverty, it is observed that poverty level have fluctuated from 60 per cent in 1992, 63 per cent in 1998 to 58 percent in 2003.

---

[7] Ethiopia: Sustainable Development and Poverty Reduction Program, Federal Democratic Republic of Ethiopia (FDRE), Ministry of Finance and Economic Development (MOFED), July 2002, Addis Ababa.

The government has launched the National Poverty Alleviation Program in 1997 with focus on four areas:

(a) Enhancing people's productivity capacity,
(b) Improving their access to quality social services,
(c) Building capacity at the community level, and
(d) Promoting participatory communication processes.

The strategy of poverty alleviation coordinating office is the central clearinghouse for all poverty-related policies and interventions. It works under the Ministry of Finance. This organization assesses the current programs, proposes new programs, seeks donor funding, undertakes field visits to meet the beneficiaries and puts the information into a database. The coordinating office urges the economic and social departments to be pro-poor in planning and resource allocation.

The government has created a 'social development fund' in the year 1998 with the assistance from UNDP, African Development Bank and other donors to provide loans and grants to legally registered organizations. The fund also helps build the capacity of civil society organizations that provide credit. The fund has helped many village level savings and credit organizations, but only six have met the requirements outlined by the central bank. The fund recognizes that the community members putting forward proposals are likely to be richer and better organized and so its grants are not being well targeted to the poor.

The poverty program in the Gambia is impressive but depends on donors for 90 percent of its financing. When donor financing ends in 2002, the fund's grant component will be reduced and phased out. The donors should also emphasize a participatory approach to development, so that the community would take responsibilities after the donors leave the project.

(a) The government has accepted the challenge of poverty reduction through:
(b) Implementing macroeconomic and sect oral policies to promote growth with equity; and
(c) Encouraging people centered development through community based programs.

The approved copy of the PRSP II also highlighted the budgetary aspect. The overall cost of the program is estimated at US$ 754 million, of which government could commit up to 30 per cent of US$ 335 million, amounting to US$ 100.5 million, based on revenue projections after debt services." he stated. He noted that donor commitments for PRSP II (2007-11) so far, amounts to US$ 174 million and therefore Gambia will need up to US$ 479.9 million to fill the financial gap. The document further stated that with the availability of Highly Indebted Poor Countries' (HIPC) resources estimated at US$ 170 million over the five-year period, the finance gap will now be US$ 310 million for the entire period of PRSP II and on average; the gap is about US$62 million per year.

Kyrgyzstan

The country was a part of Union of Soviet Socialist Republic and it achieved independence in December 1991. Kyrgyzstan is situated on the Tien-shan Mountains. It has China, Kazakhstan, Uzbekistan and Tadzhikistan as neighbors. It is developed in livestock breeding and bee keeping. It has many industries too.

Kyrgyzstan is the one of first CIS countries to adopt national program on overcoming poverty-Araket-in early 1998. Araket's traditional income measure of poverty shows that 51 per cent of the population was poor in 1997. Hence, the program aims at elimination of income poverty and raising people's standard of living as the goal of country's ongoing reforms. The country needs donor support for capacity building. The target is to reduce poverty by 10 per cent by 2015. That would imply both rapid growth and reduced inequality.

Araket's orthodox approach to poverty reduction combines employment intensive growth with human resource development and adds a safety net for abysmal poor. It distinguishes people able to work (to be integrated into the economy through growth and social services) and such vulnerable groups as children, retired people and the disabled (to be reached through targeted social assistance). The emphasis is that poor should help themselves. They should earn through their labour. Poverty reduction is closely identified with employment. The labourers are paid in kind (flour or oil) rather than cash. And the subsidies for housing and communal services appear to benefit the better off. The central government, local governments and civil society organizations are all capital starved.

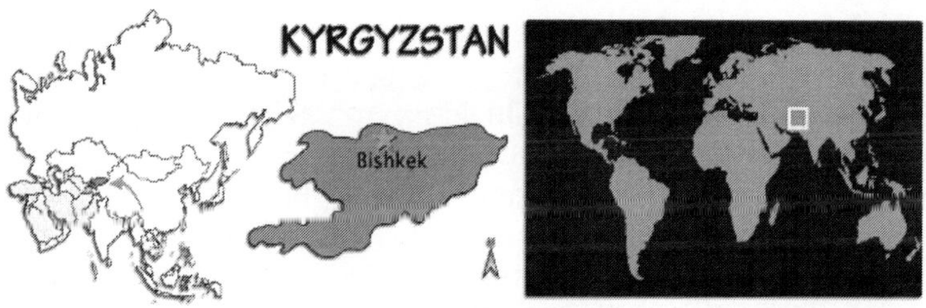

Kyrgyzstan

Another problem is that Araket overlaps the national programs for employment, women, health and education. The structure of approach to various issues should be clearly identified. Poverty reduction should be a key goal for all plans and programs including mid-term development plans. The poverty program needs an explicit budget. Hence, the Poverty Alleviation Fund was created in 1998. But this organization suffers from lack of funds and well-managed organizational activities. Communities now apply ashar (a traditional means of mutual help) to identify common development priorities and give the communities a bigger say in choosing development projects.

MALI

The Republic of Mali is a land locked state in West Africa. The area was a part of the great Mali Empire until the 15th century. In 1904, it became a French colony named as French Sudan. In 1946, it was a part of French Union. In June 1960, it became independent and was named as Sudanese Republic. Senegal federated with this country and then withdrew from Mali Federation. The Sudanese Republic changed its name to the Republic of Mali on September 22, 1960.

The country is poor in natural resources. Only 20 per cent area of Mali is cultivated. Rice, millet, groundnut and cotton are the main crops. Livestock farming is the most important occupation. Processing of hides and skins is the chief industry. River fishing is extensive. Mali exports dried and smoked fish.

Poverty is widespread in Mali. In 1994, about 70 per cent of people were income poor. But UNDP reports that 58 per cent of people suffer from different forms of human poverty. More than 50 per cent people lack access to drinking water and 75 per cent of people are illiterate. Mali is a debt-trapped country. During 1994-99, the economy of the country has been favourable with the restoration of democracy. The tensions among ethnic groups have subsided. During 1999, the economy faced new problems because of declining world cotton prices and a devastating electricity crisis.

So the government ministries, regional governments, civil societies and external donors have agreed upon the new national poverty program 1998-2002 for poverty reduction in different sectors. The Ministry of the Economy, Planning and Integration has been identified as the nodal organization for implementing the programs. The sustainable human development-monitoring unit provides day-to-day co-ordination.

The government of Mali has a budget of $ 373 million for the program's priority activities and almost 70 per cent of this amount has been earmarked for investment in infrastructure such as rural roads, schools and health centers. The external donors contribute 80 per cent of the total budget on priority activities and the rest is to be financed by the government. Mali receives debt relief from the Enhanced HIPC Initiative. The debt relief is expected to be US $250 million as the first lot. Mali abides by the International Monetary Fund's Structural Adjustment Facility. If debt relief is channeled into funds for poverty reduction and used efficiently, the income-poor people will be reduced to 60 per cent, illiteracy to 47 per cent and safe drinking water facility to 30 per cent. It is a fact that 31 per cent of non-poor people in Mali receive about 52 per cent of all social spending.

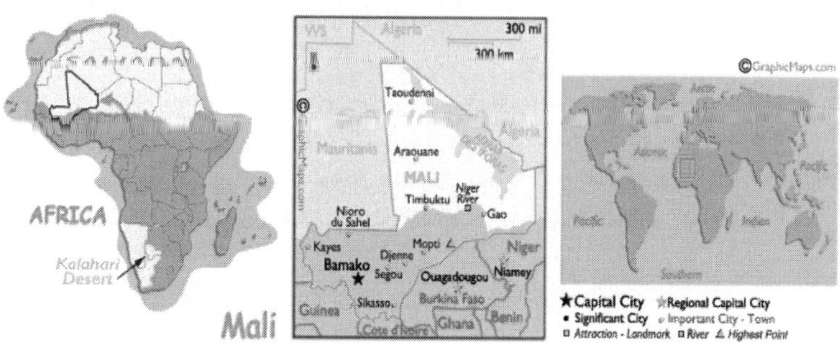

Mali

There exists high incidence of poverty among women. The Plan of Action for the Advancement of Women (1996-2000) is being integrated into National Poverty Program with UNDP support. Evaluation studies indicate that investment in community health centers, community schools, village saving and loan banks are the most successful initiatives. The people of Mali emphasize on well-drilling projects and income generating activities for peace, safety and alleviation of poverty.

Mauritania

The Islamic Republic Mauritania is situated on the Atlantic Coast of the West Africa bulge. The country was under French rule up to 1958. First it became autonomous in 1958 and then it achieved full independence on November 28, 1960. The country renounced sovereignty over its share on Western Sahara. About 47 per cent of geographical land is desert and people are nomadic.

The main profession of the people is rearing of cattle and sheep. People grow dates and grains. Fishing is also an economic activity. Fish processing and iron mining are the small-scale industries. The country has deposits of iron and copper. Mauritania has very low human development ranking 149th of 174 countries on the human development index. About 50 per cent of people are poor, 60 per cent of people are illiterate and 40 per cent of children are malnourished.

The National Poverty Alleviation Program (1998-2001) of Mauritania has two objectives:

(a) Promoting income-generating activities, especially for the self-employed, small entrepreneurs and members of co-operatives, and
(b) Increasing the poor's access to social services, particularly education, health care, water and sanitation.

The project cost of the program was $ 292 million and the target was to reduce the incidence of poverty by 18 per cent by 2001. The government of Mauritania has established the commissariat for human rights, poverty alleviation and social inclusion with the support of UNDP in mid-1998. The Commissariat receives funds from state government, external donors, the private sector and local communities and functions with relative autonomy. One commissioner (rank of minister) heads the commissariat and is assisted by an Advisory Board with representatives from economics, planning, finance, education and environment departments. The government has adopted regulations for savings and loan associations that enable them to offer micro-finance services and mobilize savings. In traditional or primitive societies, people save through purchase of land, cattle or jewelry, but in advance societies, if financial institutions are available at short distance, people save money in cash, cash certificates, and shares in mutual funds or government securities or in companies.

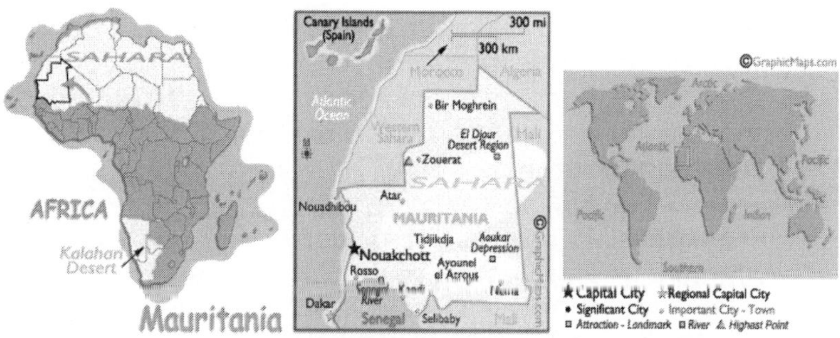

Mauritania

The Regional Priority Action Program with a fund of $12.5 million develops micro-enterprises and builds schools, health clinics, wells and roads. The drinking water projects have lowered the price of water and raised its quality. An impressive feature of many Mauritania's poverty reduction projects is their participatory design and execution. In Mauritania, the formulation, financing and execution of social habitant projects involve a partnership of local communities, civil society organizations, bilateral donors and the commissariat. Moreover, the French International Development Agency has donated 10 million francs for a social fund of poverty alleviation in 1998. This amount is being utilized for generation of employment and income through construction of roads and community centers in remote areas.

Strengths: In Mauritania, participatory approach is followed. The local communities are involved in building and maintaining community education and health facilities. Local people are recruited to maintain water pumps and health centers. They also share the building costs. The government also informs about poverty reduction projects and programs. The government supports the civil society organizations and these organizations emphasize on agricultural production, fishing, cattle rearing and micro-credit.

Weakness: The planning, monitoring and evaluation (PME) system in Mauritania is the weakest element in poverty reduction programs. Targeting of programs, data collection and expenditure surveys needs improvement in the country to guide poverty reduction programs.

Progress: Mauritania has now low budget deficit, low inflation, and more saving-investment ratio. Moreover, Mauritania achieved higher rate of GDP growth, export growth and low current account deficit. Despite a dispersed populace, primary school enrolment reach 90 per cent and school access 93 per cent and more social indicators have increased in the past two years.

Mongolia

The Mongolian People's Republic lies in central Asia with Russia to the North and China to the South, East, and West. It is one of the oldest countries. Much of the Gobi desert falls within Mongolia. The great Mongol warrior Genghis Khan (1162-1227) founded the Mongol World Empire. It became an independent country in 1921.Collective livestock farming is the principal occupation of the inhabitants. State farms practice large-scale agriculture. Former USSR and East European nations support industry. Mongolia was admitted to the World Trade Organization in July 1996. Mongolia adopted National Poverty Alleviation programs on May 25, 1994 with a view to reduce the income-poor people to 10 percent of total population. The Government of Mongolia created a Poverty Alleviation Fund of U.S. 15.7 million with assistance from the World Bank, UNDP and bilateral donors.

Poverty was unknown to Mongolia till 1991. The breaking down of former USSR, collapse of trading relations with Soviet Block and transformation of its closed economy to market-based economy caused Mongolians in poverty trap. About 25 per cent of population was under poverty by 1994 and it increased to 36 per cent by 1998.

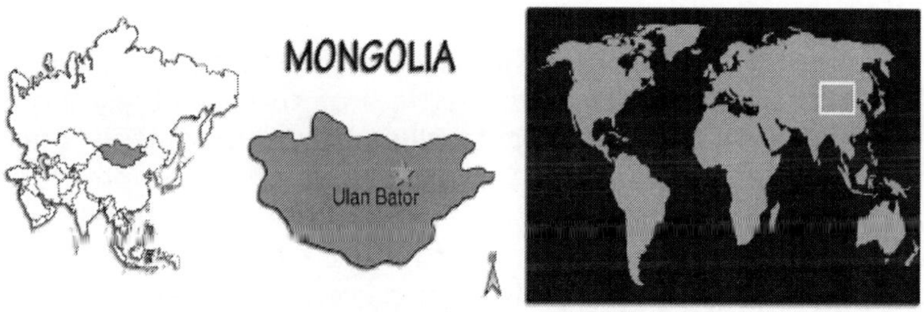

Mongolia

The Poverty Alleviation Fund created by the government emphasizes on decentralized decision-making and community participation. The Poverty Alleviation Fund (PAF) is divided into four independent but complementary sub-funds, each with specific activity areas and target groups.

These are:

(a) Local Development Fund;
(b) Income Generation Fund;
(c) Women's Development Fund; and
(d) Targeted Assistance Fund

Bulks of the funds have gone for micro-loans. These micro loans are utilized for trading, carpentry, dress making, vegetable growing, boot making and herd restocking. Micro credit is also utilized for repairing and rebuilding schools, health clinics and rural infrastructure by the organizations representing vulnerable groups. The Poverty Alleviation Fund has disbursed US $ 12.7 million for the implementation of over 13 thousand small-scale poverty alleviation projects throughout the country. Moreover, at least 30,000 poor households have escaped from poverty through income generating schemes. The UNDP has helped to set up a Women's Development Fund to provide micro loans to women and female-headed households. The donors also support a Targeted Assistance Fund to complement the government's ongoing Social Assistance Fund by providing food, fuel and clothing to the poorest.

The micro loan program is available to poor people in every urban and rural districts of the country. About 20 per cent of poor families have increased their income by the year 2000. The micro loan program has raised the interest rate and shortened the duration to one year. Micro start Mongolia – a UNDP supported program also gives credit in small amounts to the poor. The Poverty Alleviation Fund has surprised the government agencies in financing the poor in Mongolia. The future can say whether external funding for micro loans is really intended for poverty alleviation or for the benefits of the donors. Hence, impact assessment of micro loans may be taken up and the government should co-ordinate the entire program for transparency and accountability.

In Mongolia, growth has been slow and inequality on the rise. The banking system remains weak and is unable to revive the economy in both rural areas and small towns. Now there exists better access to health care and basic education. The enrolment of students in schools has increased, and infant and maternal mortality has decreased. Hence, the government of Mongolia needs to upgrade and revitalize the banking system, check the growing trend of inequalities and the increasing trend of poor families through appropriate macro and micro economic policies and pro-poor programs. The government should undertake long-term plans and annual plans on the basis of research studies and feed backs from Planning, Monitoring and Evaluation Cells in each sector of its activity.

II. Implementation of the Country Strategy and Program

A. Progress in Poverty Reduction

Progress towards MDG targets is similar to when the CSP was endorsed. However, the Government is making more efforts to direct development initiatives toward achieving the MDGs and targets. Mongolia is actively participating in the United Nations (UN) Millennium Project. The UN and Government teams are working together in developing a MDG-based national development strategy and sector strategies aligned with MDGs. The first round of training and planning exercises has been completed.

B. Progress in the Country Strategy and Program Focus Areas

Of the outcomes in the CSP results matrix; progress has been marked in financial sector development, alignment of skills and education with market demand, better education opportunities, and lower geographical isolation. Important initiatives since the

CSP have included the establishment of a financial regulatory commission, associated with an ADB financed program; the development of a secondary mortgage market, also stimulated by ADB supported work; a program for vocational education jointly funded by ADB and German development cooperation through GTZ; the completion of a section of the road connecting the Russian Federation with the People's Republic of China (PRC) through Mongolia and the commencement of work on other sections of the road; and the adoption of a heath sector master plan and initial steps to implement it. The most encouraging progress in ADB's areas of strategic focus has been in the education sector, where the Government has developed a sector master plan. In 2006, an ADB TA project that aims to support the master plan and a sector-wide approach will be presented to the Board. Regional cooperation and integration will benefit from the central corridor highway, supported by project loans for the second and regional roads projects; a regional TA project (RETA) on HIV/AIDS prevention; and greater regional cooperation in the preparation of the Western Regional Road Development Project.

However, progress in some other areas has been less encouraging. The new administration has reassessed its area development strategy, which has delayed progress. A proposed ADB project for 2006 was refocused to increase the pro-poor impacts of urban services through better harmonization with other funding agencies and this also led to delays. Progress toward an agriculture sector strategy has been slow but is back on track with ADB support and it is expected that the proposed 2007 loan for the Agriculture and Rural Development Project will be guided by the strategy. Also, while the CSP drew attention to the increased availability of rural finance, there has not been sustained progress in making available term finance for agricultural production and agro-enterprises. Progress in developing rural cooperatives under the Agriculture Sector Development Project (ASDP) has been mixed and the development of value chains and private rural enterprises has been less than satisfactory. These areas will receive renewed attention in the proposed Agriculture and Rural Development Project.

C. Private Sector Development

ADB continues to support the enabling environment for private sector development through both loan and TA operations. The Financial Regulation and Governance loan, approved in late 2005, will support the regulation and further development of non-bank financial institutions, improve corporate governance in commercial banks, and help to further develop Mongolia's capital markets. The Customs Modernization Project planned for 2006 will facilitate the flow of external trade, reduce corruption, and assist in improving the investment climate. The Agriculture and Rural Development Project in 2007 will assist the private sector to develop export markets and develop new instruments for private sector lending. Identification of potential projects for investment through the private sector window will continue to focus on the financial and infrastructure sectors to build on ADB's first private sector operation - an investment in Trade and Development Bank. SME financing and power generation projects for export of electricity are current areas of focus

D. Highlights in Coordination of External Funding and Partnership Arrangements

All major external agencies have accepted the education master plan of the Government as the basis for future funding. The Government of Japan and ADB have submitted Mongolia's proposal to the Education for All—Fast Track Initiative. Agreement has been reached with German development assistance (Deutscher Entwicklungsdienst) and GTZ over parallel financing for the proposed ADB-supported Urban Development and Housing Project and with GTZ for parallel financing for the Agriculture and Rural Development Project.

ADB's co financing strategy will be guided by two recent developments: the potential availability of more grant funds and more government interest in financing infrastructure through external financing. Building on experience in the urban development and education sectors, ADB is identifying investments for which grants or private sector funding may be available and investment gaps that need to be funded by ADB. It is also designing ADB assistance so that it can serve as a platform for funding from other sources. ADB is assisting the Government in developing strategies for the education, agriculture, and transport sectors that could be the basis for aid coordination. In responding to the Government's desire to widen its funding sources, the first part of ADB's strategy will be to assist the Government to identify appropriate areas for externally financed investments, such as an export-earning enclave project, probably in the energy sector. The Government has also expressed interest in issuing a sovereign bond. An ADB guarantee may help to reduce borrowing costs and ADB could provide such a guarantee if the use of proceeds can be mutually agreed. ADB will continue to advise the Government on its bond issuance plans.[113]

Nepal

The Kingdom of Nepal [114] is a land-locked Asian country in the Himalayan mountain range. It is bounded by Tibet and Indian states. The members of Rana family became the Prime Ministers from 1846 to 1951 and virtually ruled the country. In 1961, 15 small territories were amalgamated into Nepal. The

---

[113]ADB Country Strategy and Program
[114]ADB Asian Development Bank

king relinquished his absolute power in 1990 and Nepal became a constitutional monarchy with multiparty democracy.

The country is full of high mountains and valleys. The country is having vast resources of natural forests. Its area reduced from 60 per cent to 30 per cent because of increase of population and increase of poverty among them. About 90 per cent of labour force are engaged in agriculture, forestry and fishing. Lumbini, the birthplace of Lord Goutam Buddha and Mount Everest, the World's highest peak are situated in Nepal. Tourism is a major source of income in Nepal.

The process of planned economic development in Nepal was started in 1956. The fourth five-year plan period (1970-1975) emphasized on building of economic and social infrastructures and the fifth five-year plan (1975-1980) targeted for increasing the production of mass-oriented goods, utilization of maximum workforce and regional integration in the country. A major portion of public sector expenditure was spent on transport, communications, electricity and industrial development. The sixth and seventh five-year plans (1980-1990) emphasized on both increasing production and productive employment. During the period, stagnant exports and high increases in imports led to trade deficits and a negative balance of payment.

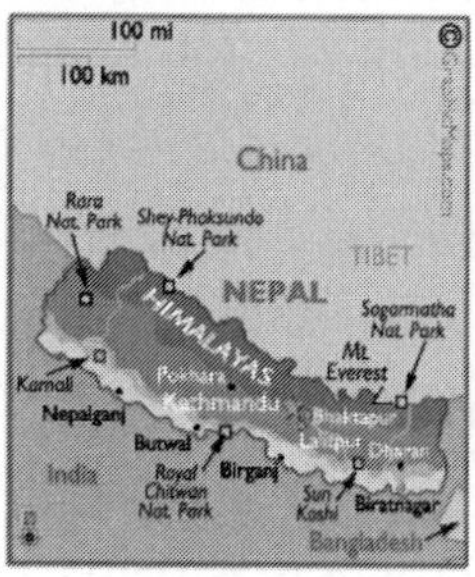

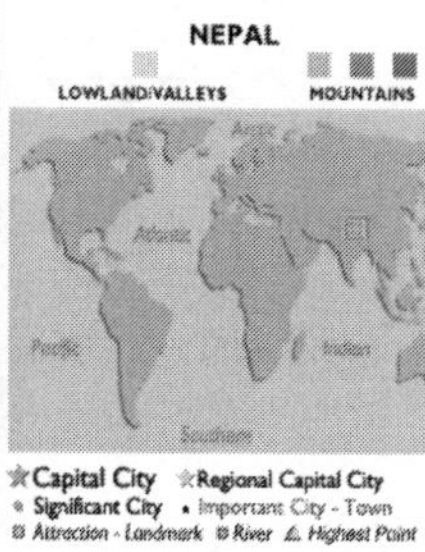

Nepal

Development Strategies:

The eighth five-year plan (1992-97) envisaged a new dimension in development approach through tackling the challenges of economic stagnation, poverty alleviation, reducing structural anomalies and controlling environmental degradation and rapid population growth. The plan targeted to provide job opportunities to 1.4 million people and to reduce absolute poverty from 49 per cent to 42 per cent of the total population. The plan further envisaged the implementation of various target group oriented sectoral and specific programs. These are:

Production and employment generating activities

(a) Development of physical infrastructure
(b) Resettlements of the poor
(c) Provision of health services
(d) Education opportunities
(e) Safe drinking water facilities
(f) Establishment of small farmer development program
(g) Production credit for rural women
(h) Leased forestry
(i) Labour-intensive public construction works
(j) Irrigation programs
(k) Decentralized local-level planning
(l) Participation of non-government organizations in poverty alleviation programs

Poverty Alleviation Programs

The Government of Nepal implemented the following steps for alleviation of poverty of the rural poor.

(a) Subsidy **:** (i). Food subsidy through National Food Corporation, (ii) Fertilizer subsidy through Agriculture

Input Corporation and (iii) Government interest and capital subsidy through Agriculture Development Bank

(b) Integrated rural development projects

(c) Food and feeding programs: Nutrition's Food Program, and Joint Nutrition's Support Pogrom - These programs could reach 2, 00,000 beneficiaries.

Targeted credit programs: Small Farmers Development Program, Production Credit for Rural Women, Intensive Banking Program, and Rural Development Banks. The basic components of all four programs are designed for community development, income generation, and provision of credit, group activities and participation in self-help activities.

(d) **Employment programs**: (i). Food-for-work program, and (ii). Special public works program

These programs create employment opportunities to the rural poor through building rural infrastructure and construction of irrigation channels during the off-farm season. The food-for-work program has generated about 1.5 million man-days of work per year. The special public works program has engaged 20,000 rural people per year. The eighth five-year plan gave emphasis on skills-generating programs such as Training for Rural Activities (TRUGA) and labour supply centers. The plan emphasized on poverty alleviation among backward ethnic and oppressed groups through income generating activities. The government also encouraged the NGOs for improvement of the socio-economic conditions in backward ethnic communities.

(e) **Settlement of land-less people**:

Nepal is implementing the Kamaiya (agricultural labourers bonded by an annual fixed wage) Abolition

Program through abolition and settlement of Kamaiya labourers. They are provided with surplus land and loan for alternate ways of living. Nepal has adopted a 20-year priority focused forward-looking agriculture prospective plan to accelerate 5 per cent growth rate in agriculture. To meet the target, the government encourages:

(a) More fertilizer use by the farmers
(b) Availability of irrigation facilities through tube wells, small canals
(c) Construction of rural roads and rural electrification
(d) Extension of appropriate agricultural technology
(e) Production of high-value crops
(f) More production in milk, meat and eggs - through "Prioritized Productivity Packages"

Industrial development in Nepal: Its contribution is less than 10 per cent of GDP. Hence, the government promulgated Industrial Enterprises Act 1992 to encourage private participation in industrial development with a minimum Government intervention.

Planning by ADB

ADB's assistance will help ease social tensions and create the foundation for sustainable poverty reduction. ADB's strategy for development assistance to Nepal—based on the development challenges and opportunities and the Government's strategic priorities set out in the Tenth Plan—will focus on:

(a) Promoting pro-poor and broad-based economic growth by connecting the rural poor, and those long excluded from the development process, to markets and economic opportunities through development of rural infrastructure facilities and services—road and air transport, telecommunications, rural electrification, irrigation, and rural finance

(b) Supporting inclusive social and human development, empowerment of the poor and disadvantaged by improving their health conditions through improved rural water supply and sanitation, and provision of basic education and vocational training needed for raising productivity and generating remunerative employment.

(c) Promoting good governance by helping combat corruption, improving delivery of local public services, and building professional management capacity to deliver results.

As crosscutting initiatives, the CSP will also focus on:

(a) Supporting the creation of an enabling environment for increased private sector participation and investment by fostering better policy, and more effective implementation of policies and regulatory reform in key sectors
(b) Addressing gender, ethnic, and caste discrimination through policy reform, targeted investments, and the mainstreaming of equal opportunity measures in key sector investments
(c) Improving social, environmental, and resettlement assessment policies, procedures, and practices as these relate to investment projects
(d) Tapping benefits from regional cooperation initiatives in the areas of transport connections and trade facilitation, energy, tourism, and communications with neighboring countries.
(e) Delivering development assistance effectively in a conflict setting is a major challenge.

Lessons learned from past ADB experience include the need to (i) keep ADB operations simple and implemental, (ii) promote local service delivery and active participation of key stakeholders to ensure that projects are demand-driven and sustainable, and (iii) work steadily to enhance public policy and institutional performance resulting in a more enabling environment for private initiatives.

To this end, (i) ADB's future assistance will be more sharply focused and results oriented, (ii) more sector-wide and programmatic approaches will be used, and (iii) participation of a wider spectrum of stakeholders and institutions in the design and implementation of all projects will be encouraged.

In addition, ADB's assistance will be increasingly harmonized with the Government's policies and procedures as well as with the assistance of other development partners. To respond to the special implementation challenges posed by the conflict, ADB assistance proposes more flexible modalities; greater community participation; more transparency of ADB operations; and a sharper focus on poverty reduction, regional equity, and the mainstreaming of social inclusion in ADB operations. This approach will address the underlying causes of the conflict and persistent poverty.

Zambia

Zambia was formerly known as Northern Rhodesia. It is situated in south central Africa and is separated from Zimbabwe by the river Zambezi. Moreover, the Kariba Dam, one of the biggest man-made dams in the world is separating both the countries. The country was under administrative control of South Africa Company from 1889 to 1924 and under British rule up to 1964. The country achieved her independence in 1964 and became a Republic.

Zambia is rich in minerals including copper, zinc, cobalt, lead, uranium and manganese. The international price of copper regulates the economy of the country. Agriculture is the main occupation of the inhabitants. The farmers cultivate crops like maize, tobacco, groundnuts, cotton, millets, cassava and sugarcane.

The committee for Campaign against Poverty in their book "Poverty Experience in Zambia" have shown that the wide spread and worsening poverty situation in Zambia in 1996 affected over 6 million people out of country's estimated nine million (UNICEF, 1996; World Bank, 1994).

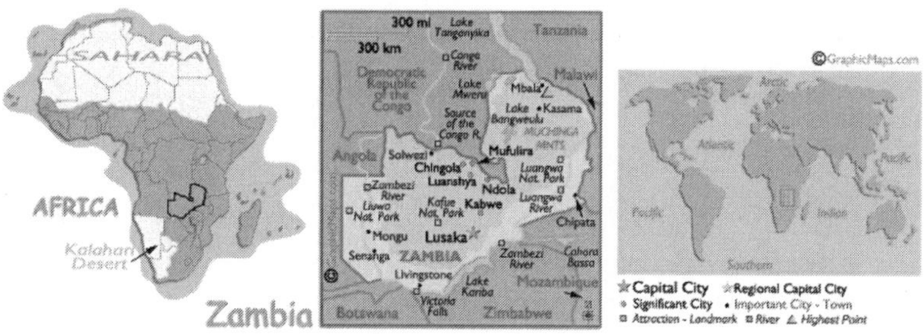

Zambia

The extent of poverty in the western province and Luapula province of Zambia is as high as 95 per cent or more. Human survival in Zambia has become a challenge to the world communities and international funding institutions. Poverty of Zambia has jeopardized in the areas of food security, health, education, sanitation and employment. Employment in formal sector has been reduced from 544,300 in 1991 to 472,000 in 1997.[115]

Social Indicators in Zambia

The country is heavily infested with HIV/AIDS and acute poverty. For both the reasons, the average life

---

[115] Mwene Mwinga (2002), " Civil Society and the Poverty Reduction Strategy Process in Zambia"

expectancy had fallen from a peak of about 54 years in mid -1980 to less than 40 years today. Signs of distress or low welfare in the form of malnutrition, disease, illiteracy, ragged clothing and dirty conditions are to be seen everywhere (World Bank, 1994; UNICEF, 1996). Chronic malnutrition in 1996 affected about 57 per cent of the poorest rural households (core rural poor) and about 41 per cent of the core urban poor (World Bank). The infant mortality rate rose from 97 deaths per 1000 births in 1980 to about 197 per 1000 in 1999, while the maternal mortality rate was 694 maternal deaths per 1000 hospital deliveries in 1996 from 200 in 1980 (World Bank, 1994). In the education sector, the primary school enrolment rate declined from over 96 per cent in the mid- 1980's to less than 80 per cent in1996, with the result that over 500,000 children were out of school (World Bank, 1994; UNICEF, 1996).

Zambian poverty is caused by:

(a) Lack of righteousness,
(b) Lack of wisdom,
(c) Lack of love,
(d) Lack of communication,
(e) Prayerlessness,
(f) Lack of peace,
(g) Lack of vision,
(h) Disorganization,
(i) Lack of gratitude,
(j) Stagnation,
(k) Mediocrity or lack of excellence and
(l) Lack of determination.

Moreover, it reports:

(a) Lack of Money is simply the physical manifestation of poverty.
(b) Poverty is a spirit, an attitude, a characteristic and very often it is a generational affair."[116]

---

[116]Gate Way to Zambia, The Zambian

PRSP in Zambia

Zambia's first PRSP has identified the following broad themes for interventions:

(a) Since poverty is wide spread in Zambia to the extent of 80 per cent of the population, pro-poor economic policies is emphasized.
(b) Zambia is dangerously dependent on foreign aid and this foreign aid is expected to contribute more than 50 per cent in the 2001 fiscal budget. It emphasizes that the country to generate its own resources and be free from high rate dependency.
(c) The PRSP suggests early solutions on non-monetary issues like voice of the people, security, safe environment, good governance, concerns for females and youths. It also emphasizes access for key services like education, health and transport for reduction of deprivations.
(d) GDP growth rate of 6 to 8 per cent per annum to achieve poverty reduction targets set for 2015. The projected growth rate is 5 percent for 2001, 2002 and 5.5 per cent for 2003.
(e) Long-term planning for development in sectors like tourism, mining, industry, energy, infrastructure, investment, capital markets and agriculture.
(f) Debt Relief
(g) HIV/AIDS and Disability issues
(h) Land development and support services;
(i) Infrastructure development;
(j) Agribusiness promotion and training;
(k) Finance and development;
(l) Technology development and dissemination;
(m) Food security and diversification

Agriculture was given priority in the budget and total allocation amounted to K41.68 billion or 35.67 per cent of total expenditure. The priority areas in agriculture include:

(a) Agricultural research
(b) Seed certification and supply
(c) Animal production
(d) Irrigation and land use planning
(e) Agricultural marketing and trade
(f) Fisheries research
(g) Agricultural extension, and
(h) Farm mechanization

Zambia gets financial assistance from IMF, World Bank, UNDP, European Union, DFID (UK), GTZ, CIDA (Canada) and USAID.[117]

Conclusion

The countries such as Benin, Burkina Faso, Ethiopia, the Gambia, Kyrgyzstan, Mali, Mauritania, Mongolia, Nepal and Zambia are poor countries, which expect prosperity in near future through foreign assistance. But the external funding may plunge these countries into "debt trap", if the investments do not yield results as expected. For example, Benin's external debt totals more than 60 per cent of GDP and its annual budget deficit are entirely financed by external resources. The external debt of Burkina Faso will be 423 per cent of exports in 1995-97 and export earnings shrank 16 per cent a year during 1990-96.

Ethiopia now makes increased investments in agriculture, food security, education, health services, HIV / AIDS, roads, water and sanitation, and gender and development for fighting poverty. The country has reached a decision point for debt relief of US $ 1930 million, which accounts for 36 per cent of the nominal debt stock as on July 7, 2001 or a common reduction factor of 47.2 per cent based on the estimated NPV of debt outstanding. In other words, HIPC debt relief is 1137 million Birr for recurring

---

[117]Poverty Reduction Strategy Paper, First Draft, Ministry of Finance and Economics Development, Zambia, September 2001.

expenditure and 2274.3 million Birr for capital expenditure in Ethiopia. The poverty program in the Gambia depended on donors for 90 per cent of its financing. The government of Kyrgyzstan is capital starved. In Mali, external donors contribute 80 per cent of the total budget on priority activities. Mongolia has created a "poverty alleviation fund" of US$ 15.7 million with assistance from the World Bank, UNDP and bilateral donors. Nepal has undertaken massive programs in production and income generating activities, and poverty alleviation programs. The country is capital starved and needs external aid. Zambia gets financial assistance from the World Bank, IMF, UNDP, DFID, USAID, CIDA and GTZ. But poverty of masses is as high as 80 per cent of the population. Poverty in western province and Luapula province is about 96 per cent of the population. If the external donors extend aid with a sole object to reduce poverty, it is quite possible through debt cancellation, increase in official development assistance (ODA) and technical guidance.

In short, poverty is the greatest challenge to the whole world and the humanity. The respective governments should sincerely try to undertake massive measures for poverty reduction programs through pro-poor, pro-rural and pro-agricultural policies. Corruption at each stage of planning and execution should be watched and there should be stringent laws for curbing corruption. Expenditure in defense sector should be minimized. The government should give maximum weight-age on 'food security' as compared to infrastructure development and defense. Food aid should be free from obligations such as buying defense equipments on loan or conversion of religion of the poor or expenditure on social welfare. The non-government organizations (NGOs) patronized by developed countries and rich people digest all donations and utilize the funds for personal advertisement and private use. The governments of poor countries should deregister all these organization or at least enquire their activities. These organizations earn money by making films on the hungry people, natural hazards, and make money by selling the photos of dying persons. The officials of governments and funding institutions are also involved these black deals. It is good news that the Committee on World Food Security is trying to restrict hunger worldwide. The Food and Agriculture Organization[118] has advised that governance of food security should aim at:

(a) Keep agriculture and food security at top of the international agenda for the eradication of hunger and malnutrition in the world;
(b) Fully understand the factors that affect world food security, the associated risks and remedial actions;
(c) Ensure close links between technical expertise and policy-making;
(d) See that the international community adopts a coherent and systematic approach to food security to respond rapidly the situations of food crisis and emergency in order to mitigate their negative effects; to stimulate investment in agriculture and rural development and mobilize the funding required ensuring the food security of local populations; and to help bolster the governance of food security in a framework of coherence and synergy of policies, strategies and actions at all levels – national, regional and international.

We feel that we can achieve food security for all and save the hungry people from starvation deaths provided the governments of low-income countries implement pro-poor, pro-rural and pro-agricultural policies in their countries.

+++++

---

[118] Report of the 36th Session of the Committee on World Food Security (CFS), Rome 18-23 November 2009

Chapter –IV

REPORTS OF COMMITTEES ON POVERTY ALLEVIATION

Hunger and self-government are incompatible: the under-nourished majority will always be ruled from above by well-fed few.

-Aldous Huxley

Starvation, hunger, malnutrition, ill health, stunted growth and disease are synonymous with poverty in all the heavily indebted poor countries (HIPC) and developing countries. Therefore, the United Nations Organizations, the World Bank, International Monetary Fund, OECD countries, G-8 and other developed countries are emphasizing on reduction of poverty since the Social Development Summit in Copenhagen in 1995. Moreover, these world organizations and developed countries have convened seminars, conferences and have drawn experiences for ascertaining the causes of poverty. They are also searching for effective policies and programs for fighting poverty in poor countries. These committees have reported the possible ways (both short-term and long-term) for alleviation of poverty in specific zones, states, and countries. The aim of poverty reduction processes is to lessen the social and economic vulnerability of the population living below the poverty line, to reduce poverty risk factors and to make better use of human capital. Salient features of some of the committees, conferences and experiences on poverty alleviation are described as follows:

1. Kyrgyzstan Experience (1991)

The collapse of the Soviet Union in 1991 caused chaotic condition in Kyrgyzstan. The Government could not provide adequate safety net for the growing number of unemployed and vulnerable groups. The budget faced severe constraints and the standard of living decreased drastically. The NGO sector was very weak and lacked experience. The UNDP undertook the following steps to strengthen the capacity of the voluntary sector so that it could become a viable partner for long-term poverty reduction, such as:

(a) Capacity building and organizational development;
(b) Self-help initiatives building upon local knowledge systems and resources;
(c) A mapping exercise of NGO capacities;
(d) Institutional strengthening;
(e) Development of community-led initiatives such as micro-credit and small-scale enterprise;
(f) Government – NGO co-ordination, and;
(g) Community-based environmental protection and rehabilitation program [119]

---

[119] KYR/94/122, Promotion of Community Based Development for Poverty Reduction in KYRGYSZTAN / UNDP

2. Dhaka Declaration (1993)

The 7th SAARC declaration pledged to implement a pro-poor development strategy, centered on the social mobilization and empowerment of poor communities in order to promote human development that can translate into an improvement in the standard of living for every one socially, politically, economically and environmentally by the year 2002. The South Asia Association for Regional Cooperation (SAARC) consists of India, Pakistan, Bangladesh, Nepal, Sri Lanka, Bhutan and the Maldives and together account for 40 per cent of the world's poor.

The Action Agenda focused on:

(a) Social mobilization that builds and empowers the organization of the poor;
(b) Decentralized agricultural development focused on household food security and basic nutritional needs;
(c) Decentralized, small-scale, labour intensive industrialization, based on appropriate technology;
(d) Human development, including universal primary education, primary health care, enhancement of women's social roles, protection of children and shelter for the poor; and
(e) Mobilization of financial resources to achieve these goals

To follow up on these commitments, each government agreed to formulate a pro-poor development plan and create an enabling environment in support of the poverty reduction efforts.[120]

---

[120] SAARC Declaration on Poverty Reduction in South Asia, Dhaka, Bangladesh - April 1993 Quoted from "UNDP-Poverty Reduction- Policy Framework for Country Strategies.

3. The Washington Consensus (1993)

The Washington Consensus of market friendly reforms refers to the following 10 objectives of policy:

(a) Fiscal disciplines;
(b) Reduction of public expenditure towards education, health and infrastructure investment;
(c) Tax reform – (broadening the tax base and cutting marginal tax rates);
(d) Interest rates that are markets determined and positive (but moderate) in real terms;
(e) Competitive exchange rates;
(f) Trade liberalization - replacement of quantitative restrictions with low and uniform tariffs;
(g) Openness to foreign direct investment;
(h) Privatization of state enterprises;
(i) Deregulation - abolishment of regulations that impede entry or restrict competition, expect for those justified on safety, environmental and prudential oversight of financial institutions; and
(j) Legal security of property rights[121]

4. Poverty Reduction in Malawi (1993)

The Government of Malawi and the UN system undertook **Situation Analysis of Poverty** in 1993.The report was the first major attempt to document key poverty factors in Malawi. It revealed that poverty in Malawi is significant and widespread, affecting 60 percent of rural and 65 percent of urban population. The most vulnerable groups include small holders with less than one hectare of land holding,

---

[121]William Son 1993, "The World Bank Report 2000-2001' P.63

casual laborers, estate workers and tenants, female-headed households, and the urban poor. The key poverty factors were identified as:

(a) Low agricultural productivity;
(b) Low non-farm income;
(c) Poor education and health;
(d) Rapid population growth;
(e) Weak institutional structure;
(f) Existing land ownership patterns;
(g) Poor access to farm inputs;
(h) Shortage of labour;
(i) Unfair pricing and marketing of smallholder crops;
(j) Inability of small holders to benefit from research; and
(k) Meager activities of Government and social organization to support decentralized and participatory development approaches

Poverty Reduction Policies

(a) Human development strategies to go beyond price-oriented reforms, focusing more on existing structural constraints and institutional weaknesses in the design and implementation of anti-poverty programs;
(b) A National Steering Committee was created to provide overall guidance and direction to a national anti-poverty program;
(c) Presidential Council on Poverty Alleviation was created to monitor 10 sectoral working groups and 24 district level exercises on poverty reduction;
(d) UNDP, UNICEF, World Bank and other donors have volunteered in the process; and
(e) Publication of annual poverty situation and dis-aggregated district level data for use in development planning, support policy and

program analysis for the national action plan for poverty elimination[122]

5. The Philippines Experience (December 1993)

The Government of Philippines set the target of reducing poverty from 41 per cent to 30 per cent between 1991 and 1998. Hence, it requested UN assistance for the formulation of a national anti-poverty strategy. The national consultants of Philippines under joint technical assistance of UN system (UNDP, UNFPA, UNICEF and WFP) prepared a document entitled "A Strategy to Fight Poverty".

The study identified the main causes of poverty as follows:

(a) Lack of employment and livelihood opportunities due to weak economic performance, exacerbated by high population growth;
(b) Concentration of wealth, incomes and access resources;
(c) Low productivity of labour;
(d) Limited access to basic social services;
(e) Poor or degraded resource base;
(f) Unresponsive and graft-ridden politics and bureaucracy, rooted in the political power of vested interest groups;
(g) Weak economic growth (which increases both poverty and inequality); and
(h) The pattern of growth has been highly skewed and inequitable resulting mass poverty of the unprivileged.

---

[122] . UNDP and Government of Malawi, **Situation Analysis of Poverty**, Lilongwe, 1993.

Suggestions:

(a) The growth strategy must emphasize a strong anti-poverty thrust
(b) People in poverty are not homogenous and will not benefit equally from broad policy measures. Hence the target should be more direct interventions to reach the hard-core poor; and

(c) The planning and implementation process should meet the survival, security and empowerment needs of the poor.[123]

6. Addis Ababa Conference (1994)

In a regional conference held in January 1994, the governments of Africa stressed that the human dimensions of development must underlie all other objectives committed themselves to an action agenda for human and social development in the African region.

The priority areas are:

(a) Alleviating poverty;
(b) Creating and sustaining productive employment and income generation;
(c) Enhancing social integration, national cohesion, peace and political stability; and
(d) Promoting democratization, human rights and popular participation.

The members of the conference recognized that "development can be sustainable only to the extent that it is human centered and the centrality of the human beings as the initiator and beneficiary of development". The African leaders pledged to forge a "new impact for human development between African

[123] .A Strategy to Fight Poverty, Manila, December 1993

governments and African people... to break the vicious circle of ignorance, poverty, unemployment and under employment, malnutrition and hunger, disease and ill-health and lack of shelter. The ultimate goal of this impact would be to ensure the peoples' overall well being through a sustainable improvement of their living standards. This requires a radical reorientation of the whole basis of development in the region through a comprehensive and integrated development strategy that fosters peoples' empowerment, investing in and building up peoples' capacities of self-reliance.

The conference decided the following steps to alleviate poverty in the region:

(a). To attack the root causes of poverty through which policies must concentrate on creating an enabling environment for raising the productivity of the labour force in the agricultural and informal sectors, where majority of people work, in order to unleash their entrepreneurial talents, creativity and productive capacity;

(b) To increase public spending on all areas of human development from its current average level of 14 percent to 30 percent of total public expenditures; the growth rate in public outlays in these sectors should be above the population growth rate

(c) To reduce the military spending by at least one-third of its present level;

(d) The conference called for urgent measures to be taken up by Africa's development partners to write off ODA debt, cancel two-thirds of Paris club debt and alleviate the burden of multilateral debt, in order to support human development efforts through the effective application of debt swaps for human development. Africa's development partners should also commit themselves to earmark at least 20 percent of ODA for human development priorities and match increased allocations that African countries will make to these fields; and

(e) Finally, African leaders expressed that for the Social Summit to become a turning point for development in the region; it should provide the world with a benchmark for improving the human condition.[124]

7. Pacific Human Development Report (1994)
(The Suva declaration)

In August 1994, the leaders of 14 pacific island countries met in Suva, Fiji, during the 25th South Pacific Forum meeting, to endorse the recommendations of the Pacific Human Development Report, a regional initiative that was supported by UNDP, in close collaboration with the UN system. The pacific HDR urged countries to assess development in terms of a range of social and economic growth but to increase the opportunities for people to lead productive and satisfying lives.

The Suva declaration urged pacific countries to take prompt and effective action to ensure that the benefits of economic growth are equally distributed for the continued improvement of people's well being (in order) to enable the majority of people to participate fully in socioeconomic life and to be the owners of the development process. The Suva declaration emphasized on:

(a) Priority areas identification;
(b) Establishing effective governance;
(c) Promoting sustainable population;

---

124 . Conference of African Ministers Responsible for Human Development, ***African Common Position on Human and Social Development in Africa***, Addis Ababa, January 1994.

(d) Advancement of women;
(e) Protection and regeneration of the environment; and
(f) Promoting health, family living and human values.[125]

8. Promoting Social agenda in Latin America and the Caribbean (Santiago de Chile Declaration)

A group of Latin American political leaders, senior planners, businessmen and civil society representatives pledged their full support and endorsement of the WSSD Declaration and Programme Action in a meeting held in Santiago de Chile in December 1994. They expressed their hope that the social summit will contribute for creating a more favorable international environment for people-centered development and poverty eradication. The members also recognized that poverty in Latin America and the Caribbean has structural causes, stemming from a profound asymmetry in the distribution of wealth and power resources, and that the active involvement of people in poverty is a requisite condition for success in fighting poverty.

The participants made a number of recommendations. Some of these recommendations are:

(a) Poverty eradication must become a top priority of development strategies and policies in the region

(b) Social policies must become state policies, and not just government policies, and they must address the structural causes of poverty, going beyond welfare or compensation into long-term development support

---

[125] . Suva Declaration on Sustainable Human Development, 1994

(c) There is a need for a new relationship between the state, the private sector and the civil society, with the state playing a facilitating role through decentralization and delegation of responsibilities in a spirit of partnership;

(d) Poverty eradication requires increased and better targeted social spending, along with a more equitable distribution of income;

(e) The activities of micro and small-scale producers and craftsmen must be supported with measures aimed at raising their productivity, in particular through the transfer of knowledge and greater access to concessional loans from the banking system;

(f)The critical role of women as agents of change in the development process must be recognized and activity supported; and

(g) Establishing of a trust fund for capacity building and institutional development of NGOs and civil society organizations. Funding for the trust fund would come from the conversion of foreign debt, through the use of debt swaps for social purposes.[126]

9. The PREDES Model in Peru (1994)

In August 1991, the Government in Peru created FONCODES, a social compensation and development fund, for the introduction of an economic stabilization package. FONCODES provides grants for social assistance and infrastructure projects, and loans for small and micro-enterprises. In general, social assistance projects are targeted at the chronically

[126] Regional Forum to Promote a Social Agenda for Latin America and the Caribbean, Santiago, de Chile, December 1994

poor, while infrastructure rehabilitation and productive ventures is intended for the newly inflicted poor. The beneficiaries manage these projects. They are benefited through technical support of municipalities, regional governments, line ministries and NGOs. Despite some achievements, an evaluation study has noted a number of problems on FONCODES:

(a) The atomistic nature of activities funded, which results from the demand-driven mechanism adopted by FONCODES;
(b) Produces "pockets of impact "rather than the broad coverage needed to attack structural poverty;
(c) An excessive emphasis on social assistance and welfare projects;
(d) Problems in the delivery, monitoring and evaluation of fund resources; and
(e) Difficulty in reaching the poorest especially in isolated rural areas and extreme fragmentation and dissension of development agents

Hence, a group of indigenous NGOs developed an alternative approach to community development, which is known as the Reconstruction and Development Program (PREDES). This program was then picked up and supported by a number of bilateral donors and UNDP for implementation.

PREDES Model

(a) To have a lasting impact in the communities through supporting activities in rehabilitating the productive base of the communities;
(b) To protect and upgrade the environment;
(c) To meet the basic needs of vulnerable groups;
(d) To strengthen grass root organizations;
(e) To adopt an area-based approach to overcome the fragmentation and dispersion of development activities;

(f) To act on a supra-communal space (the district and the province) and to promote inter-agency co-ordination at the planning and implementation stages of the program; and
(g) To attempt the link emergency actions (social assistance) to development (support to income and employment generation)

The institutional backbone of the PREDES model[127] is the District Development Committee (DDC), an autonomous decision-making body. PREDES utilizes a large share of program resources in development-oriented activities, such as small-scale irrigation and income generating projects. PREDES is having greater success in reaching the poorest people. Projects tend to be typically rural, with many of them originating in marginal and violence-prone areas. PREDES undertakes delivery of inputs, quantitative targets and has made a remarkable impact on the quality of development.

10. Poverty Alleviation in Rural Indonesia (1994)

Indonesia was one of the poorest countries in the world with a GNP per capita of only $ 50 in the 1960s.Nearly 60 percent of its population was living in absolute poverty. In the 1970s, the government embarked upon a policy of broad-based economic growth through extensive support to the agricultural sector, coupled with substantial investments in social infrastructure. The Government also implemented Integrated Area Development Program (IADP) and the Income Generation Program for small farmers and the landless as anti-poverty strategy. UNDP supported the **Income Generation Program** for over ten years. The small-farmer groups in some

---

[127] Thematic Evaluation of UNDP poverty Elimination and Grassroots Participation Program, Report of the field mission to Peru, October 1994

2000 villages were provided with micro-credit and had achieved great success.[128]

By 1993, the incidence of poverty in Indonesia decreased to only 14 percent of total population. It was difficult to identify and reach the remaining "pockets of poverty". Hence, the Government launched a new poverty reduction program, called ***Inpres Desa Tertinggal*** (IDT) in 1993. The IDT reversed the "top-down" approach to planning and introduced community participation for determining local needs and priorities.

The UNDP was requested to fund for **socio-economic baseline study** and "social preparation" in nearly 300 of the least developed villages on a pilot basis. Using a participatory rural appraisal, the project made a map of the socioeconomic conditions of these villages. The Belgian government also co-funded the project. The IDT program covered about 50 percent of the 2000 villages participating in the small farmers program. The IDT program also assisted in the establishment of self-help groups. The role of UNDP in alleviating poverty in rural Indonesia is practically remarkable through financial assistance and technical guidance. It undertook comprehensive review of the country's poverty alleviation program over the last 25 years, supported Central Bureau of Statistics and the National Planning Board for developing a more accurate database for targeting and monitoring the IDT villages.

11. The Mongolian Issues on Poverty (1994)

Mongolia started its transition to a market based economy in 1989 and thereby its social conditions deteriorated. As a result, 26 percent of the population became poor and 6 percent as very poor. The UNDP-financed study indicates that the following groups are more vulnerable to poverty, such as:

---

[128]**UNDP Indonesia**, December 1994.

(a) Children with a single or no parents
(b) Disabled persons
(c) The elderly persons
(d) Female-headed households with many children
(e) Certain categories of unemployed people

Moreover, the study also indicated

(a) Poverty is high in both urban and rural areas; the situation is particularly serious in the rural sector;
(b) Low livestock prices affect herders' income;
(c) Poverty causes impact on women, partly because of rapid increase in female-headed households;
(d) 72 percent of single heads of households, mostly female, are below the official poverty-line; and
(e) Women are also over-represented among the unemployed.

The national poverty assessment laid the basis for the formulation of the Poverty Alleviation Programme (PAP) in Mongolia. This program targeted for elimination of the worst forms of poverty and reducing number of people in poverty from 26 percent to 10 percent over a six-year period.

Program of Action

(a) Strengthening the institutional capacities of Government, at both the central and local levels, for policy management and poverty monitoring
(b) Promoting human capital development through better access to health and education opportunities;
(c) Alleviating female as well as rural poverty;
(d) Strengthening the basic social safety net
(e) Promotion of income and employment activities among small herders and the livestock sectors;

(f) Restructuring the rural economy by developing conditions for growth in the rural sector, chiefly through:

(1) Market development and upgrading of basic infrastructure
(2) Targeting the poorest households for special credit and welfare schemes to guarantee fodder, livestock and draught animals; and
(3) Promoting small-scale rural industries, especially in agro-processing, as well as rural non-farm activities.

The poverty alleviation program further contemplates the creation of four decentralized poverty alleviation funds, which will serve as the primary vehicle for allocating resources for priority needs at the local level. These are:

An employment promotion funds, providing credit for the development of small-scale enterprises and skill and business training;

(a) A local development fund to support labor-intensive public works projects for development of infrastructure and the financing of small-scale capital projects;
(b) A women's development fund to deliver special credit and business support schemes for women; and
(c) A social assistance fund which will provide direct transfers to allow people in poverty to meet their basic needs, focusing on pre-school education, basic health care and skill training.

Program Implementation: will be decentralized, with most activities carried out at the local and grassroots levels, directly by local Governments or through NGOs, co-operatives or communal institutions. There will be Poverty Alleviation Councils in each province, district and at the national level.

Mongolia's Poverty Alleviation Programme (PAP) is characterized by multi-donor collaboration process involving key bilateral donors, multilateral institutions and UN agencies .It is seen as central to development planning in the country in the coming years.[129]

12. Zimbabwe's Poverty Alleviation Action Plan (1994)

The Government of Zimbabwe introduced economic stabilization and adjustment policy package in early 1990s. Then felt an urgent need for poverty sensitive macro-economic policies and development programs to tackle the problem of mounting poverty in Zimbabwe. For tackling the problem of mounting poverty in Zimbabwe, the Government first introduced economic stabilization and adjustment policy and then poverty sensitive macro-economic policies and development programs. The Government also requested UNDP technical assistance for the design of a comprehensive Poverty Alleviation Action Plan (PAAP).[130]

The main components of PAAP are:

(a) Implementation of community-based activities in social welfare provision and infrastructure rehabilitation through labor-intensive public works programs;
(b) Implementation of sustainable livelihood initiatives in selected disadvantaged areas, focusing on women, youth and vulnerable groups;
(c) Direct support to informal sector and micro-enterprise development initiatives; and

---

[129] Government of Mongolia, Poverty Alleviation Program, Ulaanbaatar, June 1994

[130] Government of Zimbabwe, Poverty Alleviation Action Plan; the Implementation Strategies 1994

(d) Capacity building and institutional development to improve the delivery of social safety nets, with special emphasis on food, security, education and primary healthcare

Program Implementation

(a) To start with a comprehensive, countrywide social mobilization process, involving a massive public information and awareness campaign to initiate community-managed social development programs and projects
(b) To undertake district-level **poverty assessment study** highlighting the following aspects
(c) The distribution of poverty for different land-use patterns and socio-economic groups;
(d) The access of disadvantaged groups to social safety nets and the labor market; and
(e) The constraints and causes of poverty as perceived by them
(f) The poverty assessment will serve as input for community selection, for formulation of PAAP strategies, policies and programs, and for monitoring of poverty trends.

Main Features of the PAAP Implementation Strategy Include:

(a) Targeting of social expenditure;
(b) Decentralization of program implementation;
(c) A participatory approach to poverty alleviation; and
(d) A partnership approach of social delivery

Key Factors of the PAAP
(a) Only the poorest and vulnerable groups in disadvantaged areas and sectors are eligible for PAAP benefits through the provision of primary health care, education, basic services,

labor-intensive public works and sustainable livelihood activities;

(b) Participatory approach but under the full control of beneficiary communities;
(c) Funds will be allocated to the beneficiaries;
(d) Community will select the executing agent with contract agreement;
(e) People's empowerment;
(f) Central Government will be responsible for facilitating, coordinating, monitoring and evaluation of program implementation; and
(g) The UNDP, UNCEF, ILO, African Development Bank, Government of Canada, Denmark, Norway and the UK have already committed for funds for the implementation of Zimbabwe's PAAP.

13. Poverty Alleviation Program in Mexico
(November 1994)

In Mexico, the Joint Consultative Group on Policy (JCGP) agencies along with UNIFEM and WHO selected poverty as the chief area for the future inter-agency collaboration in the country.

The study highlights the following facts:

(a) Poverty is widespread in Mexico and there exists extreme disparities in its spatial distribution
(b) 60 percent of all people in poverty live in cities and incidence of poverty is higher in rural areas, and
(c) The indigenous people, migrant workers and small holders engaged in agriculture are most sufferers.

How to Combat Poverty

(1) Labor friendly economic growth through the promotion of productive employment;

(2) Redistribution of income through compensatory programs for the poorest households; and
(3) Technical assistance for capacity building for the design and implementation of pro-poor growth policies and targeted social welfare programs through
(a) Employment and income generation programs;
(b) Emphasis on small rural producers and micro-enterprises in the informal urban sectors;
(c) Support to decentralization for strengthening the capacity of local governments and civil organizations to design, manage and evaluate the anti-poverty programs;
(d) A safe mother hood initiative; and
(e) Water and basic sanitation program.

14. Promoting Community Development in Sudan (1995)

The Government of Sudan and UNDP launched Area Development Schemes (ADS) in five poorest areas of Sudan to increase community incomes and self-reliance during droughts in a sustainable manner.

Working of ADS
(a) Local organizations like Village Development Committees, Framers' Unions or Women's Groups are created and strengthened
(b) Through the use of social animation techniques, the communities' express their local needs and arrive at a list of priorities by consensus, This process increases their awareness and capacity for self management in the planning, design and implementation of development activities;
(c) The baseline survey is to be undertaken in the planning phase and is followed by social animation and mobilization process;

(d) During the second phase, the full range of program activities is launched. The program offers 3 types of projects:
(e) Investment packages, which recover their costs through profit-making activities and technical studies;
(f) Pilot projects, which strengthens the infrastructure for future investment packages and Social service;
(g) Creation of an accessible system of rural credit;
(h) Selection of self-financing projects;
(i) The ADS provides seed money to initiate the revolving fund;
(j) The Village Development Committees (VDCs) mobilize community involvement, assist in the preparation and appraisal of credit applications, and monitors the utilization and repayment of the loans;
(k) The members of the VDCs are elected; and
(l) Over time, community organizations will gradually take over full responsibility for planning, implementing, managing and monitoring their own development.[131]

15. Fourth World Conference on Women, New York (1995)[132]

In 1995, the fourth world conference on women was held in New York. The platform for action of women observed that more than 1 billion people in the world today, the great majority of whom are women, lived in unacceptable conditions of poverty, mostly in the developing countries.

[131] UNDP Series on Sustainable Human Development, Country Strategies for Social Development, 1995
[132] Platform for Action of the Fourth World Conference on Women, New York, 1995

Poverty has various causes, including structural ones. It may be caused by an economic recession, which results in the loss of livelihood, or by utter destitution of people who fall outside family support systems, social institutions and safety nets. Poverty also has various manifestations, including lack of income and insufficient productive resources to ensure a sustainable livelihood; hunger and malnutrition; ill health; limited or lack of access to education and the basic services; increasing morbidity and mortality from illness; homelessness and inadequate housing; unsafe environments; and social discrimination and exclusion. Poverty is also characterized by lack of participation in decision-making and in civil, social and cultural life. It occurs in all countries, enemas poverty in developing countries and as pockets of poverty amidst wealthy in developed countries. All types of conflict, displacement of people and environmental degradation cause poverty. Unmanageable levels of external debt push the country into debt trap.

The **gender disparities** in economic power sharing are also important contributing factors to the poverty of women. Migration and consequent changes in family structures have placed additional burdens on women, especially those who provide for several dependants. Macroeconomic policies need rethinking and reformulation to address such trends.

In order to eradicate poverty and achieve sustainable development, women and men must participate fully and equally in the formulation of macroeconomic and social policies and strategies for the eradication of poverty. The eradication of poverty cannot be accomplished through anti-poverty programs alone. It will require democratic participation and changes in economic structures, in order to ensure access for all women to resources, opportunities and public services.

16. DAC Development Partnership Strategy: Shaping the 21st Century: The Contribution of Development Co-operation (1996) (International development Goals)

At the end of the twentieth century, the members of the Development Assistance Committee (DAC) of the Organization for Economic Co-operation and Development (OECD) feel that the time is ripe to reflect on the lessons of development co-operation over the last 50 years and to put forward strategies for the first part of the next century. This report sets forth the collective views on these matters of development ministers, heads of aid agencies and other senior officials responsible for development co-operation. [133]

In the year 2000, four-fifths of the people of the world will be living in the developing countries, mostly with improved conditions. But the number in absolute poverty and despair will still be growing. However, the industrialized countries have a strong moral imperative to respond to the extreme poverty and human suffering that still afflicts one billion people. The members also have a strong self-interest in fostering increased posterity in the developing countries. Our solidarity with the people of all countries causes us to seek to expand the community of interests and values needed to manage the problems that respect no borders from environmental degradation and migration, to drugs and epidemic diseases. All people are made less secure by the poverty and misery that exist in the world.

The record of the last 50 years, form Marshall Plan aid to the network of development partnerships now evolving, shows that the efforts of countries and

[133] This report was adopted at the Thirty-forth High level Meeting of the Development Assistance Committee, held on 6-7 May 1996.

societies to help them have been the main ingredients in their success. But the record also shows that development assistance has been an essential complementary factor in many achievements: the green revolution, the fall in birth rates, improved basic infrastructure, a diminished prevalence of disease and dramatically reduced poverty. Properly applied in propitious environments, aid works. Co-operation within the United Nations, the international financial institutions, the OECD and other global and regional institutions has greatly enhanced these efforts and shaped an evolving multilaterally in which all countries hold a vital stake.

The members of the Development Assistance Committee of the Organization for Economic Co-operation and Development have learned that development assistance will only work where there is a shared commitment of all the partners. They have seen the results in countries, which have grown, prospered and achieved industrialization; they no longer depend on aid but participate in the global economy. They have seen also the countries in which civil conflict and bad governance have set back development for generations. They have learned that success takes time and sustained international and local effort can march towards economic development.

As the OECD looks ahead, the members see an overwhelming case for making that effort. As a crucial part of this undertaking, the international community needs to sustain and increase the volume of official development assistance in order to reverse the growing marginalization of the poor and achieve progress towards realistic goals of human development. Domestic preoccupations in member countries should not jeopardize the international development effort at a critical juncture.

Today's investments in development co-operation will yield a very high return over the coming years. The OECD believes that ways must be found to finance multilateral development co-operations that are adequate, efficient, predictable and sustainable. The full implementation of current agreements to pay arrears and create workable financing systems is an essential part of efforts to ensure that the United Nations and the multilateral development banks avoid sever crisis and continues to play their vital roles. The OECD also recognizes that those responsible for public money are accountable for its effective use. The OECD has a duty to state clearly the results expected and how these can be achieved. It is time to select, taking account of many targets discussed and agreed at international forums, a limited number of indicators of success by which their efforts can be judged. The OECD is proposing a global development partnership effort though which they can archive together the following ambitious but realizable goals.
These are:

Economic Benefits:

(a) A reduction by one-half in the proportion of people living in extreme poverty by 2015;
(b) Universal primary education in all countries by 2015;
(c) Demonstrated progress towards gender equality and the empowerment of women by eliminating gender disparity in primary and secondary education by 2005;
(d) A reduction by two-thirds in the mortality rates for infants and children under age 5 and a reduction by three-fourths in maternal mortality all by 2015;
(e) Access through the primary health-care system to reproductive health services for all individuals of appropriate ages as soon as possible and no later than the year 2015

Environmental sustainability and regeneration:

The current implementation of national strategies for sustainable development in all countries by 2005, so as to ensure that current trends in the loss of environmental resources is effectively reversed at both global and national levels by 2015.

While expressed in terms of their global impact, these goals must be pursued country by country through individual approaches that reflect local conditions and locally owned development strategies. Essential to the attainment of these measurable goals are qualitative factors in the evolution of more stable, safe, participatory and just societies. These include capacity development for effective, democratic and accountable governance, the protection of human rights and respect for the rule of law. The OECD will also continue to address these less easily quantified factors of development progress.

Effective international support can make a real difference in achieving these goals. This is far from saying that they can be achieved by aid alone. The people and governments of the developing countries themselves will make the most important contributions for development, as in the past. But where this effort is forthcoming it needs and deserves strong support from the industrialized countries. The OECD commits to do the utmost to help to the poor countries.

(a) By a willingness to make mutual commitments with DAC members, development partners, supported by adequate resources;
(b) By improving the co-ordination of assistance in support of locally - owned development strategies; and
(c) By a determined effort to achieve coherence between aid policies and other policies which impact on developing countries.

These approaches were set out in broad terms in the statement of policy that the OECD adopted in 1995 entitled Development Partnerships in the new global context.[134]

The report builds this statement and proposes specific new practical measures to achieve the vision of partnership for development.

The OECD intends to improve the effectiveness of development co-operation. A rich process of dialogue and decisions is underway - within the OECD, in the Interim and Development Committees of the World Bank and IMF, in the regional development banks, in the G7, and in the United Nations systems. This heightened international focus on development co-operation reinforces conviction of the OECD that development matters. The success or failure of poor people and poor countries in making their way in an interdependent world will have a profound influence in shaping the 21st century. The OECD offers proposals in this report with confidence that international co-operation can be effective in supporting development, and that the results will be well worth the effort they will demand of members of Development Assistance Committee. The stakes in a stable, sustainable future for this planet and all that will inhabit it are far too high for them to forego that effort.

17. World Food Summit
(Rome Declaration on World Food Security)[135]
13 – 17 November 1996, Rome, Italy

---

[134]The text of the statement is an annex to this report. It is analyzed and discussed in the 1995 DAC report Development Co-operation Efforts and Policies of the Members of the Development Assistance Committee (OECD, 1996).

[135] World Food Summit, Rome Declaration on World Food Security), 13 – 17 November 1996, Rome, Italy

The Heads of State and Government gathered at the World Food Summit at the invitation of the Food and Agriculture Organization of the United Nations to reaffirm the right of everyone to have access to safe and nutritious food. They pledged for to be consistent with the right to adequate food and the fundamental right of everyone, to be free from hunger. They pledged for common and national commitment to achieving food security for all and to an ongoing effort to eradicate hunger in all countries, with an immediate view to reducing the number of undernourished people to half their present level no later than 2015.

They considered it intolerable that more than 800 million people throughout the world, and particularly in developing countries, do not have enough food to meet their basic nutritional needs. This situation is unacceptable. Food supplies have increased substantially, but constraints on access to food and continuing inadequacy of household and national incomes to purchase food, instability of supply and demand, as well as natural and man-made disasters, prevent basic food needs from being fulfilled. The problems of hunger and food insecurity have global dimensions and are likely to persist, and even increase dramatically in some regions, unless urgent, determined and concerted action is taken, given the anticipated increase in the world's population and the stress on natural resources.

They reaffirmed that a peaceful, stable and enabling political, social and economic environment is the essential foundation, which will enable States to give adequate priority to food security and poverty eradication. Democracy, promotion and protection of human rights and fundamental freedoms, including the right to development, and the full and equal participation of men and women are essential for achieving sustainable food security for all.

Poverty is a major cause of food insecurity and sustainable progress in poverty eradication is critical to improve access to food. Conflict, terrorism, corruption and environmental degradation also contribute significantly to food insecurity. Increased food production, including staple food, must be undertaken. This should happen within the framework of sustainable management of natural resources, elimination of unsustainable patterns of consumption and production, particularly in industrialized countries, and early stabilization of the world population. They acknowledged the fundamental contribution to food security by women, particularly in rural areas of developing countries, and the need to ensure equality between men and women. Revitalization of rural areas must also be a priority to enhance social stability and help redress the excessive rate of rural-urban migration confronting many countries.

They emphasized the urgency of taking action now to fulfill their responsibility to achieve food security for present and future generations. Attaining food security is a complex task for which the primary responsibility rests with individual governments. They have to develop an enabling environment and have policies that ensure peace, as well as social, political and economic stability and equity and gender equality. They express deep concern over the persistence of hunger, which, on such a scale, constitutes a threat both to national societies and, through a variety of ways, to the stability of the international community itself. Within the global framework, governments should also cooperate actively with one another and with United Nations Organizations, financial institutions, inter - governmental and non-governmental organizations, and public and private sectors, on programme directed toward the achievement of food security for all.

Food should not be used as an instrument for political and economic pressure. The members reaffirm the importance of international cooperation and solidarity as well as the necessity of refraining from unilateral measures not in accordance with the international law and the Charter of the United Nations and that endangers food security.

They recognize the need to adopt policies conducive to investment in human resource development, research and infrastructure for achieving food security. The members pledged that they must encourage generation of employment and incomes, and promote equitable access to productive and financial resources. They agree that trade is a key element in achieving food security. They resolved that 'we agree to pursue food trade and overall trade policies that will encourage our producers and consumers to utilize available resources in an economically sound and sustainable manner. We recognize the importance for food security of sustainable agriculture, fisheries, forestry and rural development in low as well as high potential areas.

We acknowledge the fundamental role of farmers, fishers, foresters, indigenous people and their communities, and all other people involved in the food sector, and of their organizations, supported by effective research and extension, in attaining food security.' Sustainable development policies will promote full participation and empowerment of people, especially women, an equitable distribution of income, access to health care and education, and opportunities for youth. Particular attention should be given to those who cannot produce or procure enough food for an adequate diet, including those affected by war, civil strife, natural disaster or climate related ecological changes. The members are conscious of the need for urgent action to combat pests, drought, and natural resource degradation including desertification, over-fishing and erosion of biological diversity.

Commitments

Convinced that the multifaceted character of food security necessitates concerted national action, and effective international efforts to supplement and reinforce national action, the following commitments were accepted:

The governments will ensure an enabling political, social, and economic environment designed to create the best conditions for the eradication of poverty and for durable peace, based on full and equal participation of women and men, which is most conducive to achieving sustainable food security for all;

The governments will implement policies aimed at eradicating poverty and inequality and improving physical and economic access by all, at all times, to sufficient, nutritionally adequate and safe food and its effective utilization;

The governments will pursue participatory and sustainable food, agriculture, fisheries, forestry and rural development policies and practices in high and low potential areas, which are essential to adequate and reliable food supplies at the household, regional, national, and global levels, and combat pests, drought and desertification, considering the multifunctional character of agriculture;

The governments will strive to ensure that food, agricultural trade and overall trade policies are conducive to fostering food security for all through a fair and market-oriented world trade system;

The governments will endeavor to prevent and be prepared for natural disasters and man-made emergencies and to meet transitory and emergency food requirements in ways that encourage recovery, rehabilitation, development and a capacity to satisfy future needs;

The governments will promote optimal allocation and use of public and private investments to foster human resources, sustainable food, agriculture, fisheries and forestry systems, and rural development, in high and low potential areas; and

The governments will implement, monitor, and follow-up this Plan of Action at all levels in cooperation with the international community.

Plan of Action

1. The Rome Declaration on World Food Security and the World Food Summit Plan of Action laid the foundations for diverse paths to a common objective - food security, at the individual, household, national, regional and global levels. Food security exists when all people, at all times, have physical and economic access to sufficient, safe and nutritious food to meet their dietary needs and food preferences for an active and healthy life. In this regard, concerted action at all levels is required. Each nation must adopt a strategy consistent with its resources and capacities to achieve its individual goals and, at the same time, cooperate regionally and internationally in order to organize collective solutions to global issues of food security. In a world of increasingly inter-linked institutions, societies and economies, coordinated efforts and shared responsibilities are essential.

2. Poverty eradication is essential to improve access to food. The vast majority of those who are undernourished either cannot produce or cannot afford to buy enough food. They have inadequate access to means of production such as land, water, inputs, improved seeds and plants, appropriate technologies

and farm credit. In addition, wars, civil strife, natural disasters, climate related ecological changes and environmental degradation have adversely affected millions of people. Although food assistance may be provided to ease their plight, it is not a long- term solution to the underlying causes of food insecurity. It is important to maintain an adequate capacity in the international community to provide food aid, whenever it is required, in response to emergencies. Equitable access to stable food supplies should be ensured.

3. A peaceful and stable environment in every country is a fundamental condition for the attainment of sustainable food security. Governments are responsible for creating an enabling environment for private and group initiatives to devote their skills, efforts and resources, and in particular investment, towards the common goal of food for all. This should be undertaken with the cooperation and participation of all members of society. Farmers, fishers and foresters and other food producers and providers, have critical roles in achieving food security, and their full involvement and engagement are crucial for success.

4. Poverty, hunger and malnutrition are some of the principal causes of accelerated migration from rural to urban areas in developing countries. The largest population shift of all times is now under way. Unless these problems are addressed in an appropriate and timely fashion, the political, economic and social stability of many countries and regions may well be seriously affected, perhaps even compromising world peace. It is necessary to target those people and areas suffering most from hunger and malnutrition and identify causes and take remedial action to improve the situation. A more complete, user-friendly source of information at all levels would enable this.

5. Availability of enough food for all can be attained. The 5.8 billion people in the world today (1996) have, on average, 15 percent more food per person than the global population of 4 billion people had 20 years ago. Yet, further large increases in world food production, through the sustainable management of natural resources, are required to feed a growing population, and achieve improved diets. Increased production, including traditional crops and their products, in efficient combination with food imports, reserves, and international trade can strengthen food security and address regional disparities. Food aid is one of the many instruments, which can help to promote food security. Long term investment in research and in cataloguing and conserving genetic resources, particularly at the national level, is essential. The link between sufficient food supplies and household food security must be ensured.

6. Harmful seasonal and inter-annual instability of food supplies can be reduced. Progress should include targeting on minimizing the vulnerability to, and impact of, climate fluctuations and pests and diseases. Timely transfers of supplies to deficit areas and the conservation and sustainable use of bio-diversity, early warning systems of climate, transfer and utilization of appropriate agricultural, fishery and forestry technologies, production, and reliable trade, storage and financial mechanisms can usher prosperity in agriculture. Natural and man-made disasters can often be anticipated or even prevented, and response must be timely and effective to assist recovery.

7. Unless national governments and the international community address the multifaceted causes underlying food insecurity, the number of hungry and malnourished people will remain very high in developing countries, particularly in Africa, south of the Sahara; and sustainable food security will not be achieved. This situation is unacceptable. This Plan of

Action envisages an ongoing effort to eradicate hunger in all countries, with an immediate view to reducing the number of undernourished people to half their present level no later than 2015, and a mid-term review to ascertain whether it is possible to achieve this target by 2010.

8. The resources required for investment will be generated mostly from domestic private and public sources. The international community has a key role to play in supporting the adoption of appropriate national policies and, where necessary and appropriate, in providing technical and financial assistance to assist developing countries and transitional countries in fostering food security.

9. The multi-dimensional nature of the follow-up to the World Food Summit includes actions at the national, intergovernmental and inter-agency levels. The international community, and the UN system, including FAO, as well as other agencies and bodies have important contributions to the implementation of the World Food Summit Plan of Action. The FAO Committee on World Food Security will have responsibility to monitor the implementation of the Plan of Action.

10. Reaching sustainable world food security is part and parcel of achieving the social, economic, environmental and human development objectives agreed upon in recent international conferences. The World Food Summit Plan of Action builds on consensus reached in these summits and is based on the conviction that although the world is faced with major food insecurity, solutions to these problems exist. If all parties at local, national, regional and international levels make determined and sustained efforts, then the overall goal of food for all, at all times, will be achieved.

11. The Plan of Action of the World Food Summit is in conformity with the purposes and principles of the UN Charter and international law and strives to consolidate the results of other UN conferences since 1990 on subjects having a bearing on food security.

12. The implementation of the recommendations contained in this Plan of Action is the sovereign right and responsibility of each State through national laws and the formulation of strategies, policies, programs, and development priorities. It should be in conformity with all human rights and fundamental freedoms, including the right to development, and the significance of and the full respect for various religious and ethical values, cultural backgrounds and philosophical convictions of individuals. They and their communities should contribute to the full enjoyment by all of their human rights in order to achieve the objective of food security for all.

18. Initiatives for Sustainable Development (ISD) towards the 21st Century (June 1997)
Achieving UNCED Targets for Environmental ODA[136]

At the United Nations Conference on Environment and Development (UNCED) in 1992, Japan announced to the world that it would increase its environmental ODA in the next five years, starting from FY 1992, to an amount between ¥ 900 billion and ¥1 trillion. In the five years from FY 1992 to FY 1996, Japan's environmental ODA has grown to ¥1.44 trillion, actually exceeding the target by more than 40 percent; Japan will continue to strengthen its efforts in environmental cooperation, mainly through its ODA programs.

[136]Initiative for Sustainable Development (ISD) towards 21st Century

Philosophy of ISD

Global Human Security: Environmental problems threaten human existence, and constitute a security issue in a broad sense.

Ownership: Developing countries assume the primary responsibility for development. In promoting environmental cooperation, there needs to be a strong and responsible commitment from developing countries.

Sustainable Development: The objective of assistance should be to realize sustainable development, paying attention to the different economic and social situations of each developing country.

Program of Actions:

(I)Air and Water Pollution, Waste Disposal

(a) Acid Deposition Monitoring Network in East Asia
(b) Assisting capacity development in environment through "Environmental Centers" (in Beijing, Jakarta, and Bangkok)
(c) Financial and Technical Co-operation (for pollution control and recycling; development of appropriate technologies through "Green Aid Plan")

(ii) Global Warming: Diffusion of technologies for energy saving and new energy

(iii) Nature Conservation, Afforestation

(a) By assisting the "Indonesia Bio-diversity Center", Japan will promote building a bio-diversity information network in East Asia.
(b) Japan will establish a coral reef conservation and research center in the Asia-Pacific region,

pursuing a regional research network in the future.

(c) Japan will promote its assistance for social forestry projects, and participatory Afforestation projects covering large areas through ODA loans. Japan will strengthen its support for the ITTO (International Tropical Timber Organization)

(iv). Fresh Water Problems: Japan has been extending active assistance to developing countries in the areas of water supply, sewage systems, and well-digging.

(v) Public Awareness, Strategy Building: Japan will further promote policy dialogue through such conferences as **"Japan-China Comprehensive Forum on Environmental Cooperation"** (a bilateral dialogue process with the participation of national / local governments and private institutions), and "Eco-Asia" (a conference of environmental ministers in the Asia-Pacific region). Japan will assist environmental education projects through grant assistance for grassroots projects. Japan takes the initiative for building an international network on strategy development for addressing global environmental issues through "The Institute for Global Environmental Strategies."

19. The Kyoto Initiative: Assistance to Developing Countries for Combating Global Warming (December 1997)[137]

At the June 1997 special session of the United Nations General Assembly on Environment and Development, Prime Minister Ryutaro Hashimoto announced Japan's comprehensive medium and long-term plan for environmental cooperation. This plan, called the "Initiatives for Sustainable Development

[137] The Kyoto Initiative

towards the 21st Century" (ISD), indicates the ways Japan will support programs in developing countries to address a wide variety of environmental problems including global warming, air and water pollution, waste disposal, deforestation and loss of marine and terrestrial bio-diversity. As the host of the 3rd Conference of Parties of the United Nations Framework Convention on Climate Change in Kyoto in December 1997, Japan presented "The Kyoto Initiative", consisting of strengthened environmental support that focuses on assisting developing countries combat global warming in the policy framework of the ISD. The Kyoto Initiative like ISD will be implemented mainly through the Government of Japan's Official Development Assistance program.

Philosophy

(a) Global Human Security**:** Global warming is a threat to the survival of mankind and a matter of security in a broad sense.

(b) Ownership and partnership: It is important that developing countries exercise initiatives in combating global warming and work with developed countries to solve global- scale problems.

(c) Sustainable Development: Japan will continue to carry out financial cooperation and to transfer appropriate technology contributing to both anti-global warming measures and economic development with the aim of achieving both development and protection of the environment. In countries where poverty is a factor in environmental degradation, Japan will support anti-poverty programs to enable people to escape from the grip of poverty.

Three Pillars of Assistance:

(1). Cooperation in Capacity Development: In the five years beginning in FY1998, Japan will train 3000 people in developing countries in the following fields, such as

(a) Air pollution,
(b) Waste disposal,
(c) Energy saving technologies,
(d) Forest conservation and Afforestation

(2) Official Development Assistance Loans on the Most Concessional Conditions: Japan will grant ODA loans with the most concessional terms available internationally (0.75 per cent interest rate, 40 year repayment period) to actively promote cooperation in such fields such as Energy saving technologies, New and renewable energy sources, and Forest conservation and Afforestation.

(3)Exploitation and Transfer of Japanese Technology and Know- how: Using technology and know-how acquired in the process of combating its own pollution and energy problems, Japan will

(a) Send teams to diagnose global warming prevention measures in manufacturing plants
(b) Set up information networks related to global warming prevention technology
(c) Develop and transfer technology suited to development countries' needs; and
(d) Hold workshops on global warming prevention.

20. G8 Köln Communiqué 1999

Deepening the Development partnership:[138]

Developing countries are essential partners in a globalize world. Developed countries are committed to working with them, especially with the poorest countries, to eradicate poverty, launch effective

[138]G8 Koln Communiqué 1999

policies for sustainable development and develop their capacity to integrate better into the global economy, thus benefiting from the opportunities offered by globalization. The members affirm:

Developed countries will continue to provide substantial support and assistance to developing and transition economies in support of their own efforts to open and diversify their economies, to democratize and improve governance, and to protect human rights.

Developed countries will strive gradually to increase the volume of official development assistance (ODA), and to put special emphasis on countries best positioned to use it effectively.

To ease future debt burdens and facilitate sustainable development, developed countries agree to increase the share of grant- based financing in the ODA, they provide to the least developed countries.

While international assistance and debt relief are clearly important, their positive effects depend on sound national efforts towards economic and structural reform and good governance, where the private sector and civil society are able to play productive roles.

Developed countries intend to step up work with developing countries and multilateral institutions to improve developing country capacity to exercise their rights and meet their obligations in the global trading system so as to ensure that they derive the full benefits of liberalized trade and thus contribute to global economic growth.

Developed countries call on the UN and the IFIs to help developing countries mobilize sufficient means for social services and basic infrastructure and continue to support and to mainstream democratization, good governance and the rule of law into country development strategies.

Developed countries reaffirm their support for the OECD mandate to finalize a recommendation on untying aid to the least developed countries. They call on OECD members to bring this effort to a successful conclusion as soon as possible.

Developed countries reaffirm their commitment to contribute to the achievement of economic and social development in Africa, Asia and Latin America. They will review the situation in that regard every year, on the basis of reports by the IFIs and the relevant regional development banks, on the alleviation of poverty.

Launching the Köln Debt Initiative:

Developed countries have decided to give a fresh boost to debt relief to developing countries. In recent years the international creditor community has introduced a number of debt relief measures for the poorest countries. The Heavily Indebted Poor Countries (HIPC) framework has made an important contribution in this respect. Recent experience suggests that further efforts are needed to achieve a more enduring solution to the problem of unsustainable debt burdens. To this end developed countries welcome the 1999 Köln Debt Initiative, which is designed to provide deeper, broader and faster debt relief through major changes to the HIPC framework. The central objective of this initiative is to provide a greater focus on poverty reduction by releasing resources for investment in health, education and social needs. In this context developed countries also support good governance and sustainable development. Developed countries are aware that new proposals will require additional substantial financing. While several means of financing are under consideration, credible progress in identifying additional funding possibilities is needed, and developed countries stand ready to help with financing solutions. In this context they recognize the importance of fair burden sharing among creditors.

Conclusion

In short, the reports of committees are based on practical approaches for reduction of poverty for specific countries. But a good number of recommendations can be adopted in all the developing countries universally. The states could re-examine these suggestions and undertake amendments of state policy for achieving better results. For this, the states would need soft loan on long-term basis. It is a fact that poverty of people for centuries and centuries cannot be eradicated over night. But starvation, hunger and malnutrition cannot wait till the result of long-term planning is achieved.

Hence, the funding institutions, world organizations and respective governments should adopt effective steps for reduction of starvation, hunger and malnutrition of the food insecure families in all the heavily indebted poor countries and developing countries as a top priority. The government sponsored poverty programs do not reach the poor and vulnerable people because the corrupt government employees and political touts hijack the allotted funds in all the developing countries.

The developed countries should undertake humanitarian activities during calamities, which are directly related to World Peace movement. All people belong to one and the same genre and all belong to one family residing in this world. We have the capacity to fight against poverty united and we can enjoy 'world peace' forever.

+++++

Chapter-V

WORLD ORGANIZATIONS AND INTERNATIONAL DONORS

Poverty makes a person vulnerable and a helpless victim deprived of social, cultural and political freedom; poverty is not just 'low income' and 'low consumption' but a multiple deprivation causing premature death, chronic undernourishment, illiteracy, illness and social exclusion. Amartya Sen, Nobel Laureate in Economics

In May 1996, the Development Assistance Committee of the OECD countries published, "Shaping the 21st Century", a policy paper calling for a global partnership to pursue a new development strategy. This policy paper incorporated the 'International Development Goals'. The United Nations Millennium Declaration (2000) committed to the Millennium Development Goals, where in all the developed countries agreed to contribute 0.7 per cent of GDP for reducing poverty and hunger worldwide particularly in HIPC and developing countries.

The specific objectives of the International Development Goals (1996) are:

(a) Reduce the proportion of people living in extreme poverty by half by 2015
(b) Enroll all children in primary school by 2015
(c) Make progress towards gender equality and empowering women by eliminating gender disparities in primary and secondary education by 2005
(d) Reduce infant and child mortality rates by two-thirds by 2015
(e) Reduce maternal mortality ratios by three-quarters by 2015
(f) Provide access for all who need reproductive health services by 2015
(g) Implement national strategies for sustainable development by 2005 so as to reverse the loss of environmental resources by 2015

The specific objectives of Millennium Development Goals (2000) are:

(a) Eradicate extreme poverty and hunger;
(b) Achieve universal primary education;
(c) Promote gender equality and empower women;
(d) Reduce child mortality;
(e) Improve maternal health
(f) Combat HIV/AIDS, malaria and other diseases;
(g) Ensure environmental sustainability; and
(h) Develop a Global Partnership for Development

These goals are expressed in global terms but must be pursued country by country. Achieving them will also require building capacity for effective, democratic, and responsive governance, protection of human rights, and respect for the rule of law. The World Bank can systematically monitor progress in achieving these goals in the countries it assists.

Achieving the social goals is not so easy. If infant mortality rates were to remain at 1990 levels, the number of infant deaths would total about 8.8 million in 2015. Reaching the target of reducing infant mortality by two-thirds would require bringing this number down to about 3 million. Similarly, attaining the primary school enrollment goal would require enrolling about 200 million more children in primary school than there are today. The present poverty situation is alarming in 54 low-income countries and not fair in 58 low-middle-income countries. Can we really fight poverty? Can the developed nations assist the developing countries to realize the basic necessities of life? Can we make a road map for peace in our world? [139]

The following facts would reveal the status of poor people during the early years of Twenty-first century. So the world organizations should undertake appropriate actions to ameliorate the sufferings of the poor for a noble cause of strengthening world peace.

(a). We live in a world where 1.2 billion people live on less than US $ 1 a day and half the world population—nearly three billion people—live on less than US $ 2 a day.

(b). The GDP (Gross Domestic Product) of the poorest 48 nations is less than the wealth of the world's three richest people combined.

(c). 32 of the world's richest people have wealth, which exceeds the income of India, Pakistan, Sri Lanka, Nepal, Bhutan, Maldives, Iran and Afghanistan.

---

[139] L. Demery and M. Walton (1998), "Are Poverty Reduction and other 21st Century Social Goals Attainable?" Goals for the 21st Century.htm

(d). Additional expenditure required for providing basic education is $ 6 billion, for water and sanitation $ 9 billion, and for basic health and nutrition $ 13 billion for every one (all) in the world, which is not available till date. But we people spend $ 400 billion on narcotic drugs and $ 780 billion on military spending in the world.

(e) Nearly a billion people entered the 21st century unable to read a book or write their names; and

(f). Less than one per cent of what the world spent every year on weapons was be needed to put every child into school by the year 2000 and it didn't happen.

The DAC members of OECD countries have opened their offices in developing countries to fulfill millennium development goals with partnership with United Nations, other governments and local governments. They work with civil societies or non-government organizations. A number of world organizations, OECD countries, other developed and developing countries and a large number of philanthropic and charitable organizations are donating funds and guiding the Heavily Indebted Poor Countries, developing countries and poor people in poverty alleviation programs. In this chapter, the activities of three world organizations and four OECD countries are discussed to explain their involvement in poverty reduction programs worldwide.

World Organizations

(a) United Nations Development Program
(b) The World Bank
(c) International Monetary Fund

OECD countries

(a) Japan International Co-operation Agency (JICA)

(b) Department for International Development of UK (DFID)
(c) Canadian International Development Agency (CIDA) and
(d) Australian Aid (Aus AID)

United Nations Development Program (UNDP)

UNDP is the world's largest agency for multilateral, technical and pre-investment cooperation. It is the funding source for most of the technical assistance provided by the United Nations system. But there exists sharp differences among different countries in economic, social, cultural, administrative and political systems. It is, therefore, a Herculean task on the part of the policy makers to devise appropriate policy measures in different countries for reduction of poverty. Hence, UNDP has opted for the following priorities for poverty eradication programs. These are:[140]

(a) Creating an enabling environment for people-centered development.
(b) Empowering all people for self-reliance
(c) Promoting broad-based and equitable growth
(d) Enhancing household food security
(e) Improving access to basic infrastructure and social services
(f) Promoting job creation and sustainable livelihoods
(g) Ensuring equitable access to credit and productive assets
(h) Expanding social protection for vulnerable people
(i) Promoting gender equity and participation of women in development
(j) Preserving, maintaining and regenerating the natural resource base

---

[140] UNDP (1995), "Poverty Eradication: A Policy Framework for Country Strategies"1995 p.

The Copenhagen Summit (1995) has summarized the main themes of all previous world conferences and has drawn a coherent and integrated framework that recognizes the multidimensional nature of poverty. It calls for inter-sectoral and holistic approach to people centered sustainable development. Therefore, UNDP has asked for priority actions, costs and time to eradicate poverty in each country. UNDP has given more weights for national governments for implementing the social summit commitments to eradicate poverty. The priority actions include:[141]

(a) National poverty mapping and assessments, with rigorous attention to the gender-dimensions of poverty
(b) Setting national goals and targets for poverty elimination, with the participation of government, the private sector of community-based organizations
(c) Capacity assessment and development
(d) Review of national policies and budgets
(e) Social mobilization, participation and partnerships
(f) Decentralization of decision- making
(g) Policy and institutional reform and co-ordination
(h) Integration of social development goals into overall planning
(i) Mobilizing resources for social development
(j) Aid coordination

But no single UN agency can meet the entire challenge by itself. The UN has a vast network in 133 countries. Therefore, it is necessary that the UN system, donor countries and Breton Woods Institutions should work with developing countries through a partnership that respects the national sovereignty and development priorities of each country. To eradicate absolute poverty and reduce

---

[141]See also UNDP 1995

overall poverty in the developing countries, both technical and financial assistance is necessary. The donors are ready to assist but they need that the assistance should be properly utilized. The UNDP can play an important role in the mobilization of resources, co-ordination among donors and utilization of funds for capacity building in the developing countries.

Using a mix of country-level and global resources, UNDP has been assisting a number of countries for planning and updating anti-poverty strategies by strengthening of existing ones. This includes support in the following areas:[142]

(a) Public expenditure reviews
(b) Poverty mapping and assessments
(c) Setting national goals and targets
(d) Dialogue between government, civil society and the private sector
(e) Assessments of national capacity for poverty reduction
(f) Reviews of policies and budgets
(g) Decentralized decision-making
(h) Strengthening institutions and co-ordination mechanisms
(i) Resource mobilization through aid co-ordination

UNDP has set the following goals to shape its efforts for poverty reduction:

(a) Fostering an enabling environment for pro-poor economic growth;
(b) Securing sustainable livelihoods for the poor through access to productive assets;
(c) Advancing gender equality and the status of women;

---

[142]UNDP, Human Development Report, 1998, pp. 18-20

(d) Ensuring sustainable food security for the poor, including regeneration of the environmental resources on which the poor depend; and

(e) Supporting pro-poor governance including empowerment of the poor.

Evaluation of UNDP'S Poverty Reduction Activities:

In 1994, a team of external consultants reviewed UNDP's poverty-reduction activities. The evaluation team recommended that UNDP to become more of a facilitator than direct implementers of development activities. Moreover, it should focus its effort on building national capacity that can counteract the underlying processes of poverty generation, instead of concentrating on the efforts. Secondly, the UNDP should focus on national poverty reduction strategies and to link these with regional and global initiatives. If it got involved in micro-interventions, and should find cost-effective ways to work through intermediaries, then it would be able to demonstrate replicable examples. Thirdly, the consultants also included factors like governance, gender and environment as thematic areas linked with poverty.

But UNDP faces its own resource constraints. It remains firmly committed to poverty eradication. It provides countries what they need most and what it is best at providing. It now focuses more on improvement of policies and building institutions rather than concentrating on micro projects. It means concentrating on providing technical advice, backed by resources, and how to make governance structures participatory, more accountable and more pro-poor.

UNDP has identified the following factors for successful implementation of poverty reduction programs:

Governance:

Governance can be more effective by promoting accountability through elections, promoting accountability in finance, access to information and communication, making decentralizations pro-poor by shifting resources to poor regions or investing more in poor regions:

(a) Meeting capacity–building needs
(b) Long term targeting in Human Development Index (HDI)
(c) Adult literacy must be increased.
(d) Proportion of children under five who are underweight must be decreased
(e) Probability of dying before the age 40 must be decreased
(f) Developing national anti-poverty plans: Policies must be pro-poor, fight inequality and empower the poor
(g) Investment in agriculture
(h) Land reform and irrigation must be given priority for poverty alleviation.
(i)Investment in rural roads
(j)Linking countries' international policies to poverty
(k)UNDP emphasizes on debt relief, international trade and making aid-work for the poor in all the heavily indebted poor countries.
(l)Pro-poor local governance
(m)Promoting participatory local governance
(n)Building local capacity for poverty reduction

The United Nations Capital Development Fund (UNCDF) seeks to finance local governments, which can be utilized for increasing productivity, natural resources conservation and participatory planning.

The poor people should have their organizations to assist themselves:

(a) The foundation of poverty reduction is self-organization of the poor at the community level.
(b) Civil society organization is encouraged to work with poor communities and to influence national policy-making.
(c) South-Asian Poverty Alleviation Program assists womenfolk in Bangladesh, India, Maldives, Nepal, Pakistan and Sri Lanka with a budget of $31 million. This program created self-help groups (SHG) and tried for empowerment of women in all the South Asian countries.

Focusing resources on the poor: This includes focusing on geographical area, rehabilitating poor areas, reaching disadvantaged social groups and targeting by type of intervention.

(a)Integrating key issues in the poverty programs
(b)Monitoring progress against poverty[143]

The World Bank

The World Bank was established on July 1, 1944 by a conference of 44 governments in Breton Woods, New Hampshire. Their dream is a world free of poverty. It is one of the world's largest sources of development assistance. Its primary focus is on helping the poorest people and the poorest countries. The World Bank Group consists of the following organizations:
(a) International Bank for Reconstruction and Development (IBRD)
(b) International Development Association (IDA)
(c) International Finance Corporation (IFC)
(d) Multilateral Investment Guarantee Agency (MIGA)
(e) International Center for Settlement of Investment Disputes (ICSID)

[143]UNDP poverty Report 2000- welcoming Human poverty

The "World Bank" is the name that has come to be used for the International Bank for Reconstruction and Development (IBRD) and the International Development Association (IDA). Together these organizations provide low-interest loans, interest-free credit and grants to developing countries. Some 10,000-development professionals from nearly every country in the world work in the World Bank's Washington DC headquarters or in its 109 country offices. The World Bank is one of the United Nations' specialized agencies, and is made up of 184 member countries. These countries are jointly responsible for how the institution is financed and how money is spent. Along with the rest of the development community, the World Bank centers its efforts on reaching the Millennium Development Goals, agreed to by UN members in 2000 and aimed at sustainable poverty reduction.

The World Bank is run like a joint stock company, with its member countries as shareholders. The number of shares, a country has, is based roughly on the size of its economy. The United States is the largest single shareholder with 16.41 per cent of votes, followed by Japan (7.87 per cent), United Kingdom (4.31 per cent), and France (4.31 per cent). The rest of the shares are divided among the other member countries. A Board of Governors represents the World Bank's government shareholders. Generally, the governors are ministers, such as Minister of Finance or Minister of Development. The governors are the ultimate policy makers in the World Bank. They meet once in a year at the Bank's Annual Meetings. An Executive Director represents every member government of the World Bank Group. The United State of America nominates the World Bank's president, as this country is the largest shareholder. He holds the office for a period of five-year and chairs meetings of the Board of Directors. [144]

---

[144]. World Bank Group: Working for a World Free of Poverty

Activities of the World Bank Group

(a). The World Bank provided $19.5 billion and worked in more than 100 developing countries, bringing finance and/or technical expertise towards helping them reduce poverty in 2002.

(b). IDA provided $8.1 billion to 62 low-income countries in financing 133 projects in fiscal 2002. A borrowing country has to pay the amount within a period of 30-40 years with a grace period of 10-years for interest-free credit. About 40 countries provide the money for this funding by making contributions every four years.

(c). In fiscal 2002, IBRD provided loans totaling $11.5 billion in support of 96 projects in 40 countries for specific programs, including poverty reduction efforts, delivery of social services, protection of environment, and promotion of economic growth for improving living standards.

(d). The IBRD raises almost all its money in the world's financial markets- $23 billion in fiscal 2002. With an AAA credit rating, it issues bonds to raise money and then passes on below interest rates to its borrowers.

(e). The World Bank has allowed debt relief to the extent of $41 billion over time to 26 poor countries under the enhanced Heavily Indebted Poor Countries (HIPC) Initiative.

(f). The World Bank, along with 189 countries and numerous organizations, has committed towards unprecedented global partnership to fight poverty. The Millennium Development Goals defined specific targets in terms of school enrolment, child mortality, maternal health, disease, and access to water to be met by 2015.

(g). The Bank has committed more than $1.3 billion to fight against HIV/AIDS programs, with half of that for sub-Saharan Africa.

(h). The Bank is currently involved in more than 1,800 projects in virtually every sector and developing country. These are as diverse as providing micro-credit in Bosnia Herzegovina, raising AIDS awareness in communities in Guinea, supporting education of girls in Bangladesh, and improving health care delivery in Mexico. The Bank is helping East Timor rebuild upon independence, rebuilding Gujarat (India) after devastating earthquake, providing cattle to farmers in Timor, building roads in Indonesia, helping agricultural development in Benin or supporting women establishing their own small businesses in Pakistan.[145]

IDA commitments

Fiscal 2006 marked the first year of IDA14 and the highest volume of IDA commitments in history. Commitments reached $9.5 billion for 167 operations, consisting of $7.6 billion in credits, $1.8 billion in grants, and $60 million in guarantees. The largest share to Africa, with $4.7 billion, constituted 50 percent of total IDA commitments. South Asia and East Asia and Pacific followed with $2.6 billion and $1.1 billion, respectively. Among countries, Pakistan represents the largest single recipient. In fiscal 2006, about 19 percent of total IDA financing was provided in the form of grants. Public administration, including law and justice, was the leading sector receiving IDA support, with $2.8 billion, or 28 percent of the total. The transportation and health and social services sectors received significant support: $1.1 billion and $1 billion, respectively. The two most prominent themes were public sector governance and financial and private sector development, accounting for 19

---

[145]World Bank publications, World Bank in Action

percent of IDA commitments each. Human development (15 percent), rural development (14 percent), and social protection and risk management (9 percent) also attracted major attention.

IBRD Lending

At $14.1 billion for 112 operations, new lending commitments by IBRD in fiscal 2006 exceeded the previous year's level by $0.5 billion. This represents the highest volume of IBRD lending in the past seven fiscal years. The share of policy-based lending was slightly higher than in fiscal 2005. Latin America and the Caribbean received the highest level of IBRD lending, with $5.7 billion, or 40 percent of total IBRD commitments, followed by Europe and Central Asia with $3.5 billion and East Asia and Pacific with $2.3 billion. Five countries—Brazil, China, India, Mexico, and Turkey— received a combined commitment volume equaling 52 percent of total IBRD lending in fiscal 2006. Among sectors, public administration, including law and justice, received the highest volume of IBRD lending ($3.1 billion), followed by transportation ($2.1 billion), and energy and mining ($2.1 billion). The thematic composition of lending in fiscal 2006 was led by financial and private sector development, followed by public sector governance and urban development.

A detailed explanation on the **activities of the World Bank Group** is presented for introspection:

1. The World Bank is the highest external donor for education

Since its education funding began in 1963, the World Bank has provided some US $33 billion for loans and credits, and it currently finances 157 educational projects in 83 countries. The Bank works closely with national governments, United Nation's agencies, donors, non-governmental organizations, and other partners to help developing countries in their efforts to reach the goals of Education for All. These goals mean ensuring that all children- especially girls and disadvantaged children are enrolled in and able to complete a primary education by 2015. A good example of the Bank's lending for education is that India District Primary Education Program, which specifically targets girls in districts where female literacy rates are below the national average. Bank funding for this program is now up to US$1.3 billion and serves more than 60 million students in 271 low-literacy districts in 18 of the 29 Indian states. In Brazil, El Salvador, and Trinidad and Tobago, Bank projects champion the role of local communities in improving the quality of education by allowing them to evaluate the performance of local schools and teachers.

2. The World Bank is the largest external funded agency for the fight against HIV / AIDS:

Each day, 14,000 more people become infected with the HIV virus; half of them are between the ages of 15 and 24. HIV/AIDS is rapidly reversing many of the social and economic gains won by developing countries over the past 50 years. As a co-sponsor of UNAIDS, which coordinates the global response to the epidemic. The World Bank has committed more than US$1.6 billion to combating the spread of HIV/AIDS around the world. The Bank has pledged that no country with an effective HIV/AIDS strategy will go without funding and, in partnership with African governments, launched the Multi-Country HIV/AIDS Program (MAP), which makes significant resources available to civil society organizations and communities. Many have developed highly innovative HIV/AIDS approaches, which others are now learning from and adapting to local conditions. In 2004, MAP provided US$1 billion to help countries in Africa expand their national prevention, care, and treatment programs. The Bank also approved US$155 million to fight HIV/AIDS in the Caribbean and continues its sup-port to HIV/AIDS programs in other regions.

Providing poor people with basic health and nutrition lie at the heart of reducing poverty and promoting economic growth. While important gains have been made in many countries during the last few decades, major challenges remain. Of the 11 million children who die each year in developing countries, around 70 percent die from communicable diseases (such as pneumonia, diarrhea, malaria, measles, and HIV/AIDS) and malnutrition. The World Bank commits an average of US$1 billion in new lending each year for health, nutrition, and population projects in the developing world. Bank funds are helping to combat malaria in 46 countries and tuberculosis in 30. In China, the Bank has helped provide iodized salt to more than 90 percent of households, which means significantly fewer cases of miscarriage and stillbirths, physical deformity, and mental retardation caused by iodine deficiency. The Bank is also helping mothers in Senegal prevent and treat malnutrition in children, and is supporting the integrated prevention and treatment of childhood illnesses in Brazil.

3. The World Bank is a leader to fight against corruption worldwide:

Corruption is the single largest obstacle to development. It increases wealth for the few at the expense of society as a whole, leaving the poor suffering the harshest consequences by taking public resources away from those who need them most. Since 1996, we have launched hundreds of governance and anti-corruption programs in nearly 100 developing countries. Initiatives range from requiring government officials to publicly declare their assets and introducing public spending reforms, to training judges and teaching investigative reporting to journalists. Our commitment to fighting corruption has helped to encourage an international response to the problem. We also continue to make anti-corruption measures a central part of our analytical and operational work. We are committed to making sure that the projects we fund are free from corruption, by setting strict guidelines and providing a hotline for corruption complaints. So far, about 100 companies have been banned from participating in projects that we finance. The World Bank Institute has also developed a major knowledge, learning and data center on governance and anti-corruption.

4. The World Bank supports debt relief:

In 1996, the World Bank and the International Monetary Fund (IMF) launched the Heavily Indebted Poor Countries (HIPC) Initiative- the first comprehensive approach to reducing the external debt of the world's poorest, most indebted countries. Today, 27 countries are receiving debt relief projected to amount to US $52 billion over time. With other forms of debt relief, the HIPC Initiative will cut by two-thirds the external debt in these countries, lowering their indebtedness to levels well below the average for developing countries overall. As part of the initiative, these countries are reorienting their budgetary priorities towards key social and human development sectors. Rwanda, for example, has set targets to increase primary school enrollment and to hire teachers. Honduras is planning to deliver basic primary and maternal/child health care to at least 100,000 beneficiaries in poor communities. In Cameroon, resources are being used to strengthen the fight against HIV/ AIDS by, among other things, expanding education to promote the use of condoms by high-risk populations.

5. The World Bank is the largest international funding agency of bio-diversity projects:

Since 1988, the Bank has become one of the largest international funding institutions for bio-diversity projects. Even though bio-diversity loss is a global concern, the greatest costs are felt by rural people in developing countries, those who are most dependent on the environment for food, shelter, medicine, income, employment, and cultural identity. For this reason, the Bank has joined Conservation International, the Global Environment Facility, the Macarthur Foundation, and the Japanese government in launching a fund that will contribute to better protection of developing countries' bio-diversity hot spots. Sixty percent of all terrestrial species' diversity can be found in these highly threatened regions, which cover only 1.4 percent of the planet's total surface area. Concern for the environment is an intrinsic part of the Bank's poverty reduction mission. In addition to environmental assessments and safeguard policies, a new environment strategy is focusing on climate change, forests, water resources, and bio-diversity. Currently, the Bank's portfolio of projects with clear environmental objectives amounts to US$14 billion.

6. The World Bank works in partnership:

The World Bank has joined a large array of partners in the global fight against poverty: for example, with the World Wildlife Fund to protect forests, and with the public and private sectors to launch the Prototype Carbon Fund to help reduce the effects of global warming. The Bank is also partnering with the Food and Agriculture Organization (FAO) and the United Nations Development Programme (UNDP) to sponsor the renowned Consultative Group on International Agricultural Research—which mobilizes cutting-edge science to reduce hunger and poverty, improve human nutrition and health, and protect the environment. Through the Consultative Group to Assist the Poorest (CGAP), the Bank is working with donors and multilateral financial institutions to improve the capacity of micro finance institutions to deliver financial services to the poorest people. A partnership to fight river blindness has successfully prevented more than 600,000 cases of blindness, has opened 25 million hectares to cultivation, and annually treats more than 35 million people for the disease.

7 The World Bank is helping to bring clean water, electricity and transport to poor people:

Almost 1.4 billion people in developing countries do not have access to clean water. About 3 billion live without basic sanitation or electricity. Infrastructure facility is inadequate or poorly developed. People need basic services for everyday life. Infrastructure is necessary to help achieve the Millennium Development Goals. Delivering safe water has a direct effect on reducing child death rates. Providing communities with electricity prevents women and children from having to spend long hours-fetching firewood for cooking and heating, and gives them more time for other activities. Children especially are able to devote more time to schoolwork. In Morocco, a road project helped to increase the number of girls who enrolled in schools from 28 per cent to 68 per cent. A rural electricity project in Ecuador is helping to improve living standards and broaden opportunities to telecommunications, electricity, and the Internet and business services through the support of the World Bank.

8. The World Bank works with civil society

More than two-thirds of development projects approved by the Bank during the past fiscal year involved the active participation of non-governmental organizations (NGOs) in their implementation, and most of its country strategies benefited from consultations with civil society. The Bank now has staff working in 70 country offices around the world who reach out to and collaborate with NGOs in a variety of areas ranging from education and AIDS to the environment. In South Asia, the Bank is consulting with civil society on gender strategies, in Eastern Europe on post-conflict assistance and governance, and in Latin America on empowerment and the social impacts of reform. A good example of civil society participation in Bank projects is in East Timor, where a Community Empowerment and Local Governance Project supports democratically elected village councils composed of youth, women, and church and farmer groups in repairing roads, providing potable water, and restarting economic activities through community projects. Involvement of civil society organizations (CSO) in projects has risen from 21 per cent of all projects in 1990 to about 72 per cent in 2003.

9. The World Bank helps countries emerging from conflict:

The Bank currently works in 40 conflict-affected countries supporting international efforts to assist war-torn populations, resume peaceful development, and prevent relapse into violence. The Bank's work addresses a range of needs, including jump-starting the economy, investing in war-affected regions, repairing war-damaged infrastructure, and targeting programs to vulnerable groups, such as widows and children. The Bank also supports the disarmament, demobilization, and re-integration of ex combatants, as well as mine survey and awareness initiatives. Among the wide-ranging and innovative projects supported by the Bank are infrastructure reconstruction and community empowerment efforts in Afghanistan and rehabilitation of street children in the Democratic Republic of Congo. The Bank also supports local development activities in southern Serbia, and training for new government employees in East Timor, and national consensus and citizen participation programs in Haiti.

10. The World Bank responds to the voices of poor people:

Conversations with 60,000 poor people in 60 countries, as well as our day-to-day work, have taught us that poverty is about more than inadequate income or even low human development. It is also about lack of voice, lack of representation. It is about vulnerability to abuse and corruption. It is about lack of fundamental freedom of action, choice, and opportunity. We believe that people who live in poverty should not be treated as a liability, but rather as a creative asset that will contribute more than anyone else to the eradication of poverty. An empowering approach to poverty reduction puts poor people at the center of development and creates the conditions that enable poor men and women to gain increased control over their lives, through access to information, inclusion and participation, accountability, and local organizational capacity. Today the Bank is supporting community-driven development projects with more than US $2.2 billion in commitments. In Indonesia, 15,000 villages and community groups are developing their own proposals to receive local funding, while in Benin, women are working together to protect the forests and make them sources of income rather than sources of fuel.

The World Bank has identified the following **strategies for poverty reduction**. These are[146]:

(a) Economic growth
(b) Reducing inequalities
(c) Making market works better for poor people
(d) Redistributing people's asset
(e) Redistributing public spending
(f) Institutional reforms
(g) Increase participation of the poor

---

146 . World Development Report, 2000-01.

(h) Make State Institutions more responsible to the poor
(i) Uphold the rule of law
(j) Decentralization
(k) Pro-poor coalition
(l) Removing social barriers
(m) Building social capital
(n) Risk management
(o) Harnessing global forces
(p) Ensuring voice of the poor in global forums
(q) Making the aid more effective
(r) Relieving the debt burden

But professor Else Oyen, Chair of the Comparative Research Programme of Poverty (CROP) in Norway, presented a critical review of the World Development Report (WDR) to CIDA' s poverty Reduction Network in April 2001. These presentations raised a number of questions, which are critical to be answered. These are:

(a) What are the ethics of poverty reduction? Who are the actors and what are their reasons behind their actions? What are the consequences?
(b) Does the World Bank have the necessary legitimacy to be a major mover in poverty reduction?
(c) What is first on the World Bank agenda: economic growth or poverty reduction?
(d) In the World Bank's opinion, how much equality can be tolerated in the paradigm of economic growth? At what stage does the equalizing process reach a level where the poor are no longer considered poor?
(e) Why does the World Bank emphasize that the poor are experts on poverty?
(f) Will "empowerment" and "Social Capital" as captured in the WDR reduce poverty? What does "empowerment of the poor" really mean? What is social capital and how is it distributed to the poor?

(g) What is not in the World Bank report?

Conflict: Redistribution and poverty reduction engender conflict. This needs to be acknowledged, and counter-strategies and processes to overcome the powerful forces working against poverty reduction need to be identified.

Empowerment: Empowerment through organized labor is absent; in spite of the fact that labor unions have been major movers for the rights of workers throughout history. The WDR is silent on the role of labor unions in partnership and the formation of social capital.

Strategies of Northern Welfare States: Why the World Bank has ignored the successful and unsuccessful experiences of poverty reducing strategies of the North? For example, Norway was one of the poorest countries in Europe around the time of Second World War, when foundation of the welfare state was laid. In 2002, as per Human Development Index, Norway stands first among 173 countries studied. An important lesson from the early development of welfare states is that the initial structuring of the social policies decides the later outcome, when economic growth took off, the institutional structures went on for further re-distribution were already in place.

Concretization of strategies: The WDR should emphasize on research, arguments, strategies and honest analysis of the effects on proposed measures for poverty reduction. It should explain how the institutions should work or what future institutional scenario can be expected to have a positive impact on poverty research.

Jeni Klugman lead economist of the World Bank responded to professor Oyen's questions. Professor Klugman has opined that:

(a) Structured adjustment has not done well. Policy prescription imposed from outside simply do not work. Hence the Bank has not offered policy prescription in the WDR because universal policies do not work.
(b) It is important to increase per capita income in order to have the resources to spend on health and education. Increasing per capita income increases pay-off.
(c) Empowerment is identified in terms of accountability and transparency but fiscal capacity is limited. Empowerment will not mean much, if people are hungry.
(d) Lesson from industrial countries may be important, but are of limited value to developing countries where the per capita income is so low. The welfare programs inherited in the transition economies are acknowledged to have been useful.

The WDR is an important stocktaking and has important implications for the Bank's work; particularly poverty reduction is the singular objective of the Bank although it is not always systematically part of the Bank's work.

Similarly, Francis Lau (1997) has criticized the World Bank and IMF severely. He opines that, "The World Bank and the IMF do not eradicate poverty: they implement Structural Adjustment Plans that lead everywhere to the dismantling of economic infrastructure, the destruction of public services, and the proliferation of poverty. The World Bank and IMF are basically anti-democratic in their nature: they handle their business in a narrow circle of closely connected officials, politicians, private-sector magnates and academics, while the people affected by these policies are left out in the street, with no say whatsoever over their destiny. If the World Bank and the IMF' s prescriptive model of development means low wages, factory closures, massive retrenchment, a falling living standard and bans on collective bargaining- then it really means disaster for millions of people who may never have heard of the names of these institutions.

Oxfam International's Submission for Review of Conditionality

Oxfam International[147] is a confederation of over 12 organizations that works with over 3000 partners in more than 100 countries to find lasting solutions to poverty, injustice and suffering. The organization welcomes the World Bank's decision to review its conditionality practice in 2005. It suggests that the World Bank as the largest multilateral aid donor should be a lead player in making aid more effective for poverty reduction. Recent World Bank efforts to reform its conditionality practices have not gone far enough. Hence, Oxfam International suggests that the World Bank should review the main areas of concern. These are:

(a) The administrative burden of World Bank conditions is still excessive.
(b) Country 'ownership' is still not respected in practice.
(c) Independent impact assessments of reform proposals need to be strengthened.
(d) The danger of falling back on selectivity
(e) The role of the IMF as key to predictability and harmonization
(f) The scope of the review should be broadened.
(g) The need to assess the Bank's analytic work
(h) Implementation of the conditionality guidelines must be monitored.

---

[147]Oxfam Submission June 2005 – Submission to World Bank

International Monetary Fund (IMF)

The International Monetary Fund as established by the Bretton Woods Agreements is a substitute for the old gold standard, and an alternative to both a system of completely free exchange rates and a system of extreme exchange control. In other words, the Fund is a mixed standard employing within itself some features of the gold standard and the paper standard. It represents an attempt at "an improved system of international currency," in Keynes's words.[148]

The IMF is an international organization of 184 member countries. It was established to promote international monetary co-operation, exchange stability, and orderly exchange arrangements; to foster economic growth and high levels of employment; and to provide temporary financial assistance to countries to help ease balance of payments adjustment. The operations of IMF, which involve surveillance, financial assistance, and technical - have developed to meet the changing needs of its member countries in an evolving world economy.

The purposes of the International Monetary Fund are:

1 To promote international monetary cooperation through a permanent institution this provides the machinery for consultation and collaboration on international monetary problems.

2. To facilitate the expansion and balanced growth of international trade, and to contribute thereby to the promotion and maintenance of high levels of employment and real income and to the development

---

[148] Kurihara, K. K. (1978), "Monetary Theory and Public Policy", Kalyani Publishers, New Delhi, P. 339

of the productive resources of all members as primary objectives of economic policy.

3. To promote exchange stability, to maintain orderly exchange arrangements among members, and to avoid competitive exchange depreciation.

4. To assist in the establishment of a multilateral system of payments in respect of current transactions between members and in the elimination of foreign exchange restrictions, which hamper the growth of world trade?

5. To give confidence to members by making the general resources of the Fund temporarily available to them under adequate safeguards, thus providing them with opportunity to correct mal-adjustments in their balance of payments without resorting to measures destructive of national or international prosperity.

In accordance with the above, the IMF works to shorten the duration and lessen the degree of dis-equilibrium in the international balances of payments of the members.[149]

The IMF is now more concerned with poverty reduction and growth facility, enhanced HIPC initiative and financing of the HIPC initiative and PRGF subsidies. The activities of the International Monetary Fund are as follows:

Poverty Reduction and Growth Facility:

The objective of the IMF's confessional lending was modified in 1999 to include an explicit focus on poverty reduction in the context of a growth-oriented

---

[149]Articles of Agreement— Article1: purposes, International Monetary Fund, Washington, DC.

economic strategy. The IMF along with the World Bank supports strategies elaborated by the borrowing country in a Poverty Reduction Strategy Paper (PRSP), which is prepared with the participation of civil society and other development partners. Reflecting the new objectives and procedures, the IMF established the PRGF in place of the Enhanced Structural Adjustment Facility (ESAF) to provide financing under arrangements based on PRSP. The loan commitment capacity of the PRGF is currently estimated to be SDR 1.1 billion a year through 2005.

The IMF sanctioned new PRGF arrangements for Armenia, Azerbaijan, Cape Verde, Cote d'Ivoire, Guinea, the Kyrgyz Republic, Mongolia, Pakistan, and Sierra Leone with commitments totaling SDR 1.8 billion; in addition, augmentations of existing commitments totaling SDR 66 million were approved for Chad, Ethiopia, Ghana, and Mali. Total PRGF arrangements during FY2002 amounted to SDR 1.0 billion, compared with SDR 0.6 billion in FY 2001. As of end-April 2002, 36 member countries' reform programs were supported by PRGF arrangements, with IMF commitments totaling SDR 4.3 billion undrawn balance of SDR 2.7 billion.

Enhanced HIPC Initiative:

The HIPC Initiative, originally launched by the IMF and World Bank in 1996, was considerably strengthened in 1999 to provide deeper, faster and broader debt relief for the world's heavily indebted poor countries. By end-April 2002, the IMF and the World Bank had brought 26 HIPC-eligible members to their decision points under the enhanced Initiative and Cote d'Ivoire under the original Initiative.

The IMF provides HIPC Initiative assistance in the form of grants or interest-free loans that are used to service part of member countries debt to the IMF. As of end-April 2002, the IMF had committed SDR 1.6 billion in HIPC Initiative grants to 27 eligible countries

(Benin, Bolivia, Burkina Faso, Cameroon, Chad, and Cote d'Ivoire, Ethiopia. The Gambia, Ghana, Guinea, Guinea-Bissau, Guyana, Honduras, Madagascar, Malawi, Mali, Mauritania, Mozambique, Nicaragua, Niger, Rwanda, Sao Tome and Principe, Senegal, Sierra Leone, Tanzania, Uganda, and Zambia). Four members (Bolivia, Burkina Faso, Mozambique, and Tanzania) reached their completion points under the enhanced HIPC Initiative during FY2002. Under the enhanced Initiative, a portion of the resources committed at the decision point can be disbursed before a country reaches its completion point. Such interim assistance from the IMF may be up to 20 per cent annually and 60 per cent in total (25 per cent and 75 per cent, respectively, in exceptional circumstances) of the committed amount of HIPC assistance. As of end-April 2002, total disbursements of HIPC Initiative assistance by the IMF amounted to SDR 688.7 million.

Financing of the HIPC Initiative and PRGF Subsidies

The financing of the IMF' s participation in the enhanced HIPC Initiative and the subsidy requirements of the PRGF are administered through the PRGF-HIPC Trust and the PRGF Trust, respectively. The total resources required for these purposes are estimated at SDR 7.5 billion, of which HIPC Initiative assistance is estimated to amount to about SDR 2.2 billion and the cost of subsidies for PRGF lending is estimated at SDR 5.3 billion. These resource requirements are to be fully met by bilateral contributions from member countries and by the IMF.

The IMF also contributes about SDR 0.8 billion by means of a one-time transfer from the SDA and by forgoing compensation from the PRGF Reserve Account for the administrative expenses related to PRGF operations for the financial years 1998 through 2004. Moreover, the IMF contributes with the equivalent amount being instead transferred to the PRGF-HIPC Trust. In addition, part of the interest surcharge on financing provided in 1998 and 1999 under the Supplemental Reserve Facility related to activation of the New Arrangements to Borrow was also transferred to the PRGF-HIPC Trust. The contributions by the IMF's membership and the IMF itself are to be supplemented by investment income earned on such contributions.

The IMF has increasingly assisted members with long-term capacity building efforts; in addition to providing them with immediate policy advice, cooperation and coordination with other bilateral and multilateral providers of technical assistance have received greater emphasis. Such coordination has helped to avoid duplication of effort and to bring in technical assistance inputs the IMF traditionally does not provide (for example, computer equipment, training equipment and day-to-day support). The IMF imposes level-based surcharges on credit extended after November 28, 2000, to discourage unduly larger use of credit trances and under Extended Fund Arrangements. The IMF also imposes surcharges on shorter-term loans under the SRF and CCL that vary according to the length of time credit is outstanding. The IMF also receives income from borrowers in the form of service charges, commitment fees, and special charges. A one-time service charge of 0.5 per cent is levied on each loan disbursement from the General Resources Account.

A refundable commitment fee is charged on Stand-By and Extended Fund Facility credits payable at the beginning of each 12-month period. The IMF also levies special charges on overdue principal payments and charges that are over-due by less than six months. The IMF employed 787 staff at the assistant level and 1846 professional staff and 343 contractual employees on its payroll as of December 31, 2001.

Japan International Cooperation Agency (JICA)

The foundations for Japan's present prosperity were built by loans from the World Bank to prepare Japan's economic infrastructure. The Shinkansen bullet train, the fourth Kurobe dam, the Tomei and Meishin expressways, and so on were all built by these loans. Japan finished its repayments to the World Bank in 1990 – really only a short while ago.

The beginning of Japan as a donor country goes back to 1954. In that year, Japan joined the Colombo Plan, which was launched to assist Asian countries with their social and economic development. This was the beginning of Japan's government – to - government technical cooperation. Japan joined the Organization for Economic Co-operation and Development in 1964 and increased its amounts for economic co-operation to developing countries. Japan became the largest ODA donor country since 1989 excepting one year (1990). Japan is a peace-loving nation and desires to play a role commensurate with its position in the world to maintain world peace and ensure global prosperity. Japan is now proud that it has the world's second strongest economy, but the country's prosperity has not been achieved by one country acting alone. Resource-poor Japan imports many materials from developing countries, and the stability of those countries is linked to the stability of Japan and the rest of the world. Japan's commitment to international cooperation is activated as a member of the international community.

Basic Philosophy of Japan's ODA:

Japan's ODA charter (adopted by cabinet resolution in 1992) sets down the basic philosophy and principles of Japan's ODA. The following are the four basic tenets of Japan's ODA philosophy:

Humanitarian consideration: The hunger and poverty that great numbers of people are suffering from in developing countries, which make up so much of the world, cannot be overlooked.

Recognition of interdependence among nations of the international community: As the interdependence among nations in the world grows stronger, the economic development of developing countries is indispensable for the peace, stability, and prosperity of the world.

Environmental conservation: Japan gives serious consideration to environmental conservation as an issue for which it is imperative that all of humankind makes efforts as a shared concern; Japan can make use of its experiences overcoming its own pollution problems.

Support for the self-help efforts of recipient countries: Japan believes that development based on the self-help efforts of aid recipients themselves leads to genuine economic independence.

(2) **Principles**

Japan's ODA will be provided in accordance with the principles of the United Nations Charter as well as the following four principles:

(a) Environmental conservation and development should be pursued in tandem
(b) Any use of ODA for military purposes for aggravation of international conflicts should be avoided
(c) Full attention should be paid to trends in recipient countries' military expenditure, their development and production of mass destruction weapons and missiles, their export and import of arms, so as to maintain and strengthen international peace and stability, and from the viewpoint that developing

countries should place appropriate priorities in the allocation of their resources in their own economic and social development; and

(d) Full attention should be paid to efforts for promoting democratization and introduction of a market-oriented economy, and the situation regarding the securing of basic human rights and freedoms in the recipient country.

Priority Regions:

Historically, geographically, politically and economically, Asia is a region close to Japan. East Asian countries, especially member countries of the Association of South East Asian Nations (ASEAN), constitute one of the most economically dynamic regions in the world, and it is important for the world economy as a whole to sustain and promote the economic development of these countries. There are, however, some Asian countries where large segments of the population still suffer from poverty. Asia, therefore, will continue to be a priority region for Japan's ODA. It is also necessary to be mindful of the poverty and the economic difficulties in the world as a whole. Japan will, therefore, extend cooperation, befitting its position in the world, to Africa, the Middle East, Latin America, Eastern Europe, and Oceania. Due consideration will be paid in particular to Least among Less Developed Countries (LLDCs).

Approach to Global Problems:

Recognizing that it is important for developed and developing countries to cooperate in tacking global problems such as the environment and population, Japan will support efforts being made by developing countries to overcome these problems.

Basic Human Needs:

To help people suffering from famine and poverty, refugees, and others, Japan will provide assistance to the BHN sector and emergency humanitarian aid, human resources development, research and other cooperation for improvement and dissemination of technologies A priority of Japan's ODA will be placed on assistance to human resources development which, in the long term, is the most significant element of self-help efforts towards socioeconomic development and is a basic factor for the nation building of developing countries. Japan will also promote co-operation for the improvement and dissemination of technologies, such as research cooperation that will add to research and development as well as adaptive capabilities of developing countries. Infrastructure Improvement: Priority will be placed on assisting infrastructure improvement, which is a prerequisite to socioeconomic development.

Structural Adjustment:

Japan will provide support to structural adjustment, so that the entrepreneurship and the vitality of the private sector in recipient countries can be fully exerted in the market Priority will be placed on assisting infrastructure mechanisms, and to their efforts for a solution to the accumulated debt problem.

(A) Measures for the Effective Implementation of Official Development Assistance:

Japan will promote intensive policy dialogues with recipient countries, with a view to collecting and analyzing relevant information on these countries, and sharing with them basic perceptions on their development policies, taking into account their requests and ideas.

To respond to the various needs of developing countries in different stages of development, Japan's ODA will take advantage, to the maximum extent possible, of the merits of loans, grants, technical cooperation and other forms of assistance. All of these forms of assistance will be organically linked together and coordinated.

When called for, there will be appropriate communication and cooperation with aid agencies of other donor countries, United Nations agencies and international financial institutions, as well as Japanese local governments and private organizations such as labour and business organizations. In particular, efforts will be made to ensure that Japan's perspective on ODA is adequately reflected in the cooperation through international organizations, while taking full advantage of the expertise and political neutrality of these organizations. There will also be cooperation with and appropriate support to non-governmental organizations (NGOs), while respecting their independence.

Japan's own development policies and experiences, as well as those of countries in East and Southeast Asia, which have succeeded in economic take-off, will be put to practical use.

In implementing environmental ODA, Japan will make the best use of its technology and know-how, which it has acquired in the process of successfully making environmental conservation and economic development compatible.

In order to contribute to the transfer of technology suitable to the level of development of the recipient countries, Japan will promote the development of relevant technologies and will provide such assistance as will enable the adequate utilization of the knowledge and technologies possessed by other developing countries.

In transferring technology and know-how, Japan will make use of those possessed by the Japanese private sector as well as by the government, and provide support for technical cooperation by the private sector.

In order to cope with transnational regional problems, Japan will cooperate more closely with international organizations and other frameworks for regional cooperation such as the Asia- Pacific Economic Cooperation (APEC).

A close relationship will be maintained between ODA, direct investment and trade, so that those three can promote the development of developing countries organically. For this purpose, ODA will be more closely linked to and be supportive of economic cooperation in the private sector through trade insurance and such organizations as the Export-Import Bank of Japan.

Cooperation and research to find and formulate adequate development projects will be enhanced. For the future improvement of its ODA, project evaluations, including third party evaluations and joint evaluations with recipients and other donors and organizations, will also be strengthened.

Regional studies of developing countries, studies of development policy, and comprehensive evaluation of ODA will be further promoted.

Full consideration will be given to the active participation of women in development, and to their obtaining benefits from development.

Full consideration will be given to the socially weak, such as the disadvantaged, children and the elderly.

Consideration will be given to redressing the gap between the rich and the poor and the gap among various regions in developing countries.

Japan's ODA activities will be conducted with full care to see that they do not lead to injustice or corruption in the recipient countries.

(B) Measures to Promote Understanding and Support at Home and abroad

The following measures will be adopted to ensure that ODA is implemented with public understanding both at home and abroad and to secure the participation of the Japanese people.

Making ODA Information Public: While taking into account such matters as diplomatic relations with recipient countries, more information regarding the ODA activities will be made available to the Diet and to the public

Enhancement of Public Relations and Development Education: Organized public relations activities and educational programs on development assistance will be promoted.

What is ODA?

Funds and technical assistance extended to developing countries by donor governments to help them deal with their problems is referred to as Official Development Assistance (ODA). According to the Development Assistance Committee (DAC) of the OECD, ODA is defined as having to meet the following three conditions. ODA must be provided:

(a) To a developing country or an international organization by the government or implementing agency of the donor country;

(b) With the main objective of promoting economic development, and welfare of the recipient country; and
(c) In case of a loan, with a grant element of at least 25 per cent (the grant element is a figure showing the concessional level of a loan; for grant aid, it is 100 per cent)

Japan's ODA takes the form of bilateral assistance (grants and loans) that is directly provided to developing countries, and contributions and subscriptions to international organizations. Bilateral ODA can be divided into grants, which carry no obligation for the recipient country to pay back, and ODA loans, through which funds are lent at concessional terms, for example, at low interest rates and with long repayment periods. Bilateral grants can be divided into "technical cooperation", the main objectives of which are human resources development and technology transfer, and "grant aid cooperation"' which includes general grant aid and grant aid for increased food production, cultural affairs, disaster relief, and so on.

Although there was a decline slightly in 1998, the budget for Japan's ODA has continued to increase. And as far as total disbursements of ODA, Japan has been the top donor country for nine years in succession since 1991.By region, 62.4 per cent of Japan's bilateral ODA goes to Asia, to which Japan naturally has deep historical and economic ties. The rest 37.6 per cent of ODA assistance goes to Africa, Latin America, and the Middle East. Japan allocated 39 per cent of aid for the development of economic infrastructure (transportation, electric power, telecommunications, etc.) followed by social infrastructure and services (20.2 per cent), and production sector (12.4 per cent) in the year 1998.

Japan's ODA amounted to $10.64 billion in 1998, 20.64 per cent of the total amount provided by all

DAC member countries, making Japan the top donor that year. This means that, on a per capita basis, each Japanese citizen contributed about $84 that year for ODA. In 1997, Japan was the top ODA donor for 55 countries, mainly in Asia and Latin America. Naturally, the bulk of Japan's ODA goes to Asia and Latin America because of Japan's deep historical ties with those regions and to Africa because of its great development needs. But accompanying the changes in the international situation in the 1990s, requests for Japanese aid from Eastern Europe and Central Asia have been increasing. The result is that Japan's ODA is expanding across regions. That, too, is linked to the diversification of areas of cooperation. Top 5 recipients of Japan's bilateral ODA are China ($1158.16 million), Indonesia ($828.47 million), Thailand ($558.42 million), India ($504.95 million), and Pakistan ($491.54 million) in the financial year 1998. In that year (1998), amount of aid by 21 DAC countries was to the extent of $51,549 million and Japan alone contributed $10,640 million.

In short, the official development assistance (ODA) of Japan consists of:

(a) Bilateral Donations

The Ministry of Foreign Affairs grants the bilateral donations for the purpose of 'grant aid cooperation'. This grant-aid is sanctioned for general purposes, fisheries, and increased food production. Bilateral donations also encourage technical cooperation such as 'acceptance of trainees', dispatch of Individual experts, dispatch of study teams, provision of equipment and dispatch of Japan Overseas Cooperation Volunteers.

(b) Bilateral Loans

The Japan Bank for International Cooperation (JBIC) grants the bilateral loans to International

Organizations for projects in the developing countries.

JICA' role

Japan International Cooperation Agency (JICA) was established on August 1, 1974 as an agency to implement Japan's technical cooperation. The motto of JICA is human development, national development, bringing people together. JICA is aware of the fact that over 1.3 billion people in the world are suffering from extreme poverty. Hence, its role is growing more vital for the sake of these fellow humans with whom all of us share. As a nation dedicated to the spread of peace, Japan has a responsibility to maintain peace and prosperity throughout the world. As part of this responsibility, the Japanese government extends ODA to developing countries based on four principles:

(a) That assistance goes toward sustainable development
(b) That aid is not put to military uses;
(c) That aid will help bring about economic and social development which will contribute to international peace and stability; and
(d) That aid will promote a market-oriented economy and good governance.

Japan's ODA puts priority on global issues such as protecting the environment and controlling population, fulfilling basic human needs, and developing human resources. Today Japan is the world's largest donor nation in terms of net ODA disbursement, providing assistance to more than 140 countries.

JICA's activities

(a) It contributes to Human Resources Development

(b) Supports for Self-help Efforts
(c) Grass-roots Cooperation with Local Communities

Moreover, JICA's activities include a wide range of cooperation options customized to meet the needs of developing countries, such as:

(a) Providing technology necessary for socioeconomic development through training in Japan
(b) Transferring Japanese technology to developing countries;
(c) Matching equipment to people;
(d) A comprehensive approach to support;
(e) Helping to formulate development plans;
(f) Acting as bridge of friendship;
(g) Infrastructure for basic human needs;
(h) Supporting private-sector economic cooperation;
(i) Vitalizing Japanese communities;
(j) Quickly moving in to assist with disaster relief;
(k) For the maintenance and development of cooperation activities; and
(l) Training the front lines of international cooperation

The technical cooperation provided by JICA takes the form of assistance in building nations and in helping to develop human resources in developing countries. JICA targets the effective transfer of technology through the 'human' element, offering support to the people of developing countries as they shape their nations with their own hands and through their own efforts[150].

---

[150]JICA – INFO-KIT, File A-1, ODA and JICA; JICA – INFO-KIT, File A-2; what is JICA? (Tokyo 151)

JICA's Program in 2009

Pakistan: President of Japan International Cooperation Agency (JICA) Sadako Ogata called on President Asif Ali Zardari here on Thursday and discussed matters relating to development projects financed by JICA in Pakistan. During the meeting they also talked about the future prospects of cooperation and financial assistance by JICA in various projects particularly in infrastructure and social sector development.

The President appreciated the assistance of JICA in various projects in Pakistan and said his country needs financial assistance to meet economic challenges and to alleviate poverty. The President expressed the hope that JICA will expand its activities in Pakistan. JICA, being the donor agency of the Government of Japan, is responsible for the execution of Japanese Official Development Assistance (ODA) to the governments of the developing countries. With some 10.3 billion US Dollars of available financial resources, JICA is working in around 150 countries including Pakistan.

JICA is supporting the Government of Pakistan through development projects in education, health, environment, disaster management, transportation, water supply and sanitation, electric power, industrial development and agriculture and irrigation. Later talking to Pakistani media, Sadako Ogata said she held a fruitful meeting with the President and the focus of the interaction was to increase the participation of JICA in projects in Pakistan. [151]

Ethiopia: With a US $58 million allocation for 2009, the Japan International Cooperation Agency will continue to support projects in the areas of agriculture, health, education, water resource

---

[151] JICA Program 2009, Tokyo, April 16, 2009

development and infrastructure. Agricultural initiatives include irrigation and rural development while health assistance will involve providing nutrition and medical equipment. JICA is still trying to develop new projects including loans and grants based on the revamped JICA strategy. During the Fourth Tokyo International Conference on African held last May 2008, the Japanese government committed to double development assistance in the region by 2012. In Ethiopia, JICA's budget should scale up in 2010. ,[152]

India: The Japan International Cooperation Agency (JICA) released US $ 4 billion (Indian Currency of 200 billion) by the end of 2009. The Indian minister visited Japan in January 2009 to smoothen out the formalities for receiving the soft loan for the dedicated freight corridor project. The first phase of the corridor would link New Delhi and Mumbai. JICA has agreed in principle to give the loan, but the Japanese are demanding that 30 percent of the work, including technical assistance, be provided by Japanese companies.

The dedicated freight corridor aims at reducing the pressure on existing railway lines, easing congestion, reducing delivery times and improving overall efficiency and productivity. Work will start on both the eastern and western corridors.[153]

(E) Department for International Development (D. F. I. D.)

The Department for International Development (DFID) is Britain's development agency. It is a Ministry of the British Government. DFID is responsible for Britain's contribution to international

---

[152] Celeste Estrella, "JICA s Assistance to Ethiopia 2009", Devex, 5th March 2009

[153] Minister, Railways, Government of India, IANS, February 13, 2009

efforts to eliminate poverty. It works in partnership with developing country governments and other international agencies. Britain wants to share the global effort to eliminate world poverty in the 21st century. The policy of the government was set out in the White Paper on International Development, published in November 1997. The central focus of the policy is a commitment to the internationally agreed target to halve the proportion of people living in extreme poverty by 2015, together with the associated targets including health care provision and universal access to primary education by the same date.

DFID seeks to work in partnership with governments, which are committed to the international targets, and seeks to work with business, civil society and the research community to encourage progress, which will help reduce poverty. DFID also works with multilateral institutions including the World Bank, United Nations agencies, and the European Commission. The bulk of their assistance is concentrated on the poorest countries in Asia and sub-Saharan Africa. DFID is also contributing to poverty elimination and sustainable development in middle income countries and helping the transition countries in Central and Eastern Europe to try to ensure that the widest number of people benefit from the process of change.

The UK government in 1997 established the enhanced focus on poverty. The government published "Eliminating World Poverty: A Challenge for the 21st Century" in 1997 and "Making Globalization Work for Poor People" in 2000. The government has been advised that poverty can be reduced through explicit and multidimensional anti-poverty strategies involving human rights, empowerment, gender equality, governance and environmental concerns. No longer is the focus of rural development purely on increasing production from natural capital but now the focus is development of the community. These[154] focuses are:

(a) Reducing hunger and poverty,
(b) Decreasing vulnerability,
(c) Understanding and responding to the complexity is a pre- condition for effective interventions,
(d) Understanding the macro-micro policy linkages which can disadvantage the poor, especially trade and subsidies, and
(e) Understanding the multidimensional nature of poverty.

However, Ellis[155] has explained that rural development recognizes sustainable livelihoods, good governance, decentralization, and participation in sector wide approaches, social protection, and poverty eradication as present development ideas and approaches. Fighting poverty in rural areas particularly in developing countries is a Herculean task. The emerging characteristics of approaches to rural development must address poverty hunger[156]:

(a) Ability to address core development imperatives, demonstrate the capacity to internalize the important macroeconomic and institutional insights which are influencing the lives of the rural poor e.g. effects of international trade and subsidies on commodities on the poor producers and consumers.

---

[154] Jane Clark (2001), "Rural strategies for Poverty Reduction- Working together effectively", Speaking notes of Senior Rural Livelihoods Adviser, DFID
[155] Ellis F (2001), "Evolving Themes in Rural Development in ODI Development Policy Review"
[156] See also Jane Clark

(b) Understanding of how poor people secure a living recognition of the assets and diverse strategies of poor households
(c) Need for broad based rural growth
(d) Understanding of the complex rural urban linkages
(e) Importance of non-farm activities in rural development
(f) Linking of macro and micro policies and implications
(g) Importance of rural services beyond those to do with agricultural production delivery in health, nutrition, education and finance

He has apprehended that an individual donor agency pursing its own agenda through discrete project activities and relationships will only; at best have a marginal effect. Poverty reduction strategies of all types emphasize working in partnership between governments, donors, civil society and private sector. Development community agrees that agriculture and trade policies formal and informal should consistent with development objectives and supportive of pro poor outcomes. Shared strategies, approaches, tools, ways of working and learning together will help coherence and effectiveness.

But strategies for achieving the international development targets through making government work for poor people encounters many challenges. The challenges of achieving the key capabilities[157] are:

(a) To operate political systems, which provide opportunities for all people, including the poor, and disadvantaged, to organize and influence state policy and practice

---

[157] Strategies for Achieving the International Development Targets, "Making Government Work for Poor People", June 2000, Consultation Document, Department for International Development (DFID)

(b) To provide macro-economic stability and to facilitate private sector investment and trade;
(c) To develop a policy framework that can meet the poverty eradication targets and to raise, allocate and account for resources in accordance with those pro-poor policies;
(d) To guarantee the equitable and universal provision of effective basic services;
(e) To ensure personal safety and security with access to justice for all;
(f) To manage national security accountably and to resolve differences between communities before they develop into violent conflicts; and
(g) To develop honest and accountable government that can combat corruption

Activities of DFID

DFID works in collaboration with both developing and transitional country's governments and international development communities with clear sets out priorities[158]. These are:

To promote and support a more systematic, coherent and collaborative process to making government work for poor people. DFID pursues these goals though collaboration at global, regional and country levels by pro-active engagement and through professional support and exchanges.

DFID's bilateral program will focus on poorer developing and transitional countries. These countries have the greatest difficulty in improving the quality of their government and warrant more support. DFID prefers to work in commonwealth countries in sub-Saharan Africa, Asia, Oceania and the Caribbean.

---

[158] Op. cited

DFID has developed expertise to support reforms in elections and parliamentary government; civil society; privatization and regulation; public expenditure management; sector-wide approaches and revenue administration. DFID has specialized in civil service reform; contracting out and public service customer focus; participatory poverty assessments; gender analysis and local institutional assessments; community security and penal reform; reconstruction of government after conflict; and aspects of anti-corruption strategies. These are the areas in which DFID can most easily mobilize expertise to support governance reform.

DFID also attaches a high priority to developing expertise to serve governments better in the following newer areas: deepening democracy to promote the participation of poor people in government and developing regulatory systems to assure the quality of private sector providers of services. DFID undertakes activities to encourage competition; promoting accessible, non-discriminatory justice; reforming security sectors and creating inclusive political structure, as part of conflict prevention efforts; restricting money laundering globally; and mobilizing the political will for reform.

DFID needs to work to deepen democracy so as to empower poor people and to combat corruption and promote honest and accountable government in all regions.

Additional regional priorities for DFID include the following government capabilities:

(1) In Africa, DFID has the mandate to create an enabling environment to attract investment and to develop pro-poor policy frameworks, which are related to resource raising and expenditure allocation. Moreover, DFID desires to reform public services so as to improve service provision; to strengthen local government; to promote security and accessible

justice; and to manage national security accountably and to prevent conflicts;

(2) In Asia, DFID takes steps to divest the state of commercial activities and to manage the enabling environment for the private sector and to challenge discrimination against women and other vulnerable groups. DFID desires to modernize revenue administration and expenditure management; to introduce a customer focus in public services; to excise corruption and brutality from police forces and to make justice more accessible;

(3) In Eastern Europe and the former Soviet Union, DFID has a mandate to help governments to create conditions for enterprises, which, generate competition and sustainable employment and take account of the social dimensions of re-structuring. DFID has a proposal to develop modern revenue systems and to improve public expenditure management and to develop a new capacity in states to deliver basic services including social protection and health as necessary. DFID is capable to de-politicize and professionalism civil services; to strengthen civil society and its partnerships with government; and to develop the independence and capacity of judicial systems in accordance with human rights; and to support the development of an independent media;

(4) In South America and the Caribbean, DFID has the mandate to create an enabling environment to modernize civil services and to develop the quality and accessibility of basic services and the capacity to regulate private sector suppliers.

(5) A successful year: 2005 was a very important year for development. The UK held the Presidencies of both the G8 (from January to December) and the European Union (from July to December). The Government used this unique opportunity to put reducing poverty, especially in Africa, at the heart of

international debate. The result was a series of agreements both to increase the volume of aid and to improve its effectiveness, which together will increase the chances of achieving the MDGs.

Asia:

Much of Asia is a success story in terms of economic growth. Yet Asia still contains millions of poor people and many more than in Africa. Aid is generally less significant to national budgets in Asia than it is in Africa, so the way in which development assistance is provided must also be appropriate.

Progress towards the Millennium Development Goals:

Income poverty is falling across Asia. The number of children dying before their 5th birthday is decreasing and the number of people being cured from tuberculosis is increasing. However, more progress is needed if all the MDGs are to be met by 2015, particularly on gender equity.

Afghanistan: The London Conference on Afghanistan in January 2006 launched the Afghanistan Compact and the Interim Afghanistan National Development Strategy. The UK pledged £500 million, of which £330 million will come from DFID under a new 10 year Development Partnership Agreement. The UK is now the second largest donor to Afghanistan.

Pakistan: Over 73,000 people were killed and 2.5 million made homeless by the massive earthquake in northern Pakistan in October 2005.The UK's total contribution of £128 million (including emergency relief) makes UK the 4th largest donor to the earthquake response.

Tsunami: DFID committed £75 million for immediate humanitarian relief following the tsunami in December 2004. It has focused on reconstruction, committing a further £65 million in 2005 to rebuild homes, restore livelihoods and get children back into school.

International Development: DFID spent £4,413 million on development aid in 2005 / 06 as against £3,862 million in 2004 / 05. DFID's total bilateral expenditure in Sub-Saharan Africa was £1,097 million and £ 943 million in Asia in 2005 / 06. India, Bangladesh and Sudan received the largest amounts of DFID bilateral aid; however excluding humanitarian assistance Tanzania was the third largest recipient. £261 million of DFID bilateral spending was channeled through UK civil society organizations. DFID's humanitarian assistance in 2005 / 06 totaled £550 million, £ 411 million of which was spent bilaterally and £140 million multi-laterally. Total UK debt relief amounted to £1,653 million, of which DFID debt relief amounted to £65 million, but non-DFID debt relief was £ 1,588 million in 2005 / 06.

White Paper of UK Government 2009

This White Paper ensures that new and additional finance is made available, over and above our aid commitment to reach 0.7 per cent of gross national income. We will also increase our investment in helping developing countries to mitigate and adapt to climate change.

Development works: The UK has been at the forefront of international efforts, which have helped lift record numbers of people out of poverty in recent years. Real incomes in the developing world have doubled. Two-thirds of countries are now classified as electoral democracies. Child mortality has almost halved and the number of children in developing countries out of school dropped by 28 million.

But despite this progress, the developing world is facing its profoundest challenge in a generation. The worst global downturn in 60 years threatens to push 90 million people into poverty. Climate change and conflict threaten the lives of the poor. This matters not just for the poor, but for us all. In an interdependent world, our future is tied together. Prosperity, security and justice can only be sustained when they are shared. Development is not just a moral cause, but is in all of our common interests.

Poverty reduction and sustainable development remain the UK's central development objectives. And investing in services that directly reduce poverty like health, education, and water and sanitation is critically important. But if we are to meet the Millennium Development Goals, this alone will not be enough. We also need to directly confront the underlying causes of low growth, climate change and conflict and fragility.

Our aspiration should be to do more and to do it differently because DFID was established not as an aid agency but as a development department to build a better world for our common future.

We need to protect the poorest through the economic downturn and ensure they build back resilient and sustained economic growth.

We should support poor countries to adapt to the impacts of climate change and invest in low carbon growth.

We need to take a new approach in fragile and conflict-affected countries, doing more to provide justice, security and jobs for the poor.

We should invest more through the international system, in return for reforms to make the institutions more accountable, responsive and representative:

(a) We need to build new and deeper relationships with emerging global powers, civil society and faith groups, and the private sector;
(b) And in everything we do, we need to increase the value for money, effectiveness and transparency of international aid.

The White Paper charts new courses. It marks our renewed commitment to the ideals of international development, but also takes us in new and fresh directions. We will work across government, the international community, and at local levels with a wide set of partners to make our commitments a reality. The challenges before us all are huge. But our response cannot be to turn away when things get tough. Instead to re-double our efforts to make a fairer, safer and more sustainable world for all people, we are lagging behind. This may jeopardize our common future.

So the UK government commits to:

On sustainable growth:
(a) helping 50 million poor people through the global downturn
(b) pressing for a fair deal on trade
(c) trebling efforts to freeze and recover stolen assets
(d) delivering our commitment to double agricultural research
(e) helping 15 countries grow their economies through support from an International Growth Centre
(f) investing £1 billion for African regional development

On climate change:
(a) pressing for ambitious & equitable global Copenhagen deal with additional public finance
(b) setting up a Climate Change Knowledge Network new trans boundary water initiatives

(c) setting ambitious renewable energy targets for multilateral investment
(d) delivering £800m for climate mitigation, adaptation and innovation
(e) piloting affordable insurance for the poor

On peaceful states and societies

(a) at least half of new UK bilateral aid will focus on conflict affected and fragile states
(b) tripling investment on security and justice new economic opportunities for 7.5m people in five major fragile countries investing in more effective UN support for peace building joint UK government strategies in fragile countries 1,000 civilians ready to be sent to countries affected by conflict While keeping our promises
(c) dedicating 0.7 percent of GNI to aid by 2013 half of future UK direct support to go to public services
(d) supporting 8 million in schools in Africa by 2010 and launch new education strategy to save 6 million mothers and babies by 2015 through supporting a new international consensus to accelerate progress on mother and newborn health giving higher priority to tackling malnutrition and launch a new nutrition strategy by end 2009

Changing international institutions

(a) increasing spend on international institutions as they successfully reform more money through UN system subject to performance
(b) pushing for the creation of a new, powerful UN agency for women
(c) pressing for EU to create single Commissioner for Development and focus re-prioritize resources to fragile states

(d) pressing for better governance and performance of World Bank, IMF and regional development banks
(e) increasing support for UN emergency response funds to meet growing humanitarian demands
(f) Changing the way we deliver increase aid transparency and independent evaluation
(g) establishing joint HMG teams in key emerging economies
(h) doubling central support to civil society
(i) introducing a new aid logo
(j) supporting 30 new businesses to boost employment through a new Business Innovation Facility
(k) Increasing support for innovative financing for health.[159]

DFID 2010

(a) UK aid to Africa is on track to increase from £1.3 billion in 2004 to £3.4 billion in 2010
(b) More than 80,000 child deaths have been prevented with delivery of 14.6 million bed nets to tackle malaria. These come from a pledge of 20 million nets by 2010 that the Prime minister made in 2008.

(F) Canadian International Development Agency (CIDA)

The Government's foreign policy statement, **Canada in the World**, released on February 7, 1995 provides a clear mandate for Canadian Official Development Assistance (ODA)[160]. The purpose of Canada's ODA is to support sustainable development in developing countries, in order to reduce poverty and to contribute to a more secure, equitable and

[159]Douglas Alexander, Secretary of State, White Paper 2009
[160] CIDA' s Policy on Poverty Reduction, Canadian International Development Agency

prosperous world. Canada's development assistance program recognizes the vital link between poverty reduction and sustainable development, and is built on a broad array of programs and policies working together in an integrated way.

Poverty results from the lack of human, physical and financial capital needed to sustain livelihoods and from inequities in access to, control of and benefits from political, social or economic resources. In an interdependent world, poverty in developing countries increasingly affects the economic, social and political welfare of developed countries. Poverty can lead to serious global problem, such as environmental degradation, political and economic instability and large- scale migration of people in search of a better life. Poverty reduction is complex and difficult, and despite considerable programming experience in CIDA, it remains a challenge. Developing the capacity of people and countries to reduce poverty is central to sustained poverty reduction. CIDA's approach to poverty reduction requires:

(a) A better understanding of the country-specific and local characteristics of poverty;
(b) A coordinated use of project, program, institutional support and policy interventions to achieve maximum impact; and
(c) A clear view of CIDA' s role and capabilities

In addressing the challenges posed by poverty, important distinctions must be made between "relief" and "reduction". Poverty relief addresses survival needs of the poor, their immediate problems, and the effects of inequities. It does not enable the poor to secure or sustain their livelihoods, or to end the ongoing cycle of poverty. Poverty reduction is a process by which the causes of deprivation and inequity are addressed. Clearly, "relief" activities can be critical in dealing with famines and other disasters - indeed, short - term survival strategies are crucial for the extremely poor. However, the challenge lies in making the transition from short- term response of relief activities to interventions, which work to reduce poverty in the long run.

In this context, the policy provides a framework for poverty reduction and guides programs in six priority areas for ODA: basic human needs; women in development; infrastructure services; human rights, democracy and good governance; private sector development; and environment

Policy

Poverty reduction will be a central focus of Canada's development cooperation. CIDA will make concerted efforts through its programs to contribute to a sustained reduction both in the number of people living in poverty in developing countries, and in the extent of their deprivation.

1. An Agency-wide definition of poverty reduction will be adopted:

Poverty reduction means a sustained decrease in the number of poor and the extent of their deprivation. This requires that the root causes and structural factors of poverty be addressed. Reducing poverty places a focus on people's capabilities to avoid or limit their deprivation. Key aspects of this are: recognizing and developing the potential of the poor; increasing their productive capacity; and reducing barriers limiting their participation in society. Poverty reduction must focus on improving the social, economic and environmental conditions of the poor and their access to decision making. Poverty-reduction activities should be carried out in a manner, which promotes sustainability, builds self-reliance, and avoids dependency relationships among donors, partners, and beneficiaries. It must be clearly recognized that the scope of poverty-reduction activities can occur at the community, local, regional, national and international levels because the constraints and opportunities facing different groups of the poor can occur at all these levels. A clear distinction must be made between these levels to address the systemic causes of poverty and to promote effective programming.

2. Poverty profiles and reduction strategies will be integrated into country or regional policy frameworks.

Efforts will be made to ensure that the strategies are complementary to those of recipient countries. A poverty profile analyzes the root causes and contributing factors of poverty, and places poverty within a country's economic, institutional and social context. It summarizes information on the sources of income, consumption patterns, economic activities, access to services and living conditions of the poor, and examines how poverty is correlated with gender, ethnic and other characteristics.

A poverty reduction strategy requires an understanding of the specific characteristics of poverty in a country or locality, the requirements for poverty reduction, and assessments of where CIDA, given its resources, can have the greatest impact. CIDA will select activities, which work to diminish constraints or improve opportunities for the largest possible number of people. The identification of constraints and opportunities common to a large number of the poor in a group or country, as well as the selection of activities to reduce poverty must be done with the full participation of people, their organizations and their governments.

3. Programming at CIDA will be consistent with the goal of poverty reduction.

CIDA programming will be assessed with respect to its impact on the poor. To be consistent with the goal of poverty reduction, programs or projects – even if they do not directly target the poor – should minimize the negative impacts on the poor, where possible, and exploit complementary activities, which can also have a positive impact on the poor. (For example, in situations where private sector development can help reduce poverty by generating income and employment growth, CIDA will assist programs that support local enterprises, particularly micro enterprises, cooperatives, and small businesses). This means that the target beneficiaries of all programming will need to be identified, as well as those who might face indirect negative repercussions; and that indicators will be developed to measure the impact of projects.

4. CIDA will concentrate on areas where it has a comparative advantage: this includes both poverty-focused and policy level interventions.

Although poverty reduction is multifaceted in nature, CIDA cannot be "all things to all people". CIDA needs to focus its efforts to find areas of comparative advantage where, given its resources, it can make significant interventions. Strategic interventions require an analysis of what CIDA's capability is and on what areas it should concentrate. There must be a constant search for complementary actions among projects, programs, institutional supports and policy interventions.

5. Programming Strategies

In light of emerging development challenges and lessons learned, and to provide a central focus and coherence across the agency in its poverty-reduction effort, CIDA will:

(a) Address the root causes and structural factors of poverty: For sustained poverty reduction, the root causes and structural factors of poverty must be addressed. This places an emphasis on improving human and productive capacities of the poor, and on removing barriers to their participation in society. Thus, a key element to sustained poverty reduction is enabling the poor to secure sustainable livelihoods.

(b) Adopt a multi-level strategy: Approaches to poverty reduction can occur at both the individual or community level, and at the systemic level. The first approach works directly with those living in or vulnerable to poverty, and addresses the constraints facing them at an individual or community level (e.g., provision of assets, training). The latter approach works at the policy or institutional level, and seeks to address the broader systemic causes and factors contributing to poverty.

(c) Use a threefold classification in addressing poverty such as: targeted poverty programs, focused poverty programs, and policy interventions.

(i) **Targeted poverty programs:**

Targeted poverty-reduction activities work directly with the poor to improve their welfare. For a project to be classified under this category, two criteria must be satisfied:

(a) The poor must be the specified target group (e.g., destitute women, rural landless); and
(b) Key interventions must be designed to lead to poverty reduction through the promotion of sustainable livelihoods and the broader participation of the poor in society through the promotion of sustainable livelihoods.

Since 1982, CARE Canada's Rural Maintenance Program in Bangladesh has provided over 60,000 rural women with full-time jobs on road crews maintaining a network of roads across the country – and is now helping them start their own businesses. Even though they earn only a few dollars a week, the jobs provide steady, reliable income for some of the poorest people in one of the poorest countries in the world. A new phase of the project is encouraging women to strike out on their own and set up small businesses. They are hired for a four-year period and during the third year of the program they are enrolled in a compulsory savings program and are given training in basic marketing skills and business management. So far, about 24,000 women have "graduated" from the program and gone into business for themselves. They have confidence in themselves and are respected in their communities.

(ii) **Poverty-focused programs**

Poverty-focused activities refer to programs and activities, which benefit the poor, but do not involve working directly with them. Examples include:

(a) Capacity building of organizations, which work with the poor;
(b) Institutional changes to address the needs of the poor; and
(c) Interventions, such as research into small-scale agricultural techniques, which could be employed by poor farmers

The criteria for programs to be poverty-focused are that they will disproportionately benefit a larger number of poor than non-poor. Since 1988, the Peru – Canada Fund has improved the lives of more than a million people in Peru and stimulated the economies of hundreds of small towns and villages in the most isolated and impoverished areas of Peru. Funding for the community projects is generated through an innovative and highly effective 'lines-of-credit' program administered by CIDA. Since its creation, the Fund has financed over 170 projects, which have directly benefited 1.3 million poor people. The value of their contribution – which is estimated at double the amount of the financing provided by the fund – is their ideas and their labor. The Peru – Canada Fund has become a model for cooperation programs by other donor countries in the region.

(iii) **Policy Interventions:**

Activities, which affect the policy environment, are also crucial to poverty reduction. Removing systemic constraints at both the national and international levels can work to address the root causes of poverty for both peoples and nations. Examples include:

(a) Promotion of equitable growth-oriented policies;
(b) Working to reorient public expenditures towards social priorities;
(c) Promoting and enshrining property rights, which are equitable to women
(d) Stimulating a national dialogue on poverty issues; and
(e) Working for international policy to reduce global poverty.

6. Combine economic growth and social Investments:

There is no automatic link between economic growth and poverty reduction. Economic growth reduces poverty when the productive capacity of the poor is matched with the physical location and the labor needs of the growth sectors. Sound economic management, openness to domestic and international trade and investments, private sector development, investment in infrastructure services and in social sectors to meet basic needs, have been key elements of national policies which have strengthened the positive links between economic growth and poverty reduction.

National governments and political leadership committed to poverty reduction play a critical role. The conditions established by government's economic and social policies are crucial to the long-term sustainability of poverty-reduction measures. Governments determine the economic policy framework, redistribute resources, provide critical social investments for the poor, and frame the legislation that establishes property rights and the legal basis for removing gender inequities.

7. Address basic human needs:

Addressing priorities such as basic education, primary health care, nutrition and family planning, water and sanitation, and shelter, play a key role in poverty reduction. Education, particularly basic education, has significant benefits for the poor by increasing incomes; it also promotes participation by educating people on social issues. Educating girls is, in particular, the single most effective development investment.

8. Achieve food security:

Food security allows people to protect and sustain their broader livelihoods – while food insecurity can lead to powerlessness, dependency, and pain and reduced physical and intellectual growth. Food insecurity reinforces the cycle of poverty. CIDA will take steps to ensure that food aid is consistent with, and better integrated into, overall poverty-reduction and food-security programming strategies. Project and program food aid, which is used as a delivery channel for bilateral programming, must be explicitly integrated into overall programming strategies to increase effectiveness. Food aid must be recognized as only one aspect of food security and poverty reduction, and must be closely integrated with other development inputs and programs. Canada can work with partners for the development of food - security strategies provided they (partner/s) would work on the transitional and rehabilitative needs, beyond the immediate relief requirements.

9. Promote participatory approaches: build networks and involve governments:

Supporting the work of local non-governmental organizations (NGOs) and the international financial institutions (IFIs) is an area in which CIDA will continue to make a contribution. CIDA can assist countries in developing anti-poverty action plans by building on existing strategies for provision of basic education, primary health care, and improving the welfare of children. CIDA prefers to work with recipient governments in building national approaches for fighting with poverty.

Canada's New Government Provides an Incentive to Get Life-Saving Drugs to Developing Countries

Mr. Jim Flaherty, Minister of Finance of Canada emphasizes on April 2007 at Mississauga that Budget 2007 creates an additional incentive for drug manufacturers to donate medicines from their inventory to the developing world. He said, "There are people in Africa and in developing countries around the world in desperate need of medicines like the ones in this very facility. It's unacceptable to Canadians that pharmaceuticals remain on shelves while people are suffering from life-threatening diseases. I encourage all Canadian manufacturers to step up and donate more medicines to worthwhile charities, getting them off the shelves and into the hands of those who would most benefit from them."

Under the Budget 2007 measure, corporations donating medicines from their inventory can claim a tax deduction equal to the cost of the donated medicines or half of the amount by which the fair market value of the donated medicines exceeds its cost, whichever is less. This is on top of the deduction corporations can already claim of the fair market value of any property donated to a registered charity or government body. This additional deduction will be available only when the donation is made to a registered charity that has received funding through the Canadian International Development Agency, and if the gift is intended for charitable activities outside of Canada. This tax incentive is just one of the Budget 2007 initiatives to reduce global poverty and contribute to international peace and security. Other measures include:

(a) Investing an initial $115 million and up to $230 million over time towards the Advance Market Commitment to create a pneumococcal vaccine, expected to save more than 5 million lives in the developing world by 2030.
(b) Providing $200 million in additional support for reconstruction and development in Afghanistan, with a focus on new opportunities for women, enhanced security and combating illegal drugs.
(c) Confirming Budget 2006's commitment to double international assistance by 2010–11 from 2001–02 levels, while setting out a plan to enhance the focus, efficiency and accountability of Canada's international aid efforts

To promote participatory development, CIDA will:

(a) Enable people to realize their own capacities and goals through participatory processes;
(b) Implement policies and programming to address the gender-poverty nexus;
(c) Contribute to donor coordination mechanisms; and

(d) Support capacity building and institutional strengthening of various groups and organizations.

CIDA would prepare periodic reports outlining achievements, progress in implementation, and priority actions for the following period. A formal evaluation of policy will be conducted within 5 years.

(G) Australian Aid (Aus AID)

The Australian Government's overseas aid program is a Federal Government funded program that reduces poverty in developing countries. The program is managed through the Australian Agency for International Development (Aus AID). Each year the Australian aid program reaches more than 58 million people living in poverty around the world, with most of its activities taking place in the Asia-Pacific region. Australia works with other governments, the United Nations, Australian companies and non-government organizations to design and set up projects, which tackle the causes and consequences of poverty in developing counties. Australia's aid program serves the national interest by fostering growth, poverty reduction, peace and stability in the region and addressing Trans-national threats to Australia's security. Five guiding themes shape Australia's efforts to assist developing countries to reduce poverty and achieve sustainable development:

(a) Governance: Promoting democratic and accountable government and effective public administration

(b). Globalization: assisting developing countries to access and maximize the benefits from trade and new information

(c) Human Capital: supporting stability and government legitimacy through improved basic services like health, education, and water and sanitation services.

(d) Security: strengthening regional security by enhancing partner governments' capacity to prevent conflict, enhance stability and manage trans-boundary challenges.

(e) Sustainable Resource Management: promoting sustainable approaches to the management of the environment, including rural development, and the use of scarce natural resources.

Supporting these themes are policy frameworks in key sect oral and program areas, notably: good governance; humanitarian assistance; peace, conflict and development; health; HIV / AIDS; food security; rural development; private sector development; human rights; information and communication technologies and environmental management. In 2003-04, an estimated $370 million, or 21 per cent of total aid expenditure will support governance programs and activities that promote open and efficient markets; enhance competition; combat corruption; secure property rights and the rule of law; protect human rights; and encourage civil society participation.

Policy Framework

Australia's Aid program outlines a new policy framework for investment in growth, stability and prosperity. It emphasizes the critical importance of good governance as the basis for successful poverty reduction and development. Australian assistance for improved governance addresses five key aspects:

(a) Improved economic and financial management

Sound financial policy frameworks and robust economic institutions are important in attracting and generating private sector activity and maximizing the benefits of globalization. Foreign aid does not and never will form the bulk of the resources for long-term development. Far greater are private sector resources. Opening up to trade and investment fuels economic growth and liberalizing global trade and investment makes a substantial contribution to reducing poverty. The World Bank has estimated that if developing countries were to adopt necessary trade reforms and become more integrated into the global economy, some 300 million people could be lifted out of poverty by 2015. Australia is providing $28 million in capacity building assistance for developing countries to access the benefits of trade and investment liberalization and participate in the World Trade Organization and regional trading arrangements.

(b). Increased public sector effectiveness

Public sector effectiveness is closely linked to sound economic and financial management. Australia has established flexible and responsive mechanisms in most major partner countries to support public sector reform.

(c). Strengthened law and justice

Effective law and justices systems promote regional security, increase international confidence and help attract foreign investment. Australia is supporting legal reform programs in Indonesia, Vanuatu, Fiji, Tonga, Cambodia and PNG. Australia is supporting a professional development-training program for all judges, magistrates and court officers in order to strengthen court operations. Australian support is also helping strengthen police forces in Solomon Islands, Vanuatu, Samoa and PNG by building organizational capacity and introducing community-policing approaches.

(d). Development of civil society

Democratic and accountable government lays the foundation for effective community participation. The Australian Government helps promote and protect human rights through supporting grass roots activities for indigenous human rights groups and building the institutional capacity of national human rights bodies. With Australian support the number of national human rights mechanisms in the region continues to grow. Strong and accountable institutions that operate transparently, that enable participation by citizens in decision making and that act in accordance with the rule of law are a key to economic growth and poverty reduction.

(e). A dynamic private sector

Effective governance creates sound fiscal, monetary and trades policies and creates a positive environment for private sector development. A dynamic private sector creates jobs and incomes, generates wealth and ensures resources are used efficiently. The importance of appropriate economic policies and institutional arrangements in maintaining the confidence of investors is well known, including in recent times in regional financial markets. Transparent decision making and effective institutions can ensure these countries can best respond to rapid movements of international capital and ensure that they continue to attract long-term investment. The policy does not attempt to pick winners in the private sector; rather it focuses on creating the conditions for private sector growth in developing countries, including:

(1) Encouraging responsible fiscal and monetary policies and creating the environment for efficient production, through appropriate trade, exchange rate and pricing policies
(2) Promoting deregulation and competition

(3) Improving the appropriate legal, judiciary and regulatory environment

Australian aid assists developing countries to undertake structural reforms to encourage the private sector to flourish. Particular attention is given to privatization of state-owned enterprises, an area where Australia has considerable experience, and making credit more accessible to entrepreneurs-particularly the very poor. By providing small amounts of credit to the poor, the majority of whom are women, they can escape poverty through their own efforts and thus enjoy a fuller and more dignified life.

Aid achievements: In 2001-2002, the aid program undertook 307 activities with governance as the primary focus, with a cost of $308.3 million. Expenditure in other sectors that contributed to governance was a further $180.5 million. These are:

(a) 20 activities aimed at strengthening law and justice;
(b) 59 activities aimed at strengthening public sector management for effective delivery of government services;
(c) 113 activities aimed at fostering the development of broader community development;
(d) 106 projects to improve economic and financial management; and

In 2001-2002, the aid was around $24.4 million on trade–related assistance in the areas of trade policy development and trading, strengthening of customs and quarantine procedures, taxation and tariff reform, trade and tourism promotion, and investment development policy.

Education: Major education programs form part of Australia's aid assistance in many partner countries.

Australia helps countries develop better quality, cost effective and community focused education services, which will lead to better education outcomes in the long term. In 2003-04, Australia will spend an estimated $270 million through the overseas aid program in the education sector. The areas of assistance will be basic education, technical and vocational education, higher education, and distance education. The Australian government and the World Bank launched the Virtual Colombo Plan in August 2001, with an Australian contribution of $200 million over five years.

Rural Development: The majorities of the world's poor live in rural areas, and are disproportionately dependent on natural resources for their livelihoods, especially resources such as forests and fisheries. A strong rural economy built on improved agricultural productivity and accompanied by the right policy settings will boost national economic growth and reduce poverty. In 2003-04, the aid program will provide an estimated $ 255 million for rural development in partner countries. The strategy focuses on reducing poverty by increasing opportunities for the poor to generate income. The strategy includes three major components:

(a) Increasing agriculture sector productivity
(b) Stimulating rural non-farm employment and
(c) Managing natural resources sustainability.

Moreover, the Australian government places a high priority on assisting developing countries with food security as part of reducing poverty and achieving sustainable development. Food Security means that food is available at all times, that all persons have means of access to it, that it is nutritionally adequate in terms of quantity, quality and variety and that it is acceptable with the given culture (World Food Summit, 1996). Freeing up markets through trade liberalization is part of the process to achieve long-term food security. In 2001-2002 the aid program spent $268.1 million on food security. This figure includes expenditure from ACIAR and other government departments. This contribution is part of Australia's pledge to provide $1 billion for food security activities for the four-year period ending 2001-02.

The Australian Center for International Agricultural Research (ACIAR) develops international agricultural research partnerships that reduce poverty, improve food security and promote sustainable natural resource management in developing countries. In 2001-02 the aid program provided $194.6 million for rural development, representing about 13 per cent of overall expenditure. An additional $ 62.9 million was provided through projects in other sectors, which benefit rural development. Aus AID supported 144 projects in the rural development sector.

Infrastructure Development: Australian support for infrastructure development focuses on:

(a) Improving poor people's access to essential infrastructure services such as water supply and sanitation, transportation and energy;
(b) Assisting the creation of enabling environments for both private and public financing and management of infrastructure; and
(c) Supporting human resources development, institutional strengthening and capacity building in the infrastructure sector.

Australia spent $197.8 million on the provision of essential infrastructure through 107 activities in 2001-02. This represents about 13 per cent of overall aid expenditure. Infrastructure priorities were also achieved through $64 million of expenditure in other sectors.

Gender and Development: Australia's aid program will work with partner countries to:

(a) Address violence against women and children, including trafficking in women and girls, and promote women's positive role in conflict situations and peace building;
(b) Enhance women's economic empowerment; and
(c) Ensure that gender equity issues are effectively incorporated into governance and infrastructure activities.

The aid program spent $567.9 million on 647 activities in which gender considerations were a significant component in 2001-02. But during 2003-04, Australia provided an estimated $55 million for activities that directly address gender equality. Australia's Aid commitment places a strong emphasis on the incorporation of a gender perspective into aid activities in the five priority sectors of Australia's aid program: health, education, rural development, infrastructure and environment, and governance. The goal of the policy is to promote equal opportunities for women and men as participants and beneficiaries of development.

Environment: Preventing environmental degradation is essential if poverty reduction and development is to be sustainable in the longer term. Land degradation, deforestation and the destruction of fisheries all directly undermine the livelihoods of the rural poor. In urban areas, overcrowding, inadequate sanitation, pollution and natural disasters affect the health of the poor, making it harder for them to earn a living. The economic costs of environmental degradation have been estimated at 4-8 per cent of Gross Domestic Product (GDP) annually in developing countries. Some environmental problems, such as land degradation and pollution, can be solved principally through domestic action. Other, such as climate change and ozone depletion, also needs to be addressed through coordinated multilateral action.

In 2001-02, $205.6 million was spent on environmental activities through Aus-AID. This included $94.2 million on activities directly promoting environmental sustainability, and $111.4 million on activities in the rural development and infrastructure sectors, which indirectly addressed environmental issues. In 2003-04, Australia provided an estimated $95 million for activities that directly addressed environmental problems in developing countries. Australia will provide bilateral support for renewable energy and improved water, waste and natural resource management. Australia's regional and multilateral support will include bio-diversity conservation, climate change mitigation and adaptation, and phasing out of ozone depleting substances. Australia contributed US $1.5 billion for ODA in 2004. This means that each person in Australia gave US $ 72.6 or AUS $ 98.7 as contribution for ODA in 2004. Australia's aid program for 2005/06 consists of sectors like emergency and multi-sector, governance, law and justice, education, rural development, infrastructure, health and HIV/AIDS.

In 2007-2008 Australia would provide $3,155.3 million worth of official development assistance of which Aus-AID will manage $2,731.6 million. All Australians contribute to Australia's aid program. Every week, each of us puts in around $2.40 to pay for our aid program - about the cost of a loaf of bread a week. This amounts to around 1percent of Federal Government expenditure compared to the 42 percent spent on social security and welfare. The ratio of Australia's aid to Gross National Income (GNI) for 2007-08 is estimated at 0.30 per cent.

Globalization and the Aid Program

A package of trade-related assistance includes:

(i) Contributions to the WTO Global Trust Fund established to ensure that developing country members of the WTO could take full advantage of the opportunities offered by the Doha Round of trade negotiations;

(ii) Additional funding to build South East Asian countries capacity in trade policy analysis and market access negotiations and additional supports for African regional trade initiatives (especially in agriculture).

(iii) Trade-related support to developing countries extends beyond direct technical assistance. Australia provides tariff and quota free access for all goods produced in the 49 Least Developed Countries from 1 July 2003. These arrangements also include East Timor.

Between 1996-97 and 2002-2003, aid funding for direct trade-related technical assistance and capacity building has increased by more than 55 per cent. Estimated expenditure will reach $31 million in 2003-04. Trade liberalization has the potential to lift millions for people out of poverty. If developing countries increase their share of world exports by five per cent, this would generate $677 billion per year – seven times as much as they receive in aid.

Australia's bilateral aid activities

Australia has development partnership with Sri Lanka, Bangladesh, Pakistan, Nepal, Maldives, India, Bhutan, Indonesia, Philippines, Thailand, Vietnam, Cambodia, Laos, China, Mongolia, East Timor, Fiji, Solomon Islands, and other countries. Australia will contribute $1 billion over five years—the largest single aid contribution ever made by Australia—to assist economic and social development in Indonesia. Priorities for the Australian aid program in 2004–05 have included:

(a) Responding to the Indian Ocean tsunami and other humanitarian and emergency situations in Bangladesh, Sudan and Southern Africa
(b) Improving security, governance and services in Solomon Islands and Papua New Guinea
(c) Working with partner governments and donors to address transnational threats such as HIV/AIDS and other pandemics, organized crime and food security
(d) Developing long-term innovative approaches to the challenges faced by fragile states in our region and beyond.[161]

Australia's aid program 2011 - 2012

Facts

(a) In 2011-2012 the Australian Government plans to spend almost $4.8 billion on development assistance. This is an estimated 0.35% of Gross National Income for the year.
(b) Australian taxpayers contribute around $3.30 per week each to Australia's aid program.
(c) The Australian Government has committed to increase Australia's official development assistance (ODA) to Gross National Income (GNI) ratio from 0.34% in 2009-10 to 0.5 per cent by 2015-16.
(d) Australian Government funding for NGOs through Aus-AID amounted to $160.45 million in 2008-09, which is around 14.5% of the total funds raised by the sector.
(e) In 2008-09 the Australian community contributed $808.8million to non-government organisations (NGO) for their overseas programs which makes up 73% of their total funds raised.
(f) In 2008-09 about 1.08 million Australian people belonged to regular supporter

[161] AusAID Project Profiles / Related information / Report on Globalization and Poverty / Australian Aid

programs, a 4.9% decrease on the 2007-08 periods.

(g) There were 12,712 volunteers contributing their time to the work of NGOs.

Why does Australia give aid?

Australia wants to be a good international citizen. That reflects a key Australian characteristic: a commitment to help people less fortunate than ourselves, a belief in a fair go for all. When there is a need there is generally a strong response with offers of money, goods, personal time and knowledge. The Australian Government's overseas aid program aims to assist developing countries reduce poverty and achieve sustainable development, in line with Australia's national interest. It is guided by the Millennium Development Goals, the internationally agreed targets for poverty reduction.

Australia gives aid to other countries because it improves our regional security. Australia helps partner governments improve law and order, prevent and recover from conflict, and manage a range of transnational threats to security such as people trafficking, illicit drugs, HIV/AIDS and other communicable diseases. By helping to build stronger communities and more stable governments Australia helps improve their ability to be stable trading partners. The core principles of Australia's aid program are:

(a) Accelerating progress towards the Millennium Development Goals;

(b) A recognition that while economic growth is the most powerful long-term solution to poverty, economic growth will not, by itself, deliver fair and stable societies;

(c) A strong emphasis on the Asia-Pacific, while also increasing our efforts in Africa and South Asia;

(d) An emphasis on the power of education to promote development; and
(e) A commitment to continue to improve effectiveness.

How is aid delivered? Australia works with partner country governments and a range of partner organisations including other Australian Government Departments, the United Nations, Australian and international companies and non-government organisations to design and set up projects which tackle the causes and consequences of poverty in developing countries. The Australian Government's overseas aid is distributed in a number of forms:

Bilateral aid: Aid given from the government of one country to the government of another country. In designing an aid program for an individual country, Australia works closely with the country's government and its communities. The idea is to make sure that each program reflects the country's development priorities, our aid policies and our capacity to assist. These programs can incorporate a wide range of activities from small community-based projects to large regional development schemes.

Multilateral aid: Aid is given by the governments of many countries and distributed through international organizations such as the United Nations, the World Bank, the Asian Development Bank and the World Food Program. Australia supports effective multilateral agencies engaged in poverty reduction and sustainable development to complement and reinforce its bilateral aid. This aid is for large scale projects which include emergency relief and funding for transnational issues such as global warming and control of disease, and large scale infrastructure projects. Australia has sought to improve the effectiveness of these organizations by focusing on donor coordination, good governance and sound economic policies.

Emergency humanitarian relief: Aid to help recovery from disasters and conflict. Australia's emergency, humanitarian and refugee programs respond quickly, flexibly and effectively, providing grants, food aid, medicines and shelter materials. Strengthening preparedness for future emergencies is also part of this response.

Partnerships with non-government organizations (NGOs): Grants to NGOs to deliver programs which address Aus-AID's priorities at a community level. NGOs undergo a strict accreditation program to prove their ability to deliver aid effectively for Aus AID.

Community involvement: Funding for volunteer and education programs within Australia.

How much aid does Australia give?

The Australian Government will provide almost $4.8 billion in Official Development Assistance (ODA) in 2011-12, an increase of $0.4 million over the 2010-11 figures of $4.4 billion. The ratio of Australia's ODA to Gross National Income (GNI) for 2011-12 is estimated at 0.35 percent. The aim is to increase ODA to 0.5 percent of GNI by 2015-16.

Which countries receive Australian aid?

Australian Government aid is strongly focussed on the Asia Pacific region but it also has a strong commitment to Africa and South Asia. Most of Australia's aid activities are conducted through bilateral aid partnerships. In 2008 the Pacific Partnerships for Development launched a new model of cooperation in which Australia and its neighbours commit to jointly achieving shared goals. This means increasingly Australia will work through, rather than alongside, different countries' own systems of government and service delivery. The top ten countries for Australia Government aid in 2011-2012 (in millions of dollars): Indonesia 558.1, Papua New Guinea 482.3, Solomon Islands 261.6; Afghanistan 165.1, Vietnam 137.9, East Timor 123.7, Philippines 123.1, Pakistan 92.8, Bangladesh 92.0 and Cambodia 64.2(Budget, Australia's International Development Assistance Program (2011-12). In 2008-09 the Australian community contributed $808.8 million to non-government organizations (NGO) for their overseas programs, a decrease of $4 million on the previous year. This figure includes funds raised from donations, fundraisers, bequests, and company donations, and makes up around 73 percent of total funds raised by NGOs. About 1.13 million people belong to regular supporter programs, a 4.9 percent decrease in 2007-08.

These funds support programs run by the NGOs in 110 countries. There were also 12,712 volunteers contributing their time to the work of NGOs. The Australian Council for International Development (ACFID) is the independent national association of about 80 Australian non-government organizations working in the field of international aid and development. It administers a Code of Conduct committing members to high standards of integrity and accountability.

What makes aid effective?

Aid can be considered effective to the extent that it assists countries to develop and to overcome poverty. Some factors that can influence the effectiveness of aid are:

(a) A sound and stable policy framework;
(b) Market based policies which encourage integration in the global economy;
(c) An emphasis on social development;
(d) Enhanced participation by the local population, and notably by women;

(e) Good governance, transparency and accountability;
(f) Support for health, education, agriculture and public infrastructure development;
(g) Policies and practices that are environmentally sustainable; and
(h) Better means of preventing and resolving conflict and fostering reconciliation.

Effective aid depends on the partnership between donors and recipients. Donors need to deliver sufficient and predictable aid without unrealistic conditions such as multiple forms of reporting or tied to purchases from the donor countries. Recipients need good governance, to address corruption, and adopt policies that sustain economic growth and improve human development. To be effective the aid program must adapt to the circumstances in each country.

The Paris Declaration on Aid Effectiveness, endorsed by over 100 countries in 2005, committed their countries and organizations on five key areas:

(a) Ownership – Partner countries exercise effective leadership over their development policies and strategies to co-ordinate development actions.
(b) Alignment – Donors base their overall support on partner countries' national development strategies, institutions and procedures.
(c) Harmonization – Donors' actions are more harmonized, transparent and collectively effective.
(d) Managing for Results – Managing resources and improving decision-making for results.
(e) Mutual Accountability – Donors and partners are accountable for development results. Is aid the answer?

The Accra Agenda for Action of 2008 is in place to accelerate the progress towards the goals of the Paris Declaration. The key components of the agenda are:

(a) Improving the way aid is delivered in 'fragile states';
(b) Being more transparent and accountable in the way aid is delivered;
(c) Developing stronger partnerships;
(d) Untying aid and using partner country systems much more to deliver aid;
(e) Encouraging new aid donors to also implement the Accra Action Agenda.

Aid is necessary to build an environment where policies and infrastructure can be in place to support other sources of finance. Aid to developing countries is only a small proportion of the total level of external financing provided to developing countries. International trade, foreign direct investment, debt forgiveness, remittances from citizens working overseas and domestic savings all contribute to the development of the country.

The global agenda: ODA

Aid is not a hand out but a hand up. By addressing the massive gap between the haves and have nots aid can help make the world a fairer and a more prosperous place. In a world tightly linked by trade and investment flows, poverty in one country diminishes the potential for prosperity elsewhere. There is an increasing international commitment to improve the quality and quantity of aid.

The United Nations has set a target for developed countries to contribute 0.7 percent of their Gross National Income in aid to developing countries. The 22 member countries of the OECD Development Assistance Committee, the world's major donors, provided $US 128.7 billion in aid in 2010. This represents an increase from 0.31 percent of members' combined gross national income in 2009 to 0.32 percent in 2010, an increase of 6.5 percent over 2009 and is the highest ODA level ever, surpassing even the volume provided in 2005 which was boosted by exceptional debt relief.

In 2010 Norway, Luxembourg, Sweden, Denmark and the Netherlands all exceeded the 0.7 percent target. In 2010 the United States was the world's largest single aid donor in volume terms ($US 30.2 billion or 0.21percentof GNI), followed by the United Kingdom ($US 13.7 billion, 0.56percent), France ($US 12.9 billion, 0.5percent), Germany ($US 12.7 billion, 0.38percent) and Japan ($ US 11 billion, 0.2percent).

Millennium Development Goals: The Millennium Development Goals commit the international community to an expanded vision of development, one that vigorously promotes human development as the key to sustaining social and economic progress in all countries, and recognizes the importance of creating a global partnership for development. The goals have been commonly accepted as a framework for measuring development progress. Goal 8 calls for an open, rule-based trading and financial system, more generous aid to countries committed to poverty reduction, and relief for the debt problems of developing countries.

Global Recession: In 2008 and 2009 the global economy experienced soaring food and fuel prices, the collapse of global financial markets, and a significant reduction in world economic demand. Global growth declined from 8.1 percent in 2007 to around 1.7 percent in 2009. The crisis had severe implications for developing countries as a result of reduced direct investment, export revenue (including tourism revenues) and remittances. Although recovery from the global recession is underway, there continue to be significant challenges to progressing growth in developing countries.[162]

Conclusion

In the foregoing analysis, we have analyzed the activities of only three world organizations and five international donors, who have capacities to change the whole world into prosperity and glory. These organizations are working on humanitarian grounds for ensuring world peace.

The world organizations and Heads of Government have organized several world summits and international conferences during recent years. They have assembled for children's summit in New York, education summit in Jomtien (Thailand), earth summit in Rio de Janeiro, population conference in Cairo, social summit in Copenhagen and world food summit in Rome. But the Millennium Summit, which declared Millennium Development Goals, has synthesized the previously agreed goals and targets for reduction of extreme poverty and has time-bound result oriented objectives.

The world organizations and international donors agreed to donate 0.7 per cent of GDP for reducing poverty and hunger worldwide. The UNDP is the largest agency for multilateral, technical and pre-invest cooperation, which can concentrate on providing technical advice, arrange funds and induce the governments for pro-poor policies. The World Bank works and dreams for a world free of poverty. It provides low interest loans for longer period with a grace period. It donates funds for HIV / AIDS programs, malaria prevention, and education of children, maternal /child health programs; works in conflicts-affected countries and tries for curbing

---

[162]http://www.ausaid.gov.au/makediff/gec.cfm

corruption worldwide. The most important activity is to arrange debt relief for poor countries. The IMF promotes international monetary cooperation, exchange stability, and faster economic growth and undertakes ease balance of payments. Debt relief and subsidies for PRGF lending are the main functions of the IMF for poverty reduction in the LDCs and developing countries.

The JICA of Japan, DFID of UK, CIDA of Canada and Australian Aid implement their government programs in different countries for poverty reduction, environmental conservation, governance, healthcare, women empowerment, policy intervention, infrastructure development and food security programs. They donate funds to the governments, finance projects and work in poor countries as per bilateral agreements.

It is predicted that by 2015, nine out of ten of the world's poorest people will live in Africa and South Asia. Around half of this number will live in countries without effective governments.

The flow of funds through grant-based financing and multilateral or bilateral debt to the debtor countries did not achieve desired goals as proposed in the original document. It is because the governments and the government machinery are inefficient and corrupt in almost all the debtor countries. Similarly the donor countries, international organizations, world institutions and even individual donors appoint corrupt agencies/persons to work on their behalf without verifying their credentials in the debtor countries. There is inefficiency and corruption in project implementation and evaluation. Therefore, poverty eradication becomes impossible or the progress is negligible. As a result, inequality in poverty regions widens and it causes social imbalances. This created a new culture in all the low-income and developing countries i.e. each individual runs after runs after free gifts, no-work culture and becomes a cheat. Foreign funding encourages corruption in all the Low-income developing countries. Hence, it is advised that both the donor countries and debtor countries must ensure that the entire amount is properly utilized for the specified purposes. Corruption should be checked and stringent action must be taken on the culprits, which can be possible through vigorous anti-corruption drive, such as:

(a) Two statutory organizations such as Vigilance Commission and Evaluation Commission must be created in all the poor countries/states to check corruption and to guide and evaluate the implementation of the international funded projects at each stage. The status of these Commissions should be at par with High Courts or Supreme Courts.

(b). Donors may be requested to donate 100 per cent funds to support primary education, healthcare and anti-malaria efforts, natural hazards, pension program of senior citizens and empowering the poor.

(c). The funding institutions should award self-liquidating long-term loan to the LDCs and developing countries for infrastructure development such as roads, ports, cold storages and warehouses projects.

(d). Debts, grants and donations of all international funding organizations and countries must be included in the annual budget of debtor states/countries, so that funds can be audited and can have accountability and transparency.

(e). All funding institutions should immediately stop grants to non-government organizations. If, however, these institutions donate funds to the NGOs, it should come under all restrictions of the local administration. The funds released to NGOs must be audited and they should be answerable to the parliaments of both donor and debtor countries. There are a large number of fraud NGOs in south Asia, sub-Saharan Africa and Latin America countries.

(f). The G8, OECD, the UNDP, the World Bank, the IMF and other industrialized countries should not finance the poor countries for unproductive ventures and politically motivated projects; and

(g).The funding institutions should sanction those projects, which can really assist the poor and their grant /loan would be utilized for pro-poor policies of the indebted countries. The donor countries/International Funding Institutions should restrict sanction of huge amount of credit to corrupt, non-transparent and ineffective governments of South Asia and African countries.

International credit, assistance, donation or even gift is immediately transferred as the private property of political leaders or government officials in all developing countries.

The government machinery and the politicians in all developing countries are pocketing the foreign funds through contract business, NGOs and through diversion of funds for political gain.

And, poverty, hunger and lawlessness are increasing in all developing countries even today.

+++++

Chapter VI

POVERTY HINDERS WORLD PEACE

When I give food to the poor, they call me a saint. When ask them why the poor have no food, they call me communist.

Dom Helder Camara

Poverty is the cause of disturbances in family, village, state and country. Poverty forces the unemployed youths to join Terrorists or Maoists camps. Poverty causes corruption in government offices. It causes conversion of religion in remote tribal areas. Poverty makes a youth unemployed, hungry and squalor. Poverty encourages school dropouts. It makes them weak and diseased. Poverty creates situations when parents sell their sons and forces them to sell their voting rights to corrupt leaders. Poverty increases inequality in the society and debars them land rights. Poverty ruins political system in democratic countries; it causes concentration of political power in the rich. The budgetary funds which could have been utilized to save the poor from hunger or suicides are diverted for internal security.

To-day, more than one billion of people is hungry. Unless the problem of hunger is not solved possibly we cannot make any peace movement for the safety and secured future of the people of this planet. Hence, poverty is the biggest challenge that faces the world today. But we feel that poverty can be reduced and the poor can be safely employed in developmental processes. We can also eradicate 'starvation deaths' completely with minimum expenditure. The rich countries and rich people have to extend their cooperation for reduction of poverty worldwide.

The reduction of poverty can solve many unsolved problems (such as war, boundary problems, insecurity of people and illegal movement etc.) facing different countries to day. Moreover, the people of this planet can enjoy peace everywhere and we can boldly say that **we have achieved world peace.**

Economic growth of a country does not guarantee that poverty of all can be eradicated in the process of development. Similarly increase of per capita income in a country does not mean that number of people under poverty line is reduced. Poverty among the masses can be reduced through pro-poor, pro-agricultural and pro-rural policies, if implemented by the government. By this procedure, the poor gets a chance to enjoy the benefits. In all the developing countries, the implementing agencies and government organizations are manufacturing fake vouchers and progress reports without actual investments in the projects for the benefits of poor. In many cases poverty is caused through faulty planning by the government itself.

It is a fact that more than 1.3 billion people are poor in this world and they need universal access to economic opportunities, basic social services and empowerment. It is also reported that 42 HIPCs accommodate only 11 percent of the poorest population of the world and the rest 89 per cent of poorest population reside in other developing and developed countries. The G8 countries give more importance to the HIPC and less importance to the developing countries. The rich countries should undertake humanitarian work to assist the poor wherever they reside. These countries give aid to the governments of low-income countries and to the non-government organizations for the benefits of the poor. But both the governments and agencies lack good governance and are leveled as corrupt institutions. These funds are simply eaten away by the officials and organizations and do not reach the poor.

The World Summit for Social Development (1995) addressed three major problems of developing countries: **poverty, unemployment and social disintegration**. **The conjunction of poverty is also alarming.**

In this chapter we have analyzed subjects like Hunger Threatens World Peace and Security, Task Force on Hunger, Millennium Development Goals 2009, Fight poverty to end insecurity 2009, G-8 summit Italy, Global Monitoring Report, G-20 Leaders Statement: the Pittsburg Summit 2009, Food for Peace Program and Charitable Dining Halls to highlight that poverty is the cause of malnutrition, hunger, disease, school dropouts, illiteracy and maternal deaths. **Poverty hinders world peace.** These persons are devoid of human rights; more so their children are the most suffers in this twenty-first century.

Hunger hinders Peace and Security

The Food and Agriculture Organization and the UN World Food Program release news on world hunger very often to assist the food deficit regions of the world. But contribution of these organizations to solve the problem of hunger is limited. These organizations simply release press notes and do paper work. Both the organizations need a drastic change in organizational setup and employ economists and specialists. The UN should also evaluate their performances in solving world hunger and audit expenditure of these organizations. Problems of hunger in some countries are as follows:

Iraq: Hunger and malnutrition pose silent threats to the Iraqi people. The UN World Food Program reported that 930,000 people were suffering from hunger in Iraq in 2007. Another 6.4 million Iraqis lived on the edge of hunger. They were barely getting enough food and without the Iraqi government's monthly food ration, they would also fall into the pit of hunger. Iraqis are struggling to receive this most basic necessity food ration and this explains that the country does not possess the pictures of a stable and successful democracy. The U.S. army undertook a number of missions in the country to help relieve hunger. The U.S. 25th Infantry Division together with Iraqi soldiers, carried out a humanitarian aid drop to help hundreds of families in a neighborhood in Baqubah.

African Countries: With some 40 million people at risk of starvation on the continent, Africa is facing an immense hunger crisis that threatens peace and security. The severity of the current food crises is certainly on a scale that threatens political stability and security. In southern Africa - Zimbabwe, Zambia, Malawi, Lesotho, Swaziland and Mozambique - over 14 million people need food aid.

Difficult weather conditions, floods and drought are only part of the reason for the food crisis. Collapsing economic systems, especially in Zimbabwe; political and ethnic violence in Sudan, Burundi, Côte d'Ivoire, and the Democratic Republic of the Congo; and the HIV/AIDS epidemic are all contributing to the multiple crises. AIDS has killed millions of young men and women in Africa, and the disease is now making it "intolerably difficult" for some countries in the southern part of the continent to resist famine. The international community should address the crisis, since there is a strong link between security and food security. Government policies are more responsible for famine.

The Zimbabwe government's land distribution policy is defective. Thousands of productive farms are now fallow lands. Monopoly procurement and imports of food grains by the corrupt government and restriction of private sector trading of food grains have paralyzed the marketing system in the country. This has resulted in commodity shortages, high market prices and accelerating inflation. This policy breeds hunger, discontentment and revolution. Humanitarian assistance, food aid, and donation of tons of high-energy biscuits to the poor are simply black marketed in poor countries. Starvation deaths are caused by the government and are man-made. Moreover, the low-income countries are poor because nature does not support them. Natural calamities like flood, cyclone, and drought, less rainfall cause more harm to the crops. (Source: Environment News and Services).

India: High child mortality rates and malnutrition remains a serious problem for more than 300 million people in India. India has 30 percent of the world's births, 20 percent of the world's maternal deaths, and 25 percent of the world's child deaths. One third of India's population lacks adequate food. More than one-half of young children (73 million) are underweight, with widespread chronic malnutrition. Poor access to health care, high rates of illiteracy, poor nutrition and health practices, complicated by high fertility and short birth intervals are causative factors for the high mortality rates. (USAID reports)

Poverty causes more hardship to women and children. The poor struggles for basic needs and is more vulnerable to abuse, violence, disease, illiteracy, human trafficking, and death. Poverty encourages migration from rural areas to urban centers, from poor countries to prosperous and politically secured countries.

The United Nations has estimated that 140 million persons resided in other countries where they were not born.

They migrated through legal/illegal immigration or through seeking political asylum. Hence, reduction of poverty has assumed the greatest challenge to save the poor from hunger and malnutrition and the poor also needs 'protection of human rights'. All should be guided that 'food aid should not be used as a weapon by the donor countries to gain anything.'

Task Force on Hunger (2005)

The U N Millennium Project focuses the MDGs as the centerpiece of national poverty reduction strategies supported by international processes. The task force[163] calls for simultaneous action in seven priority areas. These are:

Global-level interventions:

The recommended interventions for **political action** in this domain include:

(a) Advocate political action to meet intergovernmental agreements to end hunger

[163]UN Millennium Project 2005, Halving Hunger: It can be done, Task Force on Hunger, UNDP

(b) Strengthen the contribution of donor countries and developing country governments to activities that combat hunger
(c) Improve global public awareness of hunger issues and strengthen advocacy organizations committed to ending hunger
(d) Strengthen developing country organizations that deal with hunger alleviation
(e) Improve monitoring and evaluation processes and practices

National-level interventions

2. Reform policies and create an enabling environment

(a) Promote an integrated policy approach to hunger reduction.
(b) Restore budgetary priority to the agricultural and rural sectors
(c) Build developing country capacity to achieve the hunger goal
(d) Link nutritional and agricultural interventions
(e) Increase poor people's access to land and other productive resources
(f) Empower women and girls
(g) Strengthen agricultural and nutrition research
(h) Remove internal and regional barriers to agricultural trade
(i) Increase the effectiveness of donor agencies' hunger related programming
(j) Create vibrant partnerships to ensure effective policy implementation

Community-level interventions

3. Increase the agricultural productivity of food-insecure farmers

(a) Improve soil health
(b) Improve and expand small-scale water management

(c) Improve access to better seeds and planting materials
(d) Diversify on-farm enterprises with high-value products
(e) Establish effective extension services

4. Improve nutrition for the chronically hungry and vulnerable

(a) Promote mother and infant nutrition
(b) Reduce malnutrition among children less than five years of age
(c) Reduce malnutrition among school-age children and adolescents
(d) Reduce vitamin and mineral deficiencies
(e) Reduce the prevalence of infectious diseases that contribute to malnutrition

5. Reduce the vulnerability of the acutely hungry through productive safety nets

(a) Build and strengthen national and local early warning systems, including advances in climate prediction at the hotspot level
(b) Build and strengthen the capacity to respond to emergency
(c) Invest in productive safety nets to protect the poorest from short-term shocks and to reduce longer-term food insecurity

6. Increase incomes and make markets work for the poor

(a) Invest in and maintain market-related infrastructure
(b) Develop networks of small rural input traders
(c) Improve access to financial services for the poor and insecure
(d) Provide a sound legal and regulatory framework
(e) Strengthen the bargaining power of rural and urban poor in labor markets
(f) Ensure access to market information for the poor

(g) Promote and strengthen farmer's and community associations
(h) Promote alternative sources of employment and income

7. Restore and conserve the natural resources essential for food Security

(a) Help communities and households restore or enhance natural resources
(b) Secure local ownership, access and management rights to forests, fisheries, and rangelands
(c) Develop natural resource-based 'green enterprises'
(d) Pay poor farmers for the environmental services they provide

Implementing the seven recommendations:

Hunger is a complex problem. Therefore, emphasis on multi-sectoral and multi-stakeholder approaches is proposed to tackle the problem simultaneously, comprehensively, and in an integrated manner. The key principles to underpin implementation of hunger reduction programs include:

(a) Identifying priority interventions
(b) Developing a national strategy
(c) Strengthening capacity
(d) Adopting a multi stakeholder approach
(e) Investment needed
(f) Synergistic entry points
(g) Task Force

The conclusion of the task force is that the hunger goal can be achieved and hunger can be eventually being eliminated from the face of the earth.

Millennium Development Goals
(September 2000)

The Millennium Development Goals[164] adopted at the Millennium Summit of the United Nations in September 2000, call for dramatic reduction in poverty, hunger and marked improvements in health, primary education, gender equality and empowerment of women, environmental sustainability and global partnership. The AIDS pandemic represents a unique challenge of unprecedented urgency and intensity. This single epidemic can undermine Africa's development over the next generation, and may cause tens of millions of deaths in India, China, and other developing countries unless addressed by greatly increased efforts. The Millennium Development Goals constitute an ambitious agenda to significantly improve the human condition by 2015. For each Goal a set of Targets and Indicators have been defined and are used to track the progress in meeting the Goals.

In September 2000, the member states of the United Nations unanimously adopted the Millennium Declaration. The international agencies including the World Bank, the IMF, the OECD countries, specialized agencies of the United Nations and the General Assembly recognized the Millennium Development Goals and accepted the goals for implementation. For each goal, one or more targets have been set, most for 2015, using 1990 as a benchmark. These are as follows:

Goal 1: Eradicate extreme poverty and hunger

(a) Halve, between 1990 and 2015, the proportion of people whose income is less than one dollar a day.

---

[164]The Millennium Project, Commissioned by the UN Secretary General and supported by the UN Development Group, The Millennium Project.

(b) Halve, between 1990 and 2015, the proportion of people who suffer from hunger

Goal 2: Achieve universal primary education

Ensure that, by 2015, children everywhere, boys and girls alike, will be able to complete a full course of primary schooling.

Goal 3: Promote genders equality and empowers women

Eliminate gender disparity in primary and secondary education, preferably by 2005,and to all levels of education no later than 2015

Goal 4: Reduce child mortality

Reduce two-thirds, between 1990 and 2015, the mortality rate among children under five

Goal 5: Improve maternal health

Reduce by three-quarters, between 1990 and 2015, the maternal mortality ratio in childbirth

Goal 6: Combat HIV/AIDS, malaria and other diseases

(a) Have halted by 2015 and begun to reverse the spread of HIV/ AIDS
(b) Have halted by 2015 and begun to reverse the incidence of malaria and other major diseases

Goal 7: Ensure environmental sustainability

(a) Integrate the principles of sustainable development into country policies and programs and reverse the loss of environmental resources.

(b) Halve, by 2015, the proportion of people without sustainable access to safe drinking water and basic sanitation

(c) By 2020, to have achieved a significant improvement in the lives of at least 100 million slum dwellers

Goal 8: Develop a global partnership for Development

(a) Develop further an open, rule-based, predictable, non- discriminatory trading and financial system (includes a commitment to good governance, development, and poverty reduction both nationally and internationally)

(b) Address the Special Needs of the Least Developed Countries (includes: tariff and quota free access for LDC exports; enhanced program of debt relief for HIPC and cancellation of official bilateral debt; and more generous ODA for countries committed to poverty reduction)

(c) Address the Special Needs of landlocked countries and Small Island Developing States (through the program of Action for the Sustainable Development of Small Island Developing States and the outcome of the 22nd special session of the General Assembly)

(d) Deal comprehensively with the debt problems of developing countries through national and international measures in order to make debt sustainable in the long term.

(e) In co-operation with developing countries, develop and implement strategies for decent and productive work for youth

(f) In co-operation with pharmaceutical companies, provide access to affordable, essential drugs in dwelling countries, and

(g) In co-operation with the private sector, make available the benefits of new technologies, especially information and communications.

Millennium Development Goals Report 2009

Aid needed to achieve development goals continues to fall below targets as economic crisis hits hard. The Secretary-General called on donors to honor commitments. With only six years until the 2015 deadline, donor countries are falling short in meeting aid commitments made in order to achieve the Millennium Development Goals (MDGs), and aid is likely to drop even further as a result of the negative economic climate.

The Millennium Development Goals Report 2009[165], launched on July 6, 2009 in Geneva has explained that the Developing countries and their partners have made significant strides in the fight against poverty and hunger, but the unprecedented economic crisis threatens to wipe out these gains.

The Secretary-General, Mr. Ban Ki-moon states in the foreword of the report, "We cannot allow an unfavourable economic climate to prevent us from realizing the commitments made in 2000. The global community cannot turn its back on the poor and the vulnerable. The goals are within reach, and even in the very poor countries, with strong political commitment and sufficient and sustained funding."

Total aid remains well below the UN target of 0.7 per cent of donors' gross national income. In 2008, the only countries to reach or exceed that target were Denmark, Luxembourg, the Netherlands, Norway and Sweden.

At the Gleneagles summit of the Group of Eight countries in 2005, and at the UN World Summit (2005), donors committed to increasing their aid. Secretary-General Ban wrote open letters to the G8

---

[165] UN Department of Public Information – DPI/2539C – July 2009

members before the Italy Summit in 2009 that annual aid to Africa remains at least $20 billion. He urged the G-8 to set out, country by country, how donors will scale up aid to Africa over the next year to make the Gleneagles commitments real.

With most OECD economies in recession, even fulfillment of previous commitments, which were expressed as a percentage of donors' national income, would imply a diminished amount of aid. For many developing countries, lower levels of aid would not only impede further progress, but could even reverse some of the gains already made.

At the same time, the ability of countries to mobilize domestic resources for development is also in jeopardy, according to the survey. Export revenues of developing countries fell in the last quarter of 2008, with the collapse of commodity prices, and debt service to exports ratios of developing countries are likely to deteriorate further, especially for those countries that enjoyed increased export revenues for the last several years.

The Millennium Development Goals report makes it clear that development initiatives consistently deliver results when sufficient and sustained funding backs political commitment:

(a) Enrolment in primary education reached 88 per cent in 2007, up from 83 per cent in 2000.
(b) Deaths of children under-five declined steadily worldwide— from 12.6 million in 1990 to 9 million in 2007 — despite population growth.
(c) In sub-Saharan Africa, where child mortality remains the highest across all regions, recent survey data show remarkable improvements in key interventions that could yield major breakthroughs for children in the years ahead. Among these interventions is the distribution of insecticide-treated bed nets that have

reduced the infection rate of malaria – a major killer of children.

(d) As a result of investments in 'second chance' immunizations, dramatic progress is also being made in the fight against measles.

(e) The estimated number of AIDS deaths worldwide appears to have peaked in 2005 at 2.2 million, and has since declined to 2 million in 2007, partly due to increased access to antiretroviral drugs in poor countries.

Despite these and other successes, the MDG Report concludes that progress has been too slow for most of the targets set in 2000 to be met by 2015, unless efforts are stepped up. Greater political will must be mustered to improve maternal health and reduce maternal mortality – the goal on which the least progress has been made -particularly in sub-Saharan Africa and Southern Asia.

Secretary-General Ban concludes:

Rather than retreat, now is the time to accelerate progress towards the MDGs and to strengthen the global partnership for development.

Managing the economic crisis can – and should – be turned into an opportunity to make the structural changes needed to forge a path towards equitable development and sustainability, including addressing the climate change problem. Nothing less than the viability of our planet and the future of humanity are at stake.

The Millennium Development Goals Report is the most comprehensive global MDG assessment to date. It is based on a set of data prepared by over 20 organizations both within and outside the United Nations system, including the World Bank and

Organization for Economic Cooperation and Development (OECD).

Overview:

The Millennium Declaration set 2015 as the target date for achieving most of the Millennium Development Goals (MDGs), which established quantitative benchmarks to halve extreme poverty in all its forms. As the date approaches, less than six years away, the world finds itself mired in an economic crisis that is unprecedented in its severity and global dimensions. Progress towards the goals is now threatened by sluggish — or even negative — economic growth, diminished resources, fewer trade opportunities for the developing countries. And the donor nations have decreased the aid flows. At the same time, the effects of climate change are becoming increasingly apparent, with a potentially devastating impact on countries rich and poor. Today, more than ever, the commitment to building the global partnership embodied in the Millennium Declaration must guide our collective actions.

The grim repercussions of the economic crisis

This report [166] presents an annual assessment of progress towards the MDGs. Although data are not yet available to reveal the full impact of the recent economic downturn, they point to areas where progress towards the eight goals has slowed or reversed.

Major advances in the fight against extreme poverty from 1990 to 2005, for example, are likely to have stalled. During that period, the number of people living on less than $1.25 a day decreased from 1.8

[166]ShaZukang, Under Secretary General for Economic and Social Affairs, The Millennium Development Goals Report 2009, United Nations, New York

billion to 1.4 billion. In 2009, an estimated 55 million to 90 million more people will be living in extreme poverty than anticipated before the crisis.

The eradication of hunger since the early 1990s was very satisfactory but it reversed in 2008 largely due to higher food prices. The prevalence of hunger in the developing regions is now on the rise, from 16 per cent in 2006 to 17 percent in 2008. A decrease in international food prices in the second half of 2008 has failed to translate into more affordable food for most people around the world.

Not surprisingly, children bear the brunt of the burden. More than one quarter of children in developing regions are underweight for their age, stunting their prospects for survival, growth and long term development. Meager progress on child nutrition from 1990 to 2007 is insufficient to meet the 2015 target, and will likely be eroded by higher food prices and economic turmoil.

These ongoing crises may also hold back progress towards gender equality, by creating new hurdles to women's employment. The International Labour Organization estimates that global unemployment in 2009 could reach 6.1 to 7.0 per cent for men and 6.5 to 7.4 per cent for women; many of them remain trapped in insecure often-unpaid jobs.

Other fallout from the global financial situation may be compromised funding for programs to improve maternal health, the goal towards which there has been least progress so far. Since the mid-1990s, most developing countries have experienced a major reduction in donor funding for family planning on a per woman basis, despite the undeniable contribution of such programs to maternal and child health.

The ability of countries to mobilize domestic resources for development is also in jeopardy. Export revenues of developing countries fell in the last quarter of 2008, with the collapse of commodity prices and exports more generally. Debt services to exports ratios of developing countries are likely to deteriorate further, especially for those countries that enjoyed increased export revenues for the last several years.

Economic necessity will doubtless continue to exert pressure on an already fragile global environment, where deforestation and the extinction of species proceed at alarming rates, and a global water crisis looms.

At the Gleneagles summit of the Group of Eight in 2005, and at the UN World Summit later that year, donors committed to increasing their aid. With most OECD economies in recession, even fulfillment of those commitments, which were expressed as a percentage of donors' national income, would imply a diminished amount of aid. For many developing countries, lower levels of aid would not only impede further progress, but could reverse some of the gains already made.

The successes so far

But the story is not all bleak. The report also portrays the remarkable advances that many countries and regions had made before the economic landscape changed so radically in 2008:

(a). Those living in extreme poverty in the developing regions accounted for slightly more than a quarter of the developing world's population in 2005, compared to almost half in 1990.

(b). Major accomplishments were also made in education. In the developing world as a whole, enrolment in primary education reached 88 per cent in 2007, up from 83 per cent in 2000. And most of the progress was in regions lagging the furthest behind. In sub-Saharan Africa and Southern Asia, enrolment increased by 15 percentage points and 11 percentage points, respectively, from 2000 to 2007.

(c). Deaths of children under-five declined steadily worldwide — to around 9 million in 2007, down from 12.6 million in 1990, despite population growth. Although child mortality rates remain highest in sub-Saharan Africa, recent survey data show remarkable improvements in key interventions that could yield major breakthroughs for children in that region in the years ahead. Among these interventions is the distribution of insecticide-treated bed nets to reduce the toll of malaria — a major killer of children. As a result of 'second chance' immunizations, dramatic progress is also being made in the fight against measles.

(d). At the global level, the world came together to achieve a 97 per cent reduction in the consumption of substances that deplete the Earth's protective ozone layer, setting a new precedent for international cooperation.

Where accelerated progress is needed:

These accomplishments demonstrate that the goals are within reach at the global level, and even in very poor countries. The MDGs must continue to provide a focus for our efforts, and the vision of a world without poverty must not be lost, even in these difficult times:

(a) Efforts to provide productive and decent employment for all, including women and young people, must be revitalized. The share of women in paid employment outside the agricultural sector has increased only marginally over the years. And in Southern Asia, Northern Africa and Western Asia, employment opportunities for women remain extremely low.

(b) The war against hunger must be embraced with renewed vigour, especially in the interests of our youngest citizens. In the countries hardest hit by the recent rise in food prices, we must implement measures to increase the availability of food, and strengthen social policies that address the negative impact on the poor.

(c) Work must be intensified to get *all* children into school, especially those living in rural communities, and eliminate inequalities in education based on gender and ethnicity, and among linguistic and religious minorities. The target of eliminating gender disparities in primary and secondary education by 2005 has already been missed.

(d). Greater political will must be mustered to reduce maternal mortality, especially in sub-Saharan Africa and Southern Asia, where negligible progress has been made so far.

(e). Rapid acceleration of progress is needed to bring improved sanitation to the 1.4 billion people who were doing without in 2006, with all its attendant consequences for the health of communities and the local environment. At the present rate of progress, the 2015 sanitation target will be missed.

(f). Efforts to improve the living conditions of the urban poor must pick up speed and extend even further. Although every region except one has made progress in this area, slum improvements are barely keeping pace with the rapid growth of developing country cities.

(g). Last, but by no means least, greater priority must be given to preserving our natural resource base, on which we all depend. We have not acted forcefully enough — or in a unified way — to combat climate change; our fisheries are imperilled; our forests, especially old-growth forests, are receding;

and water scarcity has become a reality in a number of arid regions.

Learning from past experience and looking ahead:

Advances are most evident where targeted interventions have had an immediate effect, and where increased funding has translated into an expansion of programs to deliver services and tools directly to those in need. This can be seen in the fight against malaria, in the dramatic reduction in measles deaths, and in the coverage of antiretroviral treatment for HIV and AIDS, which increased tenfold over a five-year time span. In contrast, progress has been more modest when it requires structural changes and strong political commitment to guarantee sufficient and sustained funding over a longer period of time.

This is likely the reason behind the poor performance of most countries in reducing maternal mortality and increasing access of the rural poor to improved sanitation facilities.

Achieving the MDGs will require that the development agenda be fully integrated into efforts to jumpstart growth and rebuild the global economy. At the top of the agenda is the climate change problem, which will have to be regarded as an opportunity to develop more efficient 'green' technologies and make the structural changes needed that will contribute to sustainable growth. Achieving the MDGs will also require targeting areas and population groups that have clearly been left behind — rural communities, the poorest households and ethnic minorities, all of whom will have a hand in shaping our common future.

It is possible provided the administrators visit the rural areas and meet the poor in the villages.

Fight Poverty to End Insecurity (2009)

The Human Rights Research and Advisory Consortium[167] is a group of fourteen organizations committed to promoting peace and human rights in Afghanistan. These organizations are working in the fields of humanitarian relief, reconstruction, human rights, peace promotion, basic education, research and advocacy. The consortium focuses its efforts on four key human rights concerns such as the right of all Afghans to peace and physical security, the right to education, to participate politically and to share in economic resources and development.

The consortium undertook a survey to influence policy changes that will promote human rights and peace in Afghanistan through ongoing research and advocacy. The findings are:

(a) **Causes of Insecurity**: The Survey Team found that causes of insecurity were mostly poverty and unemployment of people. Lack of employment opportunity has resulted in lack of security. When there is no work for people to do, they resort to crime. The other reasons were weak government, negative influence of neighboring state, resurgence of Taliban, corrupt government officials, fear of powerful warlords, corrupt police officers and military personnel, and criminal gangs.

(b) **Rising Crime:** A majority of the respondents stated that gun violence; Taliban related violence, suicide attacks and criminal gang activity have increased in local area. Disarmament, Demobilization, Reintegration (DDR) and Disarmament of illegal Armed Groups are partially successful.

---

[167]Riona Nicholls and Marit Glad (2008) The Human Rights Research and Advisory Consortium (2008), Fight Poverty to End Insecurity – Afghan perception of Insecurity, March 2009

(c). **Lack of confidence in law** enforcement bodies: Confidence is too low. Moreover, deep distrust of police integrity and abilities increases considerably when issues such as ethnicity and socioeconomic clash are considered. The international military patrols worsen actively security measures.

(d). **Root Causes of Insecurity**: The causes are poverty and unemployment of youths, insurgent activity, corruption within the security forces, and the negative influence of neighboring states.

(e). **The Security of Children**: The security of school going children is at risk. It is more risk for girl child as compared to boys. In south Afghanistan, police refuses to protect the girls on their way to school.

(f). **Lack of confidence in government disarmament initiative:** The main factor for insecurity is the presence of warlords (ex-commanders) as they are more powerful than the police and army. These army officers continue as power divide loyalties between the state and non-state actors. The warlords (ex-commanders) are not getting chances to rejoin the army, so they rejoin the armed groups. The ex-commandants do not trust in the governments' ability to maintain security.

(g). **Inefficient and corrupt police officers:** The salaries of police officials are low. So they overlook the crimes and are involved in them. The police patrol the main roads of the district and do not enter to the villages due to their insufficient numbers. They also don't have enough equipment so their operations are not effective. Police officers claimed that corruption was institutionalized and otherwise police were often compelled to act according to their supervisors' corrupt orders. The police themselves are the reason for some of the insecurity.

(h). **International Military Forces**: These military forces have improved security in Afghanistan but people don't accept their actions in night searches. The female members feel that their cultural norms are violated. People desire that the International Military Forces should train the Afghan forces to carry out household searches at night.

(i). **Poppy cultivation** has brought poverty and misery to the public in some provinces. The insurgents and armed groups use all the profits gained from the business. And they are responsible for insecurity and instability in the province.

Recommendations

HRRAC calls for:

(a) Increased donor focus on poverty reduction and creation of income opportunities.

Afghans have identified poverty and unemployment as the most significant underlying cause of insecurity in Afghanistan. HRRAC calls on donors to substantially strengthen measures to alleviate poverty, to promote civilian, rather than military, efforts to achieve this and to ensure that this is widely communicated both within Afghanistan and in donor countries.

(b) Increased focus and resources allocated to improve the functioning of the Afghan National Police.

Afghans identify the police as of variable quality and in some cases adversely affecting security conditions. Particular attention must therefore be given to improve the ANP's capacity and functioning. Corruption must be combated, including breaking links with local militias and criminals. The recommendations of the Special Rapporteurs of the United Nations Human Rights Council on extra judicial, summary or arbitrary executions regarding the Afghan National Police should be followed.

(c) An independent review of disarmament programs, tougher implementation of reformed disarmament initiatives and the rejection of initiatives that aim to re-arm communities.

Afghans identify the failure of the disarmament process as one of the reasons for the deteriorating security situation. Thus, the Government of Afghanistan and the international community should increase their focus on removing arms from Afghanistan, not adding them.

(d). Long-term, coordinated and pro-poor counter narcotics approaches must be supported. To realize this, the only viable option is a gradual, comprehensive and pro-poor approach, mainstreamed within rural development initiatives, combined with stronger law-enforcement measures against traffickers - not small poppy farmers. Quick-fix strategies, such as crop eradication, may yield short-term gains but can lead to great hardship for the poorest and weakest in the process - small-scale farmers and their families.

(e). ISAF should focus on its security mandate and on insecure areas.

Afghans recognize the role that international military forces play in providing security in Afghanistan. Consequently, they assert that international military forces should concentrate their efforts in insecure areas and on activities relevant to their mandate. The International Forces must put Afghan security first.

HRRAC also stresses the need to decrease civilian casualties in international military operations and to ensure greater respect for local traditions and culture, particularly in night raids.

G–8 L'AQUILA (Italy) Summit – 2009

July 8-10, 2009

G8 Pledges $20 billion For Food Security to Poor Nations:

G-8 members pledged $20 billion over three years to finance agriculture projects in poor countries and help fight hunger and food price volatility. The U.S.-sponsored food security plan aims to provide poor farmers in developing countries with seeds, fertilizers and the infrastructure needed to boost food production as a long-term solution to combat hunger and spiking food prices. Until now, most of the money to combat hunger in poor countries, especially in Africa, has been in the form of food donations or emergency aid as a short-term fix when famine strikes. In a fact sheet issued after the close of the G8 summit here, the new administration of U.S. President Barack Obama administration said it would provide at least $3.5 billion of the funds over the three-year period. The total figure was originally set at $15 billion, but Italian Premier Silvio Berlusconi said a further $5 billion was collected.

This was possible for the help from all the 30 or so countries at the L'Aquila global summit, which included key emerging nations like China, Brazil and India. Although aid campaigners welcomed the food security plan, they questioned whether all of the money would be new and pressed leaders to ensure that promises are kept this time.

Priority actions should include improving access to better seeds and fertilizers, promoting sustainable management of water, forests and natural resources. The number of people going hungry every day has reached 1.02 billion in 2009.

The U.S. Department of Agriculture economists have also made dire projections, citing affordability. The food security initiative also aims to prevent the sharp rise in prices seen last year, which sparked riots in some countries. Though many crop prices have since fallen back, the unrest helped make the complex issue of food security a major focus for G8 political leaders, who are concerned about social and political consequences. The world consumed more grain than its farmers could produce for most of this decade, thanks to surging food demand from a growing middle class in emerging nations such as China and India. Even large harvests last fall and the global recession this year haven't returned prices of many crops back to their normal levels. Since June 2008, international prices have come down but average prices are still 25 percent above the levels of 2005 and 2006 in real terms.[168]

In short, the G-8 countries have planned to fight with 'world hunger' in 2009. Food safety can check starvation deaths but cannot fight against poverty. Unless the G-8 countries pledge more funds for poverty reduction, the poor countries will not be able to fight poverty. Similarly, debt burden can only be reduced to zero, if they allow debt relief 100 percent. The poor countries would depend upon the developed countries for a longer period for donations, food-aid, and credit.

Global Monitoring Report 2009

A Development Emergency Overview

The Development Committee, a joint Ministerial Committee of the World Bank and the IMF, studied the transfer of real resources to the developing countries during the financial crisis 2008. This study was undertaken to evaluate the achievement of Millennium Development Goals at mid-point of 2008.

---

[168] Luca Di Leo, Dow Jones Newswires, G8 Pledges $20 billion For Food Security To Poor Nations, G–8 L'AQUILA (Italy) July 10, 2009

A Crisis upon Crisis

For poor countries, this is a crisis upon crisis. It comes on the heels of the food and fuel crises. The triple jeopardy of the food, fuel, and financial crises is pushing many poor countries into a danger zone, imposing rising human costs and imperiling development prospects.

With the seizing- up of the international financial markets in 2008, emerging market countries were the first among developing countries to feel the impact of the financial crisis, given their heavier reliance on private capital flows. Private capital flows to the developing world are seeing their sharpest slump ever, with net flows likely turning negative in 2009—a more than $700 billion drop from the peak in 2007. Many low-income countries are also affected by the private credit crunch; private flows to these countries, including several in Africa, which had increased in recent years, are now falling. But these countries are expected to be hit particularly hard in 2009 by a second round of impacts reflecting the global recession and declining world trade: world gross domestic product (GDP) is projected to decline in 2009 for the first time since World War II and world trade is projected to register its largest decline in the post-war period.

The impact of the global financial crisis on developing countries is reflected in sharp reductions in their projected GDP growth to rates that are the lowest since the 1990s. Average projected GDP growth in developing countries in 2009 is now only about a quarter of what was expected before the financial turmoil intensified into a full-blown crisis in the latter half of 2008 and a fifth of that achieved in the period of strong growth up to 2007. For developing countries as a whole, growth is now projected to fall to 1.6 percent in 2009, from an average of 8.1 percent in 2006– 07. Growth in Sub- Saharan Africa is projected to slow to 1.7 percent in 2009, from 6.7 percent in 2006– 07, breaking the momentum of the region's very promising growth revival of recent years. Even these low projections are subject to further downside risks. Countries in Eastern Europe and Central Asia that entered the global crisis with weaker macroeconomic fundamentals are most severely hit, with average growth in the region in 2009 now projected to be negative. Average growth in Latin America and the Caribbean also is projected to be negative in 2009. The current growth projections, adjusted for terms-of-trade changes, imply declining real per capita incomes for more than 50 developing countries in 2009.

Impact on Poverty Reduction and Other MDGs

The sharp slowdown in growth can seriously set back progress on poverty reduction and other MDGs. Food price increases between 2005 and 2008 pushed around 200 million more people into extreme poverty, and about half of them will remain trapped in poverty in 2009 even as food prices recede from their peaks. While food prices have fallen since mid-2008, they remain high by historical standards, and the food crisis is by no means over. The slowdown in growth resulting from the financial crisis will add to the poverty impact of high food prices. The International Labour Organization projects that some 30 million more people around the world may be unemployed in 2009, of which 23 million could be in developing countries. A worse- case scenario envisages as many as 50 million more people becoming unemployed in 2009. Poverty impact of the growth slowdown may range from 55 million to 90 million more extreme poor in 2009. This was not expected before the crisis. These numbers will rise if the crisis deepens and growth in developing countries falters further.

Countries that suffered economic contractions of 10 percent or more between 1980 and 2004 experienced more than 1 million additional infant deaths. It is estimated that the sharply slower economic growth resulting from the current financial crisis may cause as many as200, 000 to 400,000 more infant deaths per year on average between 2009 and the MDG target year of 2015, which translates into1.4 million to 2.8 million additional infant deaths during the period. In poor countries, education outcomes, such as school enrollment, also tend to deteriorate during economic crises—especially for girls.

The long-run consequences of the crisis for human development outcomes may be more severe than those observed in the short run. For example, the decline in health status among children who suffer from reduced (or inferior) food consumption can be irreversible, retarding growth as well as cognitive and learning abilities. Estimates suggest that the food crisis has already caused the number of people suffering permanent damage from malnutrition to rise by 44 million. The financial crisis will exacerbate this impact as poor households respond to decreases in income by further cutting the quantity and quality of food consumption.

The overall outlook for the MDGs, already a cause for serious concern, has become still more worrisome. Strong economic growth in developing countries in the past decade had put the MDG for poverty reduction within reach at the global level, but the triple punch of the food, fuel, and financial crises creates new risks. In the medium term, the proportion of people in extreme poverty in the developing world is still expected to decline, at a slower pace than envisaged before the crisis because of the slowdown in economic growth.

The food crises, and now the global financial crisis, are reversing past gains in fighting hunger and malnutrition. Before the onset of the food crisis in 2007, there were about 850 million chronically hungry people in the developing world. This number rose to 960 million people in 2008 and is expected to climb past 1 billion in 2009, breaking the declining trend in the proportion of hungry people in the developing world and seriously jeopardizing the goal of halving this proportion by 2015. These trends call for maintaining the momentum of recent efforts to boost agricultural investment and productivity.

Even at the MDG halfway point, around 75 million children of primary school age were not in school; 190,000 children under five died every week from preventable disease; 10,000 women died every week from treatable complications of pregnancy; more than 2 million people died from AIDS annually, close to 2 million from tuberculosis, and about 1 million from malaria; around 1 billion people suffered from hunger and twice as many were undernourished; and about half of the developing world lacked access to basic sanitation—grim numbers that would be far lower if the world were on track on the MDGs. The world can, and should, do better. Acceleration of progress requires a shared commitment to pursue this development agenda with greater vigor and urgency.

A Development Emergency

A global crisis must be met with a global response. Much of the attention initially was understandably focused on the impact of the crisis and the policy response in developed countries and in major emerging market countries that are closely integrated with international financial markets. But as the crisis has engulfed other, lower- income countries, it has become truly global. It has become clear that the impact on these countries, and the resulting grave risks to development prospects, must be addressed as part of a global response to the crisis. The challenge for the international community is to overcome the global financial crisis and respond to the deepening human and development crisis in poor countries.

The development emergency that now confronts many poor countries calls for commitment to a set of actions that signal a clear resolve to avert the potentially large human costs of the crisis and assist these countries to lay the ground for a recovery of strong growth and accelerated progress toward the MDGs. The stakes are high, and the need for action urgent.

Leaders of the Group of Twenty (G- 20), at their summit held in London on April 2, 2009, made important progress in coordinating a global response to the crisis. The summit's outcome showed a clear concern with the serious development dimension of the crisis. Agreements reached at the summit have laid a good foundation for follow- up. Other major meetings in the period ahead— the Spring Meetings of the World Bank and the International Monetary Fund (IMF), the UN International Conference on the Global Financial Crisis and its Impact on Development, and the G- 8 summit—can build on the progress made at the G- 20 summit by elaborating a fuller agenda and developing momentum in implementation.

The crisis calls for a reaffirmation of the world's commitment to the promise of the MDGs, in the spirit of the international cooperation that gave birth to the MDGs at the turn of the century and to the Monterrey framework for the mutual accountability of both developing and developed countries for the achievement of these goals. It is fitting, therefore, that the G- 20 leaders stated in their London summit communiqué "we reaffirm our historic commitment to meeting the Millennium Development Goals." In the current context, internal cooperation for development is needed more than ever.

Priorities for Action

At the same time, strong and urgent actions are needed to counter the impact of the global crisis on poor countries and help them restore strong growth and recover lost ground in their progress toward the MDGs. The report sets out six priorities for action.

(a) Ensure an adequate fiscal response to support economic growth and protect poor and vulnerable groups from the impact of the crisis—consistent with maintenance of macroeconomic stability.
(b) Shore up the private sector and improve the climate for recovery and growth in private investment, including paying special attention to strengthening financial systems.
(c) Redouble efforts toward the human development goals, including leveraging the private sector role.
(d) Scale up aid to poor and vulnerable countries hit hard by the crisis.
(e) Maintain an open trade and finance system—including quick action on the Doha Round.
(f) Ensure that the multilateral system has the mandate, resources, and instruments to support an effective global response to the global crisis.

Ensuring an Adequate Fiscal Response:

As many as 90 percent of developing countries are assessed to be highly or moderately exposed to the impact of the crisis, as they face slowing growth, high levels of poverty, or both. Three- quarters of the exposed countries lack the fiscal capacity to finance programs to curb the effects of the downturn.

Scaling Up Aid to Poor Countries:

The urgency for donors to deliver on their aid commitments cannot be overemphasized in the current context. Official development assistance (ODA) from members of the Development Assistance

Committee (DAC) of the Organization for Economic Co-operation and Development (OECD) rose by about 10 percent in real terms in 2008. This is a welcome development, following declines in ODA in both 2006 and 2007. In real terms, ODA from DAC donors in 2008 were about $29 billion short of the Gleneagles target of $130 billion per annum by 2010. ODA to Sub- Saharan Africa was about $20 billion short of the2010 target of $50 billion per annum. Donors should scale up rapidly to deliver on these commitments. Although the crisis has put donors' fiscal positions under increased pressure, the additional sums needed to meet the Gleneagles commitments amount to a fraction of the support they have provided to rescue individual financial institutions in their countries and a miniscule proportion of the fiscal stimulus packages they have announced.

Indeed, the crisis calls for going beyond the commitments made at Gleneagles as the needs of poor countries have increased sharply. One option for additional support is the proposal by president Zoë lick of the World Bank that developed countries invest 0.7 percent of their stimulus package, or about $15 billion based on the packages announced to date, in a Vulnerability Fund to help developing countries. The fund would support three crisis- response priorities in developing countries that lack the resources to act on their own – strengthening social safety nets, funding investments in essential infrastructure, and supporting financing for small and medium entrepreneurs, and micro finance institutions. The resources would be channeled through multilateral and bilateral agencies, in programs backed by safeguards to ensure that they are well spent.

Private aid has emerged as an increasingly important player in development finance. The OECD estimated private international giving at $18.6 billion in 2007, but this is widely considered to be an underestimate.

Alternative estimates place private international giving from the United States alone at $34.8 billion in 2006. The sources of private giving are various—foundations, corporations, and civil society organizations of different types. The rising role of private assistance has spawned innovative public private partnerships in development activities, especially in health, education, and climate change. There is some concern that the financial crisis may interrupt the rising trend in private aid. Nonetheless, private aid today represents a source that, if effectively deployed, can be an important complement to public aid and a partner in development.

Maintaining an Open Trade and Finance System

The international community has recognized the importance of addressing the crunch in trade finance in a coordinated fashion. The G- 20 leaders agreed at their London summit to ensure the availability of at least $250 billion of trade finance over the next two years through their export credit and investment agencies and through the multilateral development banks (MDBs) — including up to $ 50 billion of trade liquidity support over the next three years through the new Global Trade Liquidity Pool introduced by the International Finance Corporation (IFC).

Empowering Multilateral Institutions

The IFIs are facing an unprecedented rise in demand for financing. With the slump in private capital flows, estimates of developing countries' financing gap in 2009 reach as high as $1 trillion. The IFIs will need to play a role in filling some of this gap, including using their leverage ability to help revive private capital flows. In this context, the G- 20 leaders at their London summit took timely action in agreeing to support a sizable increase in resources available to the IMF and the MDBs.

The G- 20 leaders agreed to support a tripling of resources available to the IMF to $750 billion. They also supported a general allocation of the Special Drawing Rights (SDRs) equivalent to $250 billion to increase global liquidity, $100 billion of which will go directly to emerging market and developing countries ($19 billion to low- income countries). The IMF has moved quickly to strengthen its lending framework, including establishing a new Flexible Credit Line to provide large and upfront financing to emerging market economies with strong fundamentals and policies, enhancing the flexibility of the regular stand-by arrangements, doubling access limits for emerging markets and low- income countries, and reforming conditionality to make it more focused and tailored to country circumstances. The IMF plans to step up it's lending to low- income countries to around $3 billion a year over the next two years—triple last year's level.

The G- 20 leaders also supported an increase in MDB lending of $100 billion to a total of around $300 billion over the next three years and agreed to ensure that all MDBs have the appropriate capital. They supported a 200 percent general capital increase at the Asian Development Bank (ADB) and a review of the need for capital increases at several other MDBs. They also agreed to support, through voluntary bilateral contributions, the World Bank's Vulnerability Framework, including the Infrastructure Crisis Facility and the Rapid Social Response Fund.

The concessional windows of the African Development Bank, the ADB, and the World Bank have received significant increases in resources through recent replenishments. Also, debt relief provided through the Heavily Indebted Poor Countries (HIPC) Initiative and the Multilateral Debt Relief Initiative (MDRI) has increased fiscal space in many poor countries. Nonetheless, the rise in the financing needs of low-income countries hit hard by the crisis would test the adequacy of available resources. An immediate need is for donors to honor existing pledges to the MDB concessional windows and to the MDRI.[169]

G-20 Leaders' Statement: The Pittsburgh Summit on September24 - 25, 2009

The G-20 Pittsburgh summit (2009) has recommended the following actions the people and countries. The statement includes on: A Framework for Strong, Sustainable, and Balanced Growth, Strengthening the International Financial Regulatory System, Modernizing our Global Institutions to Reflect Today's Global Economy, Reforming the Mandate, Mission and Governance of the IMF, Reforming the Mission, Mandate and Governance of Our Development banks, Energy Security and Climate Change, Strengthening Support for the Most Vulnerable, Putting Quality Jobs at the Heart of the Recovery, and An Open Global Economy. In the present analysis, we have mentioned on only aspect for the vulnerable.

Strengthening Support for the Most Vulnerable

1. Many emerging and developing economies have made great strides in raising living standards as their economies converge toward the productivity levels and living standards of advanced economies. This process was interrupted by the crisis and is still far from complete. The poorest countries have little economic cushion to protect vulnerable populations from calamity, particularly as the financial crisis followed close on the heels of a global spike in food prices. We note with concern the adverse impact of the global crisis on low income countries' (LICs)

---

[169] Extract from "Global Monitoring Report 2009", Development Committee, Joint Ministerial Committee of the World Bank and the IMF, DC 2009 - 0002, April 16, 2009

capacity to protect critical core spending in areas such as health, education, safety nets, and infrastructure. The UN's new Global Impact Vulnerability Alert System will help our efforts to monitor the impact of the crisis on the most vulnerable. We share a collective responsibility to mitigate the social impact of the crisis and to assure that all parts of the globe participate in the recovery.

2. The MDBs play a key role in the fight against poverty. We recognize the need for accelerated and additional concessional financial support to LICs to cushion the impact of the crisis on the poorest, welcome the increase in MDB lending during the crisis and support the MDBs having the resources needed to avoid a disruption of concessional financing to the most vulnerable countries. The IMF also has increased its concessional lending to LICs during the crisis. Resources from the sale of IMF gold, consistent with the new income model, and funds from internal and other sources will double the Fund's medium-term concessional lending capacity.

3. Several countries are considering creating, on a voluntary basis, mechanisms that could allow, consistent with their national circumstances, the mobilization of existing SDR resources to support the IMF's lending to the poorest countries. Even as we work to mitigate the impact of the crisis, we must strengthen and reform the global development architecture for responding to the world's long-term challenges. We ask our relevant ministers to explore the benefits of a new crisis support facility in IDA to protect LICs from future crises and the enhanced use of financial instruments in protecting the investment plans of middle income countries from interruption in times of crisis, including greater use of guarantees.

4. We reaffirm our historic commitment to meet the Millennium Development Goals and our respective Official Development Assistance (ODA) pledges,

including commitments on Aid for Trade, debt relief, and those made at Gleneagles, especially to sub-Saharan Africa, to 2010 and beyond.

5. Even before the crisis, too many still suffered from hunger and poverty and even more people lack access to energy and finance. Recognizing that the crisis has exacerbated this situation, we pledge cooperation to improve access to food, fuel, and finance for the poor.

6. Sustained funding and targeted investments are urgently needed to improve long-term food security. We welcome and support the food security initiative announced in L'Aquila and efforts to further implement the Global Partnership for Agriculture and Food Security and to address excessive price volatility. We call on the World Bank to work with interested donors and organizations to develop a multilateral trust fund to scale-up agricultural assistance to low-income countries. This will help support innovative bilateral and multilateral efforts to improve global nutrition and build sustainable agricultural systems, including programs like those developed through the Comprehensive African Agricultural Development Program (CAADP). It should be designed to ensure country ownership and rapid disbursements of funds, fully respecting the aid effectiveness principles agreed in Accra, and facilitate the participation of private foundations, businesses, and non-governmental organizations (NGOs) in this historic effort. These efforts should complement the UN Comprehensive Framework for Agriculture. We ask the World Bank, the African Development Bank, UN, Food and Agriculture Organization (FAO), International Fund for Agricultural Development (IFAD), World Food Programme (WFP) and other stakeholders to coordinate their efforts, including through country-led mechanisms, in order to complement and reinforce other existing multilateral and bilateral efforts to tackle food insecurity.

7. To increase access to energy, we will promote the deployment of clean, affordable energy resources to the developing world. We commit, on a voluntary basis, to funding programs that achieve this objective, such as the Scaling Up Renewable Energy Program and the Energy for the Poor Initiative, and to increasing and more closely harmonizing our bilateral efforts.

8. We commit to improving access to financial services for the poor. We have agreed to support the safe and sound spread of new modes of financial service delivery capable of reaching the poor and, building on the example of micro finance, will scale up the successful models of small and medium-sized enterprise (SME) financing. Working with the Consultative Group to Assist the Poor (CGAP), the International Finance Corporation (IFC) and other international organizations, we will launch a G-20 Financial Inclusion Experts Group. This group will identify lessons learned on innovative approaches to providing financial services to these groups, promote successful regulatory and policy approaches and elaborate standards on financial access, financial literacy, and consumer protection. We commit to launch a G-20 SME Finance Challenge, a call to the private sector to put forward its best proposals for how public finance can maximize the deployment of private finance on a sustainable and scalable basis.

9. As we increase the flow of capital to developing countries, we also need to prevent its illicit outflow. We will work with the World Bank's Stolen Assets Recovery (STAR) program to secure the return of stolen assets to developing countries, and support other efforts to stem illicit outflows. We ask the FATF to help detect and deter the proceeds of corruption by prioritizing work to strengthen standards on customer due diligence, beneficial ownership and transparency. We note the principles of the Paris Declaration on Aid Effectiveness and the Accra

Agenda for Action and will work to increase the transparency of international aid flows by 2010. We call for the adoption and enforcement of laws against transnational bribery, such as the OECD Anti-Bribery Convention, and the ratification by the G-20 of the UN Convention against Corruption (UNCAC) and the adoption during the third Conference of the Parties in Doha of an effective, transparent, and inclusive mechanism for the review of its implementation. We support voluntary participation in the Extractive Industries Transparency Initiative, which calls for regular public disclosure of payments by extractive industries to governments and reconciliation against recorded receipt of those funds by governments.[170]

Food for Peace Program

Ryan Swanson (2004)[171] has expressed that even in the 21st century, with its technological advances; the quest for food security remains a daunting challenge. There is some reason for optimism, however, as the United States and many other countries have put in place programs to fight hunger throughout the world and significant success has been achieved. But even with these victories, there is still much work yet to be done.

Although fertile soil and proficient farmers have consistently provided for the United States' domestic food needs, U.S. leaders have long recognized that the problem of food scarcity knows no national borders. On one hand, basic humanitarianism demands that hunger elsewhere cannot be simply ignored. But also, and perhaps more practically speaking, today's international economy determines that problems rarely stay confined to one particular country or region. The reverberations of food scarcity

---

[170] Pittsburgh summit, media center, No. 129639

[171] Ryan Swanson (2004), Fighting world Hunger: US food policy and the food for peace program, Ag Exporter, October 1, 2004

in one country make their impact felt in food markets around the world. The U.S. government designates millions of dollars and tons of food each year for food aid.

The United States has a long history of providing assistance to needy countries around the world. Following World War I, the American Relief Administration, led by entrepreneur and soon-to-be President Herbert Hoover, distributed more than 4 million tons of food and supplies to starving people in Europe, especially the Soviet Union. The Berlin Airlift of 1948 came in response to Joseph Stalin's closure of all roads and railroads into Berlin in June 1948. For nearly one year, British and American forces responded by delivering by plane all food and other necessary materials to sustain the isolated city. The delivery of over 500,000 tons of food eventually broke Stalin's blockade.

Similarly, William Lambers (2009)[172] has opined that Mr. Barrack Obama, the President of the United States should follow Eisenhower's 'Food for Peace' policy for the hungry mouths of the world. As President Obama tackles enormous foreign policy challenges, he would be well-advised to extract good ideas from past administrations and carry forward this "better part of history." At least one example comes from the Eisenhower administration, a time when the Cold War and nuclear weapons' fears dominated the world scene. During this turbulent period, President Eisenhower called for a peace conference. Representatives from different countries gathered to discuss topics like school lunches. Yes. That's right. This was not the typical peace

---

[172]William Lambers (2009), "Food For Peace: Eisenhower's Unsung Initiative Can Be Obama's Most Powerful Tool for Peace" interview with UN World food Program Officials, February 9, 2009

conference. It was not about disarmament, but rather food to fight hunger abroad.

In May 1959, Argentina, Canada, Australia, and France joined the United States at a conference to explore using food "in the interest of reinforcing peace." And today Obama should not relent in his own exploration of Food for Peace when crafting his foreign policy.

Fighting hunger was a part of the Eisenhower administration strategy right from the get-go. Just months into office, riots broke out against Soviet and Communist domination in East Germany. Where there is chaos, you are certain to find food shortages and this was certainly the case for East Germany. The U.S. responded quickly with 15 million dollars worth of shipments to Berlin to fight hunger. Eisenhower stated, "We asked no remuneration, no return, and no exchange of goods. We just put it there for humanitarian purposes."

Harold Stassen, one of Ike's assistants during the crisis, wrote: "The East Germans remembered who fed them when they starved and remain grateful to this day....the window of freedom those millions of East Germans glimpsed during this period, and their brutalization by the Soviet oppressors, laid the foundations for the political events of 1989. The whole world can thank Dwight Eisenhower for reaching out to "feed the hungry Germans."

The following year Eisenhower signed Public Law 480, known today as **Food for Peace**. This became the mechanism for sending U.S. surplus food abroad to fight hunger. But Food for Peace was not well-known, making it harder to gain public support and input, not to mention showcasing it as America's best public diplomacy tool.

Food for Peace coordinator Don Paarl berg tried to spread the word including having Eisenhower make an address on September 1st, 1960. In the speech, Ike noted, "The world cups its ear to hear the rattling of rockets. It listens less closely to the sounds of peace and well-being which emanate from the slow but steady improvement in world health and nutrition."

While the young Food for Peace program was unsung during Ike's day, there is no reason for that oversight today. Obama and the technological organization that won his election can also bring world hunger issues to the very forefront of America's agenda. Like Ike, Obama can give a Food for Peace address to highlight the current global hunger menace, its threat to American security, and America's tools to fight it.

For a long-term, Mr. Obama should appoint a "hunger czar" as stipulated by the Global Food Security Act.

Having a white house advisor on global hunger issues would be critical to making sound foreign policy judgments in Afghanistan, Sudan, Iraq and many other countries. As long as hunger and poverty exist in those countries, there cannot be peace.

The Obama administration should work with the international community to build a global school lunch program and a separate feeding program for infant children. These may not be headline-grabbing initiatives, but they are the most important in terms of peace building. We saw that after World War II when the school lunches provided by the U.S. Army, UNRRA, Catholic Relief Services, UNICEF and others served as a foundation for rebuilding Europe.

In the Food for Peace years, school lunches were critical in helping many countries like Italy and Japan. A "school lunches for peace" partnership with the charity CARE was developed during Ike's years and into the Kennedy administration. CARE helped provide school meals to many countries including

Poland, Korea, and India. Today, Gaza, the West Bank, Afghanistan, Colombia, Iraq, Sudan and many others are in need of universal school feeding.

There will be some who will question why the United States should worry about hunger abroad when it has problems of its own at home. With the ongoing financial crisis, it's easy to ignore the desperate needs of those in faraway lands.

After World War II, the "Greatest Generation" did not take that approach and helped Europe and Asia fight hunger. Secretary of State George Marshall, realizing that hunger and chaos abroad threatened America's security, stated, "We can act for our own good by acting for the world's good." Today, Nancy Roman of the World Food Programme writes, "To allow, now, the financial crisis to become the excuse for tossing up our hands and watching hunger multiply is foolish at best, tragic at worst."

These facts reveal that United States has practiced food aid to the hungry nations and hungry people since World War I. All religions also speak that food aid is the best aid. We feel that if corruption on food movement is minimized, we can avoid hunger, starvation deaths and loss of peace from all low-income and developing countries. But the respective governments must watch the movement of donated food materials, as there is every possibility that it enters into black markets in the deficit countries. We have further observed that government machinery do all mischief in handling the donated food materials and rich people take advantage in this distribution process at the cost of hungry people.

Charitable Dining Halls

The World Food Program (WFP), guided by the 1996 Rome Declaration on World Food Security, is committed to the goal of halving the number of food unsecured people by 2015. Founded in 1963 as the food aid arm of the United Nations, WFP is the world's largest international food aid organization. In 1998, WFP food aid reached approximately 75 million of the world's hungry, distributing more than 2.8 million metric tonnes of basic food essentials. In short, World Food Program has been doing a soul search since its inception since 1963 in its keenness to provide the most appropriate interventions to enhance food security of the poorest. Where people have less or no access to food and are poor, hungry and malnourished, WFP offers the most direct intervention in food-aid. There should be united approach to feed the hungry mouths of all the food insecure families all over world and particularly in South Asia, sub-Saharan Africa and Latin America. We desire a hunger-free world.

WFP uses food to enable those caught in the hunger trap to access development opportunities. It also strives to enable households, which can no longer depend on natural resources for their food security, to make a shift to more sustainable livelihoods. WFP's commitments to women set a bold agenda to ensure "women's well-being and the empowerment". In order to avoid the serious consequences of nutritional deprivation of young children and expectant and nursing women, WFP provides food aid for women and children.

Food aid is also used to encourage women's participation in development activities to gain assets. WFP works in close collaboration with the governments in their efforts to eradicate hunger and malnutrition by supporting their programs. WFP also believes in building the capacity of local institutions and creating partnerships with other development agencies for optimizing resources and increasing impact. Moreover, WFP encourages local entrepreneurship, advocates eco-restoration and creates alternate livelihoods for lasting advantages to the poor.

The motto World Food Program is:

A world in which every man, woman and child has access at all times to the food needed for an active and healthy life. Without food, there can be no sustainable peace, no democracy and no development.

WFP activities seek to:

(1) Improve the nutrition and quality of life of the most vulnerable at critical times in their lives
(2) Help the hungry and poor to build assets and become self-reliant; and
(3) Save lives of refugees and internally displaced in emergency situations.

WFP has partnered with UNESCO, the World Bank, and Japan's Overseas Economic Cooperation Fund, ILO, SIDA, UNICEF, UNFPA, UNDP and other donor organizations for resource sharing. It also makes partners with national governments, NGOs and private sectors for bringing development opportunities to the poor. As 320 million people of India are considered food-insecure and consume less than 80 per cent of minimum energy requirement, the Food and Agriculture Organization has classified India as a low-income, and food-deficit country. Moreover, one-fourth of the world's hungry resides in India. Hence, the WFP has undertaken its activities in India with the following objectives:

(a) Improve nutrition and quality of life for the most vulnerable at critical times in their lives
(b) Make sustainable improvements in household food security for the poor, especially for women and children, and invest funds in development for long-term security;
(c) Strengthen channels for locally produce food grains and support local entrepreneurship; and

(d) Advocate for eco-restoration through participatory methods and development

Working of World Food Program

WFP has identified that hunger occurs where there is concentrated poverty, resource degradation, recurrent food shocks and lack of mainstream development. Therefore, WFP targets food security of poor women, particularly mothers, and children at risk. It looks after the poor forest-dependent population, scheduled caste and scheduled tribe people living below poverty line. [173]

Other focuses are:

(a) Reducing hunger
(b) Solving micro-nutrient deficiency
(c) Increasing access to maternal and child health care
(d) Food- for –Work
(e) Working for better food at a lower cost
(f) Responding to humanitarian crisis
(g) Creating alternative livelihoods
(h) Funding human development
(i) Promoting the sustainable use of natural resources
(j) Increasing food security through irrigation
(k) Generating new income
(l) Constructing community assets
(m) Teaching new skills
(n) Giving access to credit and creating leadership
(o) Investing in girls and women's education
(p) Supporting local markets and economies, and
(q) Studying project impact

---

[173] Reducing Hunger Tackling Poverty-Food Aid Intervention in India(1999), World Food Program-Country Program Report 1997-2002, pp 1-26

Amartya Sen (2003)[174] has observed that the mid-day meal scheme in India has made a promising start around the country, imparting positively on school participation, particularly by girls, ending classroom hunger and fostering social equity, as students tend to mix with each other. But the programs are working on shoestring budgets, frugal menus, inadequate infrastructure and poor logistics ensuring that these meals disrupted classroom activity. In many villages, oppressed class people are not allowed to cook mid-day meals. It is also reported that nearly half of all children are malnourished. In 2003, 50 million school children were getting these meals in India and within a year or so the program would cover all – 100 million – children. He has also observed that school mid-meal is an extraordinarily important issue as it is related to both education and nutrition and argues that all arguments against it "the cluster of benefits" could be turned on their heads. He has pointed out that feeding along with schooling has a long history around the world. It is a fact that the extent of under-nourishment among children in India is higher than most parts of the world, including sub- Saharan Africa.

Conclusion

The Millennium Development Goals has identified gender inequality, lack of primary education, clean drinking water and healthcare, environmental degradation and defects in planning as the causes of high incidence of poverty. Hence, the funding institutions are donating funds and assisting the heavily indebted poor countries to generate opportunities for the poor citizens to cross over the poverty line. But people with absolute poverty are hardly benefited with programs and policies of the

[174] Sen, Amartya (2003), " Hunger in Classroom", Times News Network, The Times of India, Bhubaneswar-National, August 2, 2003, P7

government and/or the funding agencies. In an Indian state (Orissa), even 22 days-old child was sold as parents were unable to take care of her in 2003 and in another case an eight-month-old child was sold for US $18 in 2006. Child sale occurs each year in different districts of Orissa (India) till now. If hunger (food) can't be solved, starvation deaths can't be permanently checked, we have to admit that there are lapses in policies, programs and implementation of poverty reduction measures.

The poor do not desire to live a poverty life. He is dragged into poverty any time. Generally persons with single parents (especially women), or persons with disability, closure of industrial houses, continuous crop failures, victims of natural hazards (such as flood, cyclone, earthquake), displaced persons, aboriginals, and death of earning members fall victims of poverty. Moreover, jobless, homeless, landless or characterless people are poor. Failure in business, users of intoxicants, high medical expenses and family problems make the people poor. Victims of frustration, despairs, apathy, cheatings, and failure may be dragged into poverty net.

We feel that empty stomach should be considered as the worst form of poverty. Other indicators of poverty like healthcare, primary education and women empowerment should not compete with food security programs during implementation of poverty reduction strategies. A hungry man has no friend, no religion, no country and even no God. It is necessary for all governments, all donors, and all philanthropy organizations to chalk out suitable measures for ending starvation-deaths worldwide. For world peace, food security must be given topmost priority as a hungry man has no ambition, no future and no dream. The state laws cannot debar a hungry man/woman to become a criminal or anti-social. But all programs of supplying food grains to the poor at cheap rate (or free food grains) can never reach the poor because the distributors are either politicians or powerful persons. The rich man knows the technique of cheating the poor.

The stocks of food grains released for the empty stomachs through food-for-work program are subsidized. Therefore, there exists a price variation in open markets and causes the food stocks to enter into black markets. Giving food grains to hungry men/women in lieu of hard work like road construction and digging ponds is not only inhumane but also ineffective. This policy is defective and needs the nod of the Human Rights Commission.

There are two alternatives for solving food insecurity and ending starvation deaths. The governments, funding institutions, philanthropy organizations, individuals and non- governmental organizations should organize or open free dining halls for the food-insecure families in each village or in a cluster of villages. Starvation deaths can be stopped cent percent if only free mid-day meal is available to each hungry man in each settlement. The donors must treat the food-insecure people as their 'Guests' to these Charitable Dining Halls.

A hungry man is unable to earn his food because he is too old or diseased or unemployed. A hungry person fails in his attempts or misses opportunities or is debarred from justice to escape from poverty. He is poor; he is unlucky; he is uncared for but God resides in him. All religions have recognized 'food aid as the best aid'. The donors should not try to make political mileage through mid-day meals programs. There should not be signboards, leaflets, and pamphlets depicting the generosity of the donors of this program because there are many food-insecure families, who prefer starvation as against begging for cooked food.

In short, facts and figures on poverty and hunger illustrate a pathetic picture, which hampers a march toward world peace. These are as follows:

(a) Only 11 percent people reside in 42 Heavily Indebted Poor Countries, but 89 percent of poorest population resides in developing and developed countries.
(b) Developing countries face major problems like poverty, unemployment and social disintegration.
(c) Poverty causes abuse, violence, disease, illiteracy, human trafficking and immature-deaths.
(d) Poverty induces migration, which results in increase of homeless squalors and lawlessness.
(e) Poverty causes insecurity, conflicts, terrorism, Maoism, Naxalism, corruption and environmental degradation.
(f) Poverty causes food insecurity, school dropouts, child mortality and pregnancy related deaths.
(g) One-fourth of world's hungry people reside in India.
(h) The Unite Nations has predicted that one billion people are hungry in 2009.
(i) The United Nations, G-8 countries, G-20 countries, world organizations are attempting to fight poverty and hunger; but these organizations are yet to solve the problem of hunger.
(j) Unless poverty and hunger are reduced considerably, world peace process cannot make a substantial progress. Hunger alone disturbs one billion people.

Policy options

Poverty is mostly inherited. But it should not be tolerated by the society. A proverb reminds us, **Poor is born in debt, lives in debt and dies in debt**. Food aid should not be used as a weapon by the donor countries to gain anything. The reduction of poverty is possible, if each citizen has a 'Pass Book' in his/her name. Similarly, charitable dining halls are not necessary, if each food-insecure family is provided only $100 per year through his/her passbook.

All transactions for charity, subsidy, grants, or donations should be made through banks or post offices or approved banking institutions for avoiding frauds or manipulations. Hence, an amount of $20 billion per year is necessary for all the food insecure people on this earth.[175]

The remittance will also encourage the have-nots to earn an income through their own labor. This income will create an aspiration, a challenge, and self-motivation to break the poverty line. The poor can boast that he owns something in his life. Moreover, a poor family cannot commit mass suicide if they possess one Pass Book with some cash in the bank. The United Nations should consider for collecting contributions from all the member-countries for their share to the extent of at least 0.1 percent of GDP to increase the fund for the Food Insecure Families (FIF) of the world. As a result, each food insecure family can get an amount of US $ 100 or more annually.

A small step to solve the problems of Food Insecure Families would be more beneficial than flooding billions of dollars in fighting poverty through Infrastructure development, advocacy or research studies. We strongly feel that the problems of poverty and food security can be solved and it can lead to world peace. And it is possible. Poor should be allowed to possess human rights to live, eat and express their feelings. Let the government hear them with patience.

---

[175] It can be calculated: 1 billion ÷ 5 X $ 100 = US $ 20 billion. We have assumed 5 persons per family. The number of hungry persons is one billion in 2009.

Chapter VII

WORLD PEACE IS POSSIBLE

Poverty is a phenomenon induced by inequality. Is inequality a necessary outcome of development? Are growth and re-distributive justice incompatible ends? Perhaps these are separate processes both dependent on the prevalent socio-economic power structure and the political system. – Hiten Bhaya

The World Bank has defined poverty as, "a poor person is someone who has less than one US dollar a day to live on (this is based on the dollar value in 1985)". The United Nations Development Program (UNDP) has developed an index for measuring poverty levels based on several criteria. The poverty index is based on longevity (percentage of the population who die before the age of 40), education (percentage of population that is illiterate), and acceptable living conditions (percentage of population that has access to health care and clean water, and the percentage of malnourished children under five years old). A multidimensional definition of poverty acts as a guide for Swedish developmental co-operation, where poverty is not just a case of low income, but also a lack of access to health care, schools, and social security. Other factors include exposure to violence, injustice, powerlessness and uncertainty in the face of unexpected situations like sickness, accidents and natural catastrophes.[176]

The government of India uses thirteen indicators to categorize the poor by scoring method. The indicators are size group of operational holding, type of houses, availability of wear clothing, food security, sanitation, ownership of consumer durable, literacy status of the highest literate adult, status of households in labor force, means of livelihood, status of children, type of indebtedness, reason of migration, and preference for assistance. The identification of the poor is to be done through door-to-door survey with hundred-percentage coverage in each village. The "below poverty line" households are thus identified for targeting them under poverty alleviation programs.[177]

Majority of poor people lives in Asia, but the highest concentration of poor people is found in Africa. Most of the poor people are rice-eaters. Poverty is more wide spread in countryside than in urban locations. The causes of high incidence of poverty are: widely prevalence of HIV / AIDS, female-headed families, ethnic minorities, people without assets, lack of employment opportunities, frequent natural calamities, corrupt government machinery, war monger countries, lack of peace and security, lack of pro-poor policies and poor agricultural productivity. Necessarily the world organizations and developed countries have opened offices in all heavily indebted poor countries and other developing countries to implement poverty alleviation programs. The specific

---

[176]Swedish International Development Agency- poverty reduction

[177]Guidelines for BPL Census, 2002

objectives of the Millennium Development Goals [178] include national strategies for sustainable development, empowerment of women and eliminating gender disparities by 2005 and schooling of all children, reducing infant, child, and maternal mortality rate, increasing healthcare and reversing the loss of environmental resources by 2015.

The food crisis, and now the global financial crisis, is reversing past gains in fighting hunger and malnutrition. Before the onset of the food crisis in 2007, there were about 850 million chronically hungry people in the developing world. This number rose to 960 million people in 2008 and is expected to climb past 1 billion in 2009, breaking the declining trend in the proportion of hungry people in the developing world and seriously jeopardizing the goal of halving this proportion by 2015. These trends call for maintaining the momentum of recent efforts to boost agricultural investment and productivity.[179]

Can the above objectives of the Millennium Development Goals be fulfilled within the time frame of 2005 and 2015? The answer will be; the objectives of Millennium Development Goals will be partially achieved.

The specific objectives adopted, as Millennium Development Goals are not the causes of poverty but these are the effects of poverty. Hence, the Millennium Development Goals can never be fulfilled even after 2015. Attacking the causes of poverty can reduce poverty more effectively.

The donor countries, international funding institutions and the United Nations Organizations should be aware of hard truths prevailing in all the heavily indebted poor countries and developing countries.

---

[178]See chapter IV and V

[179]Global Monitoring Report, April 16, 2009

These organizations should evaluate their own activities, performances, capabilities, and impact of their assistance in poor countries.

Difficulties in poverty reduction programs:

The World Food Summit (1996) had set the target of reducing the number of the food insecure by 20 million per year. The United Nations Summit (2000) endorsed this target with the declaration of "Millennium Development Goals". However, Food and Agriculture Summit of FAO (2000) has noted that the number of hungry people was reduced by less than 6 million per year. So the question is, "What has gone wrong in the procedure of tackling the reduction of food insecure?"

Poverty cannot be reduced without benefiting the poor directly. It is also difficult to reach the poor people of developing countries by the donors. All the people born or brought up in HIPC or developing countries are not poor. There are billionaires and millionaires in poor countries, who have been benefited through politician-contractor-businessmen nexus.

In poor countries, democracy, fair election, transparency in administration, justice for all, equality in opportunity, good governance, and even the Constitution of a country are interpreted in favor of the administration and rich people.

Unless food security is ensured for the (poor) family, enrolment of all children in primary schools becomes a utopian thought. The mid-day meals in schools cannot attract children for a longer period. A hungry child needs food and is less interested to read mathematics.

A hungry woman needs food first then medicines. Hence, infant mortality, child mortality, and maternal mortality cannot be checked through medicines, doctors and hospitals and cannot access reproductive health services without food security. The healthcare program should follow food security program.

Mostly poor people reside in inaccessible forest, hilly or swampy areas. They are away from industrial towns, cities, or employment generating institutions. They live in forests and live on forest produce; they cut forest plants; they destroy forest resources by fire; they kill forest animals and they are the causes of environmental loss. The loss of environmental resources can be reversed through food security, employment opportunities, education facilities, and plantation programs. Unless food security or employment opportunities are available to each family, environmental losses cannot be checked.

The governments of developing countries could not stop engagement of child labor and bonded labor till date.

Pumping more assistance to the HIPCs or developing countries for poverty reduction will lead to corruption. Similarly cheap and long-term loan will create more number of millionaires among the politicians, businesspersons and government officials in those countries. The conditions of poor people cannot change, if foreign assistance is routed through corrupt government machinery. Corruption has become a way of life in developing countries. Amassing wealth through corrupt practices does increase social prestige as against social boycott or hatred in all the Heavily Indebted Poor Countries. The government officials and politicians utilize all techniques to grab subsidies, gifts, free foods, and aid earmarked for the poor.

The donations of donor countries are utilized as per the advice of the donors; the budgets of the poor countries are prepared on the advice of the donor countries; and the poor countries borrow from International Funding Institutions or the World Bank to repay the interest of the previous borrowings. The advice of the donor countries has landed the poor countries to get into debt trap. Conditionality, high level discussions, press clippings, donor's visit along with officials of the World Bank, review meetings and expression of interest to donate funds cannot mitigate the sufferings of the poor unless the real poor are directly benefited through generation of employment and earnings.

People are dying without food; Ministers are enjoying life as emperors. Some governments are busy in manufacturing Anti-Ballistic Missile (ABM), Cruise Missile and Weapons of Mass Destruction (WMD) and selling war equipment to other countries. The Presidents, Prime Ministers, or envoys of different countries are searching for allies worldwide and are making extensive tours to convince their counterparts that their journeys are purely for world peace. It is misleading. People have not voted the political party to wage wars, to manufacture war equipments or to make few people millionaires at the cost of the country and people; but the political leaders in the democratic countries make it.

Suggestions of the Secretary General of UNO

Kofi Annan (2002), the Secretary General of the UNO has highlighted five key areas where he hoped concrete results could be achieved water and sanitation, energy, health, agriculture and bio-diversity. Rt. Hon Clare Short has stressed that action on each of these is important for achievement in poverty reduction worldwide. These are:

Water and sanitation: The political declaration and program of action should recognize the importance of access to freshwater and sanitation to the lives of the poor. One billion people lack access to safe drinking water, and 2.4 billion people currently lack access to sanitation. Agreeing a new target to halve the proportion of people without access to sanitation – to complement the existing Millennium Development Goal on access to freshwater – would be a good achievement.

Energy: Energy can play in nationally owned poverty reduction strategies. The Global Village Energy Partnership would seek to create a 10-year work program to reduce poverty and enhance economic and social development through the accelerated provision of modern energy services to those without access. It would bring together developing and industrialized country governments, public and private organizations, multilateral institutions and other key stakeholders to address the links between energy and poverty reduction in rural areas, and improve delivery of energy services.

Health: The Millennium Development Goals for health has targeted reducing of child mortality by two thirds, reducing maternal mortality rate by three quarters, and reversing the spread of HIV / AIDS, malaria and tuberculosis - all by 2015. For this, the Global Fund has received pledges of around $ 2 billion over five years.

Agriculture: It contributes in poverty reduction through economic growth, sustaining livelihoods and delivery of environmental services. Hence, actions are required by developing countries to improve rural roads, access to markets, seeds and fertilizer, credit and land security, supported by actions by developed countries to reduce the current iniquitous system of tariff barriers and subsidies.

Bio-diversity: Bio-diversity is linked with poverty reduction. Whether for food, medicine, shelter or income generation, poor people throughout the world depend on bio-diversity. Forests provide poor people with a range of goods and services. Hence, illegal logging and associated trade should be banned. This trade, which is based on corrupt and abusive misuse of forests, denies a livelihood to millions of poor people, it robs governments of billions of dollars, which could be spent on development programs, and it provokes and sustains conflicts. It is a problem shared by producer and consumer countries alike. It requires actions by governments, business, consumers and civil society.[180]

Views of the President of the World Bank

James D. Wolfensohn, the President of the World Bank has expressed: "Before September 11, development issues were always at the end of the G8 summit agenda. Now they come first. Now rich countries acknowledge that poverty is a serious issue, which is close to us, especially after the September 11 event. That day we understood that poverty was no longer encircled by the boundaries of a wall. In fact, that wall, which we believed to be far away from us, collapsed together with the Twin Towers. All of a sudden, Afghanistan got the heart of New York, Wall Street, and the Pentagon. And poverty is related to terrorism.

Governments need to turn the rhetoric about poverty into action. This has to be done at two levels. (1) By countries themselves that are trying to develop and they need to have an environment, which is equitable, and which has legal and judiciary systems that work to protect people's rights. You need a financial system that is transparent. Moreover, you need to fight corruption so that people do not steal money, which is necessary for development. And you need to help build the government itself. Those are the things you need to get it done. In addition, governments need programs for education, health,

---

[180]Rt. Hon Clare Short, "Poverty Reduction and Sustainable Development – the Challenge for Johannesburg", A speech in Development Policy Forum, QEII Conference Center, London File: /A\ Poverty Reduction and Sustainable Development – the Challenge for Johannesburg.htm

and infrastructure as well as programs to protect their culture and history. (2) Rich countries should also provide assistance in terms of money and people. And it's important that they should open their markets for trade so that the poor countries can export."[181]

Views of Researchers

Research scholars in economics, planning, sociology, anthropology, statistics, and funding institutions, donor countries and non-governmental organizations have suggested that proper planning and implementation of pro-poor policies can mitigate the sufferings of the poor. The availability of micro-credit, employment generating activities, food security, and development in agriculture, investment in human capital, attitude and activities of foreign funding institutions, involvement of NGOs, effective governance, and debt relief measures can assist the poverty reduction programs.

Moreover, low cost technology to small producers, fairer political process in democracy, land rights, safety net for poor, non-farm occupations, improving sustainable environment and community forestry have resulted better performances in poverty reduction programs. Promotion of small-scale enterprises, export promotion, rural development, agro-industry, and abolition of estate monopoly are necessary for success of poverty reduction programs. The government must hear the voices of the poor. This process can assist, console and change the state policy for the benefits of the poor.

---

[181]Wolfensohn, James D. (May 24, 2003) "Poverty is Related to Terrorism", interview with La Republica (Italy), Office of the President, The World Bank Group, Washington, DC, Press Release

Authors' Suggestions

1. Food Security

Not all poor meet starvation deaths. Families without any source of income come under extreme poverty category. The refugees, landless old-aged laborers, female-headed families, physically handicapped, chronic patients, disaster-affected families and idle persons are likely to come under extreme poverty. These persons have no aspiration, no future, no income and they do not have food security. These persons are likely to meet untimely deaths; they die without food, without medicines, without care and without money. These people have never received government aid to cross poverty line. They need assistance throughout their life in order to survive. They need assistance for survival and to avail chances to cross the poverty line within a couple of years.

There are as many as 854 million food-insecure inhabitants in the world. In other words, 171 million food- insecure families need food aid (taking an average of five members per family). If only US $ 100 per family is directly donated to these families per year, starvation deaths can be completely checked or reduced to an expected level. In short, we expect that the UNDP or another world organization to arrange an amount of US $ 17 billion per year for these unfortunate brethren for their survival. If the world organizations, the G8, and the OECD continue the food security program up to end of 2015, about 50 per cent of food-insecure families (85 million families) will attend the status of food-secured families by 2011 and all food-insecure families will be food-secured families by 2015, These families must be selected carefully in different countries. There exist enough chances to include non-poor in this category through government machinery, non-government organizations and politicians. Hence, checking and cross checking may be made to identify the food-insecure families in the entire world. The amount must be credited to the accounts of the food-insecure families without any intermediary.

2. Bank Account

Now, in most of the countries, the citizens have 'photo identity cards' to prove their identity that they belong to a particular country. Each adult person should possess Bank Account, Land Account and Health Card in this twenty- first century. If a person does not touch money, save money, deposit money, draw money and does not enter to a bank premises, he (she) cannot cross poverty line even if the world community pour sufficient aid to the developing countries. A bank account will induce the poor to save; to apply for loan to start a retail shop; to make him (her) free from the clutches of itinerant moneylenders; to deposit his (her) savings; to deposit government assistance; and to receive bank loan. And the poor can say to his (her) family members **"We have money in our bank"**. This satisfaction and self-confidence will make him (her) to think and plan for a better future. A bank account can induce the poor to get rid of poverty.

Moreover, relief grants, gifts, other government assistance, cooperative loan, and old age pension can be transacted through their bank accounts. The amount may be credited directly in the bank account of the beneficiary to avoid corruption at official level and wastage of time in procuring the benefits. Subsidy in food-grains earmarked for the poor must be completely stopped, as this creates black marketing, smuggling and hoarding. The subsidy amount earmarked for the poor may be credited in their accounts. This will help them to save time and they can purchase quality food-grains in open markets.

3 Group Insurance Schemes

In all the developing and heavily indebted poor countries, the poor is not covered under any insurance scheme. The poor sell labour and earn for the family members. Attack of forest animals, snakebites, malaria, dehydration, sunstroke, accidents, black fever, HIV/ AIDS, starvation, pneumonia, and natural calamities like fire, flood and cyclone, cause extreme hardship to the poor and their family members. He works in adverse situations and undertakes risky jobs. He is illiterate, untrained, underfed and un-cared for in the society. He works (manual labour) for the benefit of others. But the society neglects the poor.

The poor man does not have the capacity to insure his life or that of his family members. The insurance companies do business for the rich man who is capable of giving premium each year. The rich person ensures his life, and also of his family members, vehicles, house property, and business and for health care. Most of the rich people pay premiums and do not claim any amount from the insurance companies in most of the years. The poor man needs insurance coverage for his family members. But most of them have not heard of the insurance coverage. Can the International organizations and funding institutions take up steps for the insurance coverage of the poor?

Suggestions

A group of rural poor people in a village or cluster of villages may be provided with one-time-group-insurance policy for untimely deaths.

All the poor living in both rural and urban areas may be insured with health care facilities each year. Those persons, who are admitted in hospitals, may be granted the amount necessary for purchase of medicines, doctor’s fees and diets.

The International funding institutions may provide funds for the insurance coverage of untimely deaths and health care for each individual. We expect that a modest beginning may be started with a per capita per year insurance premium of US $ 2 for untimely death and US $ 1 for health care for all people living less than US $1 per day (1.2 billion people). This program may be started globally at a time and can be managed by an international insurance organization. It is expected that the insurance coverage for premature death may be only US $ 200 and for heath care only US $ 50 per affected person. As a good venture for the entire poor people worldwide, it is suggested that the program may continue for a period of 5 years. After that, the local committees or the state government may continue to finance the insurance programs. Each year the 'insurance premium' would be US $ 2.4 billion for all the 1.2 billion poor people and the medical treatment of the poor will be another US $ 1.2 billion. In short, it is necessary to allocate US $ 3.6 billion for the life insurance and medical treatment of all the poor people of the world each year.

If these funding institutions desire to include all persons living on less than US $2 per day (2.80 billion people) for the insurance coverage for untimely deaths and health care, the insurance premium would be US $5.6 billion and the medical treatment of the poor will be another US $ 2.8 billion. In short, it is necessary to allocate US $ 8.4 billion for the life insurance and medical treatment of all the poor people of the world each year.

A friend in need is a friend indeed. A poor man needs cash for hospitalization of kith and kin and for funeral ceremony of the deceased. We hope that group insurance and hospitalization bill for the poor will be more helpful to the poor. This will debar the poor to procure high-interest-credit from the unscrupulous moneylenders, who could have made him a lifetime-bonded laborer.

4. Debt Relief

Clare Short opines, "Millennium Development Goals are carefully chosen. Therefore, they are achievable. The international community must significantly increase the development efforts. This means fairer trade rules that allow developing countries to access our markets; and it means increasing development assistance, improving how that assistance is delivered, and focusing it on poverty reduction. Moreover, domestic savings, foreign direct investment, export earnings, debt relief and aid are necessary to eradicate poverty, achieve sustained economic growth and promote sustainable development". He has explained that good governance (both political and economic) in developing countries, commitment of OECD countries to provide more and better aid, a sustainable exit from debt, better trade access, and a stronger voice for developing countries in international decision-making can increase the targeting on the reduction of poverty. He has further emphasized that international aid of US $ 55 billion per annum could increase efficiency (value) by 50 percent through effective pro-poor policies. At Monterrey, the European Union and the United States made pledges of increased aid, which we estimate will lead to an increase in development assistance from a total of US $55 billion in 2003 to US $67 billion a year by 2006.[182]

Suggestions

The PRSP for all poor state / country may be prepared for future planning and debt relief. It will be more appropriate to prepare PRSP for a specific agro-climatic zone or specific societal group or

---

[182]Op. cited

administrative unit. Therefore, it will be more effective to eradicate poverty in that zone or for that group.

The UN agencies have contributed to a number of PRSPs and now engaged in preparation of PRSPs in almost 60 countries around the world in areas from trade to macroeconomic policy to monitoring to coordination. Our suggestion is that let the poverty pockets of all the developing countries prepare their PRSPs initially with local economists and planners. The basic reports can be totally up-dated, modified, enlarged and reoriented by the UNDP or Global Funding Institutions. Local partnership with UN system or the World Bank or the IMF can be more effective than imposed.

5. Basic Needs

Basic needs cover food, clothing, shelter, education and healthcare. The poor is devoid of these necessities as per his/her requirement to lead a normal life. The International Funding Institutions, governments, local institutions and donors should keep a watch on the poorest people who are prone to commit suicide or fighting with starvation deaths without any consideration of caste, creed, religion, or place of birth. These people need sympathy, consolation and aid. There are many families who don't possess any wealth such as a piece of land, a small hut, wear dresses, few quantities of rice or wheat, even utensils and mats to sleep. They are starved in money and materials. But they are docile and innocent. They pray God for early deaths. They are the sons and daughters of the Almighty; their pity cannot be described or evaluated. Can the Noble Laureates, political leaders; the G8, The OECD, the UNDP and poverty economists find ways to save the lives of the poorest people? Can the poor fulfill their basic needs? The state laws provide two meals, medicines, clothing, mosquito nets, drinking water, electricity and blankets to the prisoners, who are sentenced jail-terms for causing nuisance to the society. But the innocent poor, who are deprived of all opportunities throughout life, are still devoid of these basic needs. The innocent people are not burden on the society; rather the society gets an opportunity to assist them.

6. Rural connectivity

Rural connectivity means accessibility of road to the people. In predominantly agricultural economies of developing countries, adequate network of roads is the linkage between rural farms and primary agricultural markets. Poverty alleviation is closely linked to rural connectivity. Enhanced mobility and access to goods and services of poor people result in livelihood security. In sub- Saharan Africa, south Asia, and Latin American countries transport planning has been neglected. Generally, the government invests more in conventional motorized transport infrastructure and in railways. But rural connectivity in developing countries is neglected where majority of inhabitants is poor or extremely poor. This has resulted in plight of poorer people and has caused lack of mobility, high level of unemployment, lack of marketing facilities, and obstacles in schooling facility of children, high mortality of children, and maternal deaths because of absence of motorized transport facilities to hospitals and health clinics.

A road to an isolated village not only improves people's access to markets and service centers; it also brings the village within easy reach of development interventions. A road to isolated village would bring dealers and traders to village interiors, or the community would be able to travel out more easily with their produce. A road creates wider market opportunities and increases the bargaining power over their economic produce.[183] Village roads help in generating employment and income. Rural roads constructed by the government through contractors or through 'food–for–work' programs are both below standard and costly. These roads are washed away through rainfalls and are not repaired for years. Maintenance of rural roads is more politicized in developing countries. The influential persons, political leaders and administrators decide the fate of the existing roads.

Suggestions

Each revenue village should have a "Village Road Committee" to look after village roads, its construction, repair, and maintenance. The state government, rural development organizations and funding institutions should advise, render assistance in planning and execution of road development and award funds to the village road committees. The efficiency of sanctioned funds is maximized through direct payment to the beneficiaries, the village road committee.

Village roads should connect each village to facilitate easy reach of bicycles, bicycle trailers, mopeds, and three wheelers. This will connect people with markets, health clinics, schools, bus stops, railway stations, post offices and ultimately the district head quarters. The Village Road Committee may take up new road construction for their benefit in the beginning and this road can be upgraded, widened, and developed by them through finance available from the government or funding institutions. The partnership between the users of road and the government must be strengthened. Unless the users are involved in road management, the quality and

---

[183] Maganya, J, S perera, R Silva, "Trails- Transport Initiative, Links and Strategies- International Transport Program" Issue No. 3

longevity of village roads cannot be maintained for a longer period. The committee should take up beautification of roads by planting ornamental trees and/or growing roadside trees to allow shed to the walking travelers.

7. Rural Agricultural Markets

Marketing of agricultural products is vitally important in any campaign to free the world from hunger for two reasons. Most of those who go hungry do so because the food they need costs more than they can afford. The second main reason for stressing the significance of marketing is its impact on production. If the producer cannot see an easily accessible market outlet where he can sell the food he produces beyond his own needs, then he has little incentive to produce it. Effective marketing is also critical for the success of development programs designed to uplift a population as a whole. In spite of the strides in industrialization, being made in many developing countries to break through the "cycle of poverty", a large section of the population must continue to depend for their living on agriculture. Any plan of economic development that aims at diminishing the poverty of the agricultural population, reducing consumer food prices, earning more foreign exchange or eliminating economic waste, has, therefore, to pay special attention to the development of efficient marketing for food and agricultural products.[184]

The government can improve the market structure and organization through regulatory measures, marketing infrastructure, declaration of administered prices, direct entry of public agencies, and promulgation of policies for exports and imports and

[184] Abbott, JC et al (1967), "Marketing – Its Role in Increasing Productivity", FAO basic study No.4, Freedom from Hunger Campaign, Food and Agriculture Organization of United Nations, Rome, P. 1

by fiscal and monetary policies, that affects the performances of agricultural marketing systems. The government can establish regulated markets for the benefits of the farmers.[185] The Food and Agriculture Organization (FAO) provides support to developing countries and the emerging economies in the improvement of marketing systems for both farm produce and inputs such as fertilizers and seeds. Emphasis is firmly placed on the promotion of marketing by the private sector and the role of the governments in developing an appropriate environment for the private sector to function efficiently. Mallick[186] has suggested, "Licensed traders should be allowed to continue since the government does not have the necessary competence to handle the entire trade in food-grains, nor can it provide alternative occupation to those who are engaged in such trading activities. The government can assist trading sector by providing accurate market information, supply of capital and entrepreneurship to improve supply elasticity."

Suggestions

(a) Rural agricultural markets: The government should take steps to create rural agricultural markets in each cluster of villages, so that the peasants, artisans, and other persons would be able to sell their marketable surplus with remunerative prices.

(b). Agricultural marketing research: It should be prioritized in all the heavily indebted poor countries and developing countries for availing funds for market development, creation of infrastructure, international

---

[185] Acharya, SS (1998), "Agricultural Marketing in India: Some Facts and Emerging Issues", Ind. Jr. of Agri. Econ. Vol. 53, No 3, July- Sept. 1998, pp 310-332

[186] Mallick, SC, " Marketing of Rice in Orissa" Research (Orissa) Publication, Bhubaneswar, P. 288

trade, forecasting of prices, remunerative prices and crop planning.

(c) Development of market infrastructure: Infrastructure increases marketing efficiency, improves storage facility, activates information services, creates agricultural processing units, renders training and extension facilities and strengthens competition among market functionaries. Development of infrastructure creates wider markets, regulates price variability, creates employment opportunity and assists the poor for mobility and earnings. Investment in roads can fight poverty, hunger and starvation.

8. Employment Opportunities

In all HIPC countries, agriculture contributes a major share in Gross Domestic Product and generates employment to the extent of two-thirds of total man-days in rural areas. However, it does not absorb all rural labourers and youths. As employment elasticity in agriculture is lower, there exists massive unemployment and underemployment in rural areas. Hence, non-farm sector should be tapped for creation of employment opportunities in poor countries along with farm sector. The possible areas for employment generation are:

(a) Construction of rural roads
(b) Construction and maintenance of irrigation channel and ponds
(c) Construction of houses, buildings, culverts
(d) Retailing of agricultural products
(e) Trade and commerce
(f) Training for acquiring skills in services sector
(g) Occupational mobility
(h) Rural manufacturing and agro-processing units
(i) Diversification of agriculture
(j) Export oriented agriculture
(k) High value crops like fruits and vegetables and
(l) Large-scale public investments

Hence, governments may take up policy reforms to generate more employment opportunities to the rural poor. A poor family cannot survive without wages.

Bhalla and Hazell [187] have suggested the following policy options:

(a) Accelerating the rates of sectoral and national economic growth
(b) Reversing the trend of deceleration of agricultural growth and public investment in agriculture;
(c) Promotional policies for labor-intensive and higher income generating allied agricultural and non-agricultural activities in rural and urban areas for domestic and export markets;
(d) Diversification of agriculture towards hitherto neglected dry land regions has the potential to lead to an appreciable acceleration in agricultural and rural employment, and to reduce poverty.

9. Land Reforms

Land is the real asset and therefore land tenure is complicated. It covers the economic, social, political, legal and local customs concerning the ownership of land. Special tenancy legislation has been developed in almost every country to safeguard the interest of the tenants. Security of tenure, rent control and permanent state of occupancy and elimination of intermediate right-holders are the aims and objectives of such legislation. Security of tenure refers to written document, duration of tenancy and acquisition of ownership by tenants. These conditions

---

[187] Bhalla, G S and P Hazell, "Rural Employment and Poverty – Strategies to Eliminate Rural Poverty within a Generation", Economic and Political Weekly, EPW Research Foundation, Mumbai (India), 38 (33), August 16-22, 2003, pp.3473-84

vary in different countries. In most of the countries, land is owned unevenly and the poor tenants are deprived of their legitimate share.

Poverty is inversely related to land ownership in agriculture dominated economy.

Most of the poor persons do not own land. The tenants, who cultivate land, do not own land. Poverty is inherited in poor countries. Moreover, land cases in poor countries have landed the poor nowhere; whatever they earn they spend in land courts for establishing their rights over their land, they cultivate. Land cases transfer rural surplus to the cities and make the peasants extremely poor. In all poor countries, there exists serious imbalance between distribution of landed property and labor power. This imbalance has to be radically corrected through proper enforcement of various land reform laws and such economic development measures as would strengthen the economic position of the vast mass of working peasantry and thereby ensure a balanced and stable growth of the entire agrarian economy.[188]

On September 1, 2003, the Government of India and University of Washington, Seattle organized a national workshop in New Delhi on; "Reforms in Land Policy for Accelerated Agricultural Growth and Rural Development". The workshop observed that land reform policies aimed to promote agricultural growth and alleviate rural poverty have had limited success in India. It suggested the potential of new reform approaches such as contract farming, legalizing procedures for land leasing, and sanctioning

[188]Report of the National Commission on Agriculture, India, Vol.15

homestead-cum-garden plots for the poor and landless to be suitably examined and plaited.[189]

Suggestions:

Computerization of land records is necessary for the benefits of the land- owners and the government. This can save the landowners from legal harassment and unnecessary expenditure in land courts. Each landowner must be provided with a "Land Pass Book" for each plot.

If Land Pass Book is provided for each plot of land, sub-division and fragmentation of land holding can be checked or forbidden by law. This can also restrict court cases; the number of plaintiffs and petitioners can be minimized through computerization of land records. The satisfaction derived by landowners to stand on their own land can't be measured in monetary terms.

Each landless family may be provided a plot of one-tenth of an acre (40 Sq. Meters) for homestead-cum-kitchen garden purpose. This land should not be transferable by law but can be inherited.

Land is the real asset and therefore land tenure is complicated. It covers the economic, social, political, legal and local customs concerning the ownership of land. There should be separate 'Land Department' in each state / country. Moreover, independent 'Evaluation Machinery' should be created in each state for the appraisal of the effects of agrarian reform programs. In addition, there should be a 'research organization' to study the impact of tenancy legislation, land management, problems on land, and its productivity.

---

[189]Hague, T., " Reform for agricultural Growth and rural Development", Economic and Political weekly, 38 (48), November 29,2003 P. 5031

Land is a factor of production and an asset that can fight poverty in all the developing countries and HIPCs. Land is a source of inspiration and it adds prestige to the owner. The satisfaction derived by standing on one's own land cannot be measured in monetary terms. There exists psychological attachment of a farmer to his land and he regards land as his mother.

10. Environment

Johannesburg provides an important opportunity to change the terms of global debate on the links between poverty, environment and sustainable development. We must be clear that protecting the environment is not an end in itself. We do not simply want to conserve the world that we have. We want improved lives for the poor of the world and a world that is sustainable for future generations. We can fuse the energy of development and environment movements so that they can work more effectively together for systematic poverty reduction and sustainable development.

The environment is crucial to the livelihoods of poor people. The poor depend on wood for their cooking and heating, they use fodder for feeding their livestock, they get medicine from the forest, they get water from streams and wells and they often build houses from natural materials. The poor suffer most when air and water are polluted. A billion people - mainly women and children are exposed to indoor air pollution from inadequate ventilation and the burning of traditional fuels, such as wood and dung.

In addition, they suffer too when seas are over fished and forests are decimated by unauthorized goons. In addition, poor people are highly vulnerable to environment disasters and the environment-related conflicts. Droughts, floods, cyclones, hailstorms and other disasters can wipe out any development gains that poor people have made. And their frequency and severity is expected to increase with climate change.[190]

Suggestions:

Environmental degradation must be checked by law and in practice.

Forest area should not be reduced at any cost in all the countries and a fixed percentage of geographical area must be earmarked as forestland.

Both private organizations and/or local inhabitants must renovate all the degraded forestland. In small forest lands, cultivation of bamboo and fruit plants like jack fruits, mango and area specific fruit plants can be encouraged for the benefits of local inhabitants

Village committees should be made partners in forest management. Forest officials cannot safeguard the forests without the involvement of local people.

The governments should encourage plantations of high-value forest trees like sandal, teak, and other non-teak plants in private, eroded and un-irrigated lands.

The amendments in forest acts would change environmental degradation and induce the inhabitants of developing countries to earn higher income. The number of poor people residing in sub-Saharan Africa, south East-Asia and Latin American countries can be drastically reduced through modifications in Forest Acts and their export earnings can be dramatically improved. The deficit of cereals in hilly areas can be met from surplus food-grains of irrigated tracts.

---

[190]Rt. Hon. Clare Short –op cited

The reserve forests may be fully managed and administered by the respective governments. Forests are created by nature. But corrupt governments and corrupt people destroy it. The forest officials and forest contractors are responsible for the loss of forest coverage.

11. Favorable Prices for Cereals

The Governments must award favorable prices for cereals to the vast majority of farmers and peasants. All farmers do not cultivate all crops. But all farmers grow cereals. The offer of favourable prices of farm-harvested cereals would encourage the farmers to stick to cultivation.

The cost of production of crops in agriculture must include interest of value of land, labor cost of family labourers, cost of hired laborers, cost of bullock power, cost of mechanization, cost of fertilizers and manures, cost of pesticides and insecticides, irrigation charges, marketing costs, storage costs, and interest on bank loan and own funds, premium for risk and uncertainty in agriculture, insurance cost, and profit over investment. The interest on value of own land is not considered during cost estimates, which is illegal. When an industrial sector charges all costs because of their bargaining power, the farmers must be allowed the same facilities. The subsidy granted to agriculture sector is mis-utilized and misappropriated in the public sectors and channels.

The government must procure the marketable surplus of cereals directly from the peasants at his doorstep. But the government employs private millers and administrators to procure paddy / wheat. Before the government starts procurement, the traders procure the cereals at throwaway prices just after harvest. In many cases the traders give advances and mortgage the produce even before the crop season.

Unless the government assures the farmers and peasants favorable prices for their agricultural produce, the farmers would continue to be poor for generations. Farmers do not get even the production cost of the cereals. All farmers of the low-income countries are debarred from justice and rights, as they are poor. The GDP in Agriculture is fast decreasing in all countries. The government allows subsidies to consumer's price of cereal to please the consumers for vote politics, but the poor peasants do not benefit by the price structure of government monopoly procurement schemes.

Hence, Government should consider parity prices for cereals in fixation of Minimum Support prices.

Five forms of parity prices could be considered in price formulation to award justice to the farmers.

These are:

(a) Input-output price parity
(b) Inter-commodity price parity
(c) Inter-sectoral price parity
(d) Price received and prices paid parity by the farmer
(e) International price parity

The government should consider salary increase of the employees in government and private organizations over the years and the benefits realized by the farmers in agriculture during the same period. It could be studied with a **Base Year**.

The farm prices face discrimination all the years. The percentage price rise of gold and percentage price rise of cereals with a base year would reveal the sufferings of the farmer community. Government policy forces the farm youths to migrate to urban areas to seek employment in road construction or in services sector.

The indebted peasants commit suicides because agriculture is a loss bearing profession and the government is deaf to hear their cries and sufferings even in twenty-first century. In India, on an average, 18,000 farmers commit suicides annually.

The government keeps the consumers' prices low in cereals for the advantage of the Government. This price policy affects the farm sector adversely. The farmers support a political party to form the government but the government adopts step-motherly attitude to farmers after the formation of the Ministry.

It is suggested that favorable prices to cereals can reduce the number of the poor people in the country/ countries. Government neglects the farmers as they are indebted and poor. All the peasants of all developing countries do not have bargain power. They suffer because they do not have organization to express their sufferings and they are eager to live for their children at the cost of their own lives, happiness and pleasure.

12. Measurement of Peace

The economic growth of a country is measured by Gross National Product (GNP), Gross Domestic Product (GDP), and by per capita income. But this calculation could neither solve poverty of people nor award peace to a region, country or the whole world. Hence, a new measurement theory is devised by the authors, which can ensure comparatively a more practical solution of solving human sufferings, and could at least try to award permanent peace to a region, country or the world.

Each Government should measure its efficiency by measuring the **Gross Domestic Peace of a Country** (G D P C). The Government can try to award peace to the citizens by studying the following factors and evaluate its performances. People of the country should also cooperate with the government in peace measurement and peace achievement.

The **Suresh–Pritam Model** for peace measurement is as follows. These factors are:

G D P C = f (S, D, H, W, C, E, O, F, P, X)

(1) Food Secured families (S)
(2) Debts sustainable families (D)
(3) Families those can bear medical, educational, social and Household bills (H)
(4) Area free from Rebellion, War and Terrorists (W)
(5) People's perception of Corruption-free politics and administration (C)
(6) Forest coverage for clean Environment (E)
(7) Employment Opportunity (O)
(8) Families without Court cases (F)
(9) Share of State Income in Budget Expenditure Proposal (P)
(10)Other Factors Contributing to Peace (X)

GDPC can also be calculated with a single factor or with a multiple of factors in percentages. But more number of factors would bring better results. The data could be drawn from official records of the government or from published reports of researchers. We can also collect latest data by observing statistical procedures. The Gross Domestic Peace of a Country can be classified as Highly Peaceful with >80 percent output, 60-80 percent as Peaceful, 40-60 percent as Moderately Peaceful, 30-40 Percent as Doubtful Peace Area and <30 percent as No-peace Zone.

Conclusion

The study aims at reduction of number of poor people spread over the length and breadth of the entire globe and particularly in the areas where more number of poor people reside. It is irony of facts that poor people do not believe that they can get rid of poverty through proper planning and execution of pro-poor policies by the government with support of developed countries.

Most of the poor people are rice-eaters. The corrupt politicians and bureaucrats divert money allocated for the poor people to their personal accounts through fraudulent practices and false vouchers.

Poverty is a global problem. Acute poverty causes starvation-deaths. Hence, the Development Assistance Committee of OECD countries, World forums, World organizations and all developed and developing countries should work in tandem to fight against poverty for a peaceful world. The world community should contribute patronage and work with a mission for a safer environment.

The World Bank, the International Monetary Fund, the UN organizations and donor countries should donate funds, guide and assist the ongoing programs of education, health care, micro-credit, training of local youths and area-specific research projects for reducing poverty in all HIPC and developing countries. Two world organizations can be created for reduction of poverty worldwide; one world organization will collect funds from different sources and another world organization can utilize funds in different poor pockets of the world with partnership of poor people and respective governments.

As corruption is a world problem, particularly in HIPC and developing countries, donations to governments cannot yield desired results in poverty reduction programs. Hence, **one-third** of the donated funds may be directly deposited in local currency in the accounts of the poor to avoid official harassment, pilferage and corruption. The donors can award the other **two-thirds** of the donated funds to the respective governments with or without matching grants of one-third for implementing pro-poor policies with proper planning, monitoring, and evaluation facilities. The governments should undertake strict supervision over the projects, so as to check misuse of funds.

The Millennium Development Goals would never achieve the targets by 2015. However, MDGs assist in poverty reduction worldwide. The goals can be fulfilled through empowering the poor.

The governments of low-income countries must ensure that each adult possesses a bank account, a land passbook, a voter identity card, and life-insurance coverage.

The government must provide pensioners' benefits to all senior citizens in each country for peaceful living in their old ages. Let the offspring be freed from carrying their parents on their shoulders, which have forgotten their responsibilities and duties toward their parents.

Each country should decide the minimum age for 'Senior Citizen Pension'. It could be done by Matriculation certificate or Birth certificate or simply by Voter's list. The lowest and the highest amount of pension paid to individuals in the country should be in proportion of 1:10. Pension amount must be directly deposited in the bank account of the beneficiaries (both old man and old woman).

All subsidies awarded by the government must be stopped as corporations, government institutions and officials are the major beneficiaries. The targeted-beneficiaries do not get an opportunity to smell the benefits. Profitable agriculture and cottage industries can generate more employment opportunities to the rural poor. It is possible by increasing the procurement prices of rice and wheat. As long as the cities increase its population, geographical area and employment opportunities, rural labourers would come to towns and cities to lead urban life. It is a sign of development, but it happens at the cost of farmers and farming.

Similarly rapid industrialization grabs agricultural land, diverts farm youths from agriculture to non-farm occupations, destroys atmosphere, and increases political corruption and decreases farm land. The government must ensure that rice and wheat requirement of the country is produced in the country itself. Dependence of cereals on other countries as a routine assignment would encourage terrorism, political turmoil, war, dacoit and nuisance and would convert the country into a desert in the long run.

The governments should not utilize funds on populist measures to grab political mileage. The government must do justice to the people with suitable policies and programs to award peace to all. The government must take all precautionary measures to check starvation-deaths, encourage rural connectivity, create rural agricultural markets and protect environment. The world organizations and funding institutions must see that the funds are properly utilized.

The funding institutions should not satisfy the needs of corrupt governments but look into the necessity of the poor people. Foreign funding is the biggest source of corruption in all the developing countries.

Long-term loans for infrastructure development have encouraged massive corruption and have put these debtor countries into debt trap forever.

The NGOs and Civil Societies are prone to corruption and need strict supervision by the government or simply these organizations should be de-recognized or declared as personal or private organizations.

All the policy measures advocated by different organizations, countries, research workers and religious forums are exceptionally good suggestions. Our ultimate goal is world peace, where terrorism is completely wiped out and no one starves. Political parties acquire huge private wealth at the cost of the people and the country. In all low-income countries corruption restricts development and increases social disorders. Corruption controls politics and controls democracy.

Hungry people are neglected in each successive government. Unemployment has created lawlessness in the countries and has created Maoists, Naxalites and Terrorists. The governments face internal and external threats and spend huge amounts on security measures. Governments spend less on essential services and neglect the peasants, agricultural labourers and hungry people. The number of poor people increases each year in all low income countries. This imposes loss of peace among the people.

In short, poverty is inversely related to world peace.

Fighting poverty is not a political or religious agenda; it is simply a human activity for its survival. When we have not created this Earth, we have no right to destroy it. Let us hope that eternal peace prevails in the world and no individual is a burden to this civilization. We are very optimistic that there could be WORLD PEACE to render justice to all people and other living beings.

Mr. Tony Blair, the former Prime Minister of the United Kingdom, has called for a fairer deal for the world's poor. He says that there will be 'no security or prosperity at home' unless rich nations deal with poverty overseas'.

Each country should consider Gross Domestic Peace of a Country (GDPC) to measure peace and prosperity of all people in a country.

Eight decades ago a poet, philosopher, great lover of humanity and Nobel Laureate advised all of us in this way:

The human world is made one; all the countries are losing their distance every day, their boundaries not offering the same resistance as they did in the past age. Politicians struggle to exploit this great fact and wrangle about establishing trade relationships. But my mission is to urge for a world-wide commerce of heart and mind, sympathy and understanding and never to allow this sublime opportunity to be sold in the slave markets for the cheap price of individual profits or be shattered away by the wholly competition in mutual destructiveness.

----- Rabindranath Tagore,
Paris, May 3, 1930

The End

AUTHOR INDEX

Abbott J C	331
Acharya S. S.	332
Adiseshia Malcoln S	19
Ahmad M	55
Ahmad N Zamias	43
Ahmad Iftikar	53
Alan S Sverrisson	61
Alam rouful	40
Aldous Huxley	131
Amartya Sen	174
Anna Tibaijuka	71
Anup Shah	32
Anwar Nasution	69
Aneka G C	49
Arena C J	49
Aiyar SSA	34
Arellano Lopez S	59
Aydin Hayri	69
Ayittely George	22
Barron M Antonieta	74
Basley Timothy	51
Belessakos Elias	64
Berry Albert	73
Bhalla G S	334
Breslin Edward D.	52
Brown James	47
Bill Peters	67

Binayak Sen	72
Boote Antony R.	63
Celeste Estrella	216
Cornelius Peter K	37
Cheru Fantu	69
Chilowa Wycliffe	39
Christou Costas	64
Chakraverty Rabindra	73
Christina Daseeking	68
Chu Keyoung	36
Coxhead Ian	54
Cleary	59
Clements Paul	57
Cohen Daniel	29
Corden W Max	62
Dashwood Hevian S	41
David Bigman	41
Dillip Mukherjee	40
Delius Peter	52
Dellas Harris	64
Dom Helder Camera	261
Douglas Alexander	228
Ellis F	218
Elbadawi Ibrahim A	65, 66
Echeverri Gent John	37, 71
Evan Timorthy G.	44
Faruqee Rashid	54
Francis Lau	197
Fujita Koichi	46
Fisccher Stanley	62
Gupta S.P	50
Ismail A Ghafar	43
Jan Bojo	81
Jane Clark	218
Jan Vandemoortele	75
Gaude J	48
George Soros	34
Ghani Ezaz	63
Goheer Nabeel A	45
Graham Carol	60
GraciaAldaz Jesus	67

Greener Robert 38
Haggblade Steven 47
Hague T 336
Houben Aerdt C.F.J 62
Hiten Bhaya 314
James D Wolfensohn 321,322
Jim Flaherty 237
Kaijage Frederick 71
Karim M. Rezaul 44
Khandker S. R. 44, 72
Khan Haider Ali 73
Khanna Kailash C 36
Killick Tony 38
Lal Deepak 49
L. Demery 176
Leo Tolstoy 18
Levy Santiago 36
Liu Aying 38
Lieten G K 61
Lopez J Humberto 76
Luca .D Lilyo 287
Luis Serven 76
Maganya J 330
Martin Dent 67
Ma Jun 53
Mitchell Deborah 37
Malik Md. Hussain 49
Mallick S. C. 49, 332
Marrit Berg 50
Marit Glad 282
Meena Mwinga 125
Mookherjee Dillip 41
Barak Husain Obama 290
Nelson Mandela 79
Orr 75
Osada Mitsu 44
Pranab Bardhan 41
Professor, Oyen 197,195
Psacharopoulous George 56
P. Hazell 47,321
Pritam Mallick 49

Petras J.F	59
Quershi S K	55
Rabindranath Tagore	347
Rahman A.	43
Rankin Katharine N	46
Ravi Kanbur	51
Rt. Hon Clare Short	321,338
Raj Sekhar D	45
Ravallion Martin	47
Rello Fernando	74
Raoetal	40
Riona Nicholls	282
R C Reddy	81
Robert Mattson	56
Robert Powell	68
Ruben Ruend	50
Ruriah K. K.	199
Russiah R.	58
Ryan Swanson	301
S Perera	330
Salih Booker	82
Samal R K	49
Shari I	58
Shaw Judith	60
Sha Zukang	274
Sharma Ruchir-	23
Sidsel Saugestad	56, 58
Silva R	330
Soto Marcelo	29
Stiglitz Joseph -E	23, 82
Stiphens Macolm	65
Svensson Jakab	41
Tanzi Vito	36
Teklu T	48
Tendler Judith	56
Tarazona Etheli	57
Travers Lee	53
Thugge Kamau	63
Vandana Shiva	26
Von-Braun Joachim	48
Vyas V S	52

Warr Peter G 54
Wahid Abu N M 43
Walton M. 176
Watzlawick H. 48
Webb Patrck 48
Weyland Kurt T I 40
West Gerald T 57
William Lambers 302
William Som 134
Yao Shujie 38

+++++

SUBJECT INDEX

Activities of DFID - 220
Activities of World Bank Group 185,187
Addis Abba Conference-137
Agriculture-53
Agricultural Development Led Industrialization 101
Atlas Methodology - 83
Austrian Aid program–239,249
Australian bilateral aid activities 249
Bank Account 324
Basic Human Needs – 207,308
Bilateral Donations – 212
Bilateral Loans – 212
Causes of Poverty - 28
Charitable Dining Halls – 305
CIDA -228
Comparative Research Program of Poverty 195
Conflict in Burkina faso-97
Climate Change in Burkinafaso-94
Debt Relief -61,327
DFID -216
DFID activities -211
Dhaka Declaration 132
Dutch disease - 24
Employment Generation 47
Employment Opportunities 333
Environment -337
FAO-130

Favourable Prices for Cereals- 339
Fight Poverty to End Insecurity – 282
Food for Work program-121
Food for Peace Program - 301
Food Security 514,323
Foreign Funding Institutions 56
Gender Disparity - 152
G8 Coln Communique-170
G8 L' Aquila Summit -286
Global Recession-257
Global Monitoring Report -287
Governance -60
Growth mirage-26
HIPC –79,172
HIPC Initiative-202
Human Capital-55
HIV / AIDs in Burkinafaso-92
Heavily Indebted Poor Countries – 79
IBRD Lending - 187
Income Classifications-82
Income Generation Programme-144
Initiative for Sustainable Development (ISD) -166
International Monetary Fund -199
International Development Goals 175
JICA activities 213
JICA – 214
JICA's role - 213
Kyoto Initiative 168
Kyrgyzstan Experience 132
Land Reforms 334
Lucas Parados-29
Micro-credit – 42
Millennium Development Goals (MDG):
91,175,256,270
Millennium Development Goals Report –273
Mongolia Issue on Poverty - 144
N G O –58,129
National Poverty Alleviation Programme-110
OECD –153,156,157
Official Development Assistance –129,256
Paris Declaration on aid effectiveness-255

Philippines Experience 136
Pittsburgh Summit – 297
Poverty in Ethiopia – 27
Poverty in India – 25
Poverty Alleviation Fund-113
Poverty Alleviation in rural Indonesia 143
Poverty Alleviation Program – 120,145,149
Poverty Reduction and Growth Facility 200
Poverty Reduction Strategy Papers 84, 79
Poverty Reduction Strategy Papers in Jambia-126
Poverty Reduction Factors in Malawi 134
PREDES Model 141,142
Poverty diet-30
Resurgent India-26
Rural Connectivity 329
Rural Agricultural Markets –331
Santiago de Chile declaration -140
SDPRP – 99
SEWA – 41
Shining India-26
Severity of Poverty – 21
Suresh - Pritam Model – 342
Suva Declaration-139
Task force Hunger-266
Training for Rural Activities-121
UNCED-166
UNDP –178
Views of Researchers-322
Washington Consensus -134
Working of World Food Programme-307
World Bank -183
World Development Report -195
World Food Summit-158
World Summit for Social Development –263
Zimbabwe, Poverty Alleviation Action Plan (PAAP) - 147

A MOVEMENT FOR A PEACEFUL WORLD

AUTHORS

Professor Suresh Chandra Mallick (b 1944) was a faculty member of the OUAT, Bhubaneswar (India) during 1968 – 2004. He is a researcher, writer, thinker and social worker. He is an Agricultural Economist with specialization in Agriculture, Poverty, Marketing, Policy and World Peace to motivate people's involvement in peace process. He held the post of Vice President, Indian Society of Agricultural Marketing during 2003 – 05. At present, he is the Chairperson of the Institute of Development Studies & Policy Research, Bhubaneswar.

Pritam Mallick (1975–2006) was extremely noble, friendly and knowledgeable and possessed extraordinary memory. He received B.A. (Honors) from Utkal University, M.A. from Central University, Hyderabad and M. Phil. Degree from Jawaharlal Nehru University and completed Ph. D. courses in JNU. He was a specialist in Monetary Economics and Econometrics. He remembered the Oxford Dictionary and Roget's Thesaurus to master English literature. He acquired deep knowledge in Astrology, Palmistry, Mathematics and Statistics. He contributed enormously for WORLD PEACE manuscripts as co-author. But his heavenly demise occurred on August 4, 2006.